BiBi

ਬੀਬੀ

The Cookbook

Chet Sharma

BiBi

ਬੀਬੀ

The
Cookbook

Stories from
my Bibi

The Streets
Shuraat

The Garden
Kethi

The Sea
Samundar

The Pasture
Shikaari

Desserts
Meetha

BiBi Essentials

Stories from our family and friends

Trevor Noah

To know a grandmother's love is to know love in its purest, most unconditional form. It's the kind of love that lingers in the air like the aroma of a slow-cooked meal, wrapping itself around you with a warmth that asks for nothing in return. To step into BiBi is to step into that very embrace.

Bibi, Gogo, Nonna, Abuela, Grandma – no matter the language, the word carries the weight of history, culture, and deep, unshakable familiarity. It's not just a name; it's a feeling. So, it feels only right that Chet's restaurant bears this name.

Technically, BiBi is a restaurant. Emotionally, it is a love letter, a physical manifestation of the warmth, generosity and care that grandmothers pour into their food. You don't just taste it – you feel it in the way the space is designed, in the way the team makes you feel at home, in the way each dish arrives at the table like a whispered secret from the past.

I'll never forget my first meal at BiBi. The impeccable presentation was the kind that makes you stop to admire it before you dig in. The flavours? As refined and precise as you'd expect from a place that has garnered such well-deserved acclaim. But what caught me off-guard was something no Michelin star or critical review could have prepared me for: the profound sense of home. Every bite, every spice, the balance of heat and depth, felt like a memory brought to life. It was as if I had been welcomed into another grandmother's kitchen, into a different lineage of love and tradition. The warmth was familiar, yet the stories told through the food were new, unfolding in ways that felt deeply personal despite never having lived them before. It was an invitation, a seat at a table that had been set long before I arrived, filled with history, care, and an unspoken understanding that food is love in its most universal form.

Every dish Chet prepared or presented, you could see it wasn't just food to him. It wasn't just about technique or accolades or even the joy of cooking. It felt like he was reaching back in time, recreating a memory, an experience, a moment that had shaped him. He carried each plate to the table not just with skill, but with reverence, because he wasn't merely carrying food – he was carrying the history of his people. There's something magical in the way he has remembered something we so often forget: that food is an edible archive, a testament to traditions, histories, and lives that have come before us. In every dish, there is a story waiting to be tasted, a past that refuses to be forgotten, and a love that continues to nourish long after the last bite.

BiBi is not just about dining; it's about belonging. If you've ever been lucky enough to know the love of a grandmother, you'll understand exactly what I mean.

Aziz Ansari

When Caucasian people recommend Indian restaurants, you must be cautious. So, when one of my friends said I had to try BiBi, I was sceptical. I'm not into 'fancy' restaurants, long tasting menus, or food that is complex for complexity's sake. I also believe that with Indian food, homemade is best. Give me food from any grandma in the world, I'm happy. It's simple in the most elegant way, time tested, comforting and tasty.

One day, walking near Mayfair, I stumbled near this place my friend spoke of – BiBi. They had a lunch special and counter seating. This all seemed relaxed and more my vibe. I walked in and asked if I could sit at the bar alone. The staff were kind and happy to have me. The chef, Chet, soon came and said hello and told me he not only knew my work, but was frequently told we looked alike (a scenario that happens to me more than you'd think).

He guided me through his beautiful lunch. First, he served me some chai, 'the true, real chai,' he said, that was savoury and mushroom based, rather than made with sugar, milk, etc. It was warming and a microcosm of my meal – incredibly thoughtful, with a humble sophistication that was respectful of tradition, but above all else, delicious. Next was some cheddar papads with a dip of mint, mango and yogurt. This instantly recognisable Indian snack was executed to a level of perfection by a guy who you were not surprised to learn had spent time at Mugaritz and The Ledbury. He then brought out the goat kebab galouti, explaining the story of a king who lost all his teeth from smoking too much opium and needed food he could chew with his gums. It was a fun piece of history and a great preamble to a fantastic dish.

The final course was a stunner – Sharmaji's Lahori Chicken. It felt like a mother's curry, with chef techniques that were not in opposition to the dish's warmth and comfort but enhanced it. Served with exquisitely executed rice, dal and roti ... I was in a state of shock, joy and excitement. This is what I wanted elevated Indian food to be – fun, but humble, not trying to outdo home food but support and expand it. When I learned what the name of this 'fancy' restaurant, BiBi, meant, it all made sense – grandma.

Hans Zimmer

Even the most delicious food tastes twice as good in the right environment, surrounded by old friends and a chef like Chet, who instantly becomes a friend for life. I'm a composer, and the people that truly understand me are chefs. We both work ridiculous hours trying to give our audience an unforgettable experience. And, we both try to find the freshest, most beautiful and surprising ingredients to prepare something not only original, but of a quality that puts a smile on your face.

We spend all day shopping and chopping, cleaning, peeling and preparing, right up to the moment that the guests (or in my case, the audience) arrive, throw our perfect ingredients into a boiling pot, and – voila – serve up an unforgettable experience, perfectly prepared and perfectly on time… P.S. I love Sharma's restaurant, BiBi!

Tom Kerridge

From the moment I made the first booking at BiBi, I was incredibly excited about my visit. There was a buzz about this fantastic restaurant, opened by a great chef with Indian heritage, that was connected through food, but also modern-day professional cookery. As you walk through the door, a sense of excitement flows throughout the restaurant. The open kitchen adds to that sense of engagement between restaurant service, kitchen and ingredients: rice from a single estate in Kerala, cooked beautifully, deep flavours, exceptional produce, in an amazing restaurant. Undoubtedly one of the finest additions to the London, but most importantly, British food scene. Chet has a wonderful restaurant that deserves all the plaudits and credits that it gets.

Ryan Chetiyawardana

Chet is one of the most inspiring (and experienced – he must have the wildest CV in the biz) chefs I know. Combined with his holistic approach to excellence and hospitality as a whole, BiBi was always going to be one of the most exciting venues, not just in London, but globally. As dear friends, I was so excited when the project came to life, but even then I was unprepared for the sheer breadth and brilliance that the restaurant brings. The commitment and wild creativity, matched with the fun, warmth and deliciousness (and, of course, the soundtrack!) means it's always top of my rec-ommendations list. It's also the only spot where I push my inability to eat spicy food to the absolute limits!

Olly Smith

When Chet appeared on BBC's Saturday Kitchen, I was blown away by his exceptional skill, deep humility, sense of humour and knowledge of wine. The dish he cooked was scrumptious and mere days later, utterly inspired, Matt and I duly made our pilgrimage to BiBi. From the moment we perched at the counter, it was one of the most gracious, tantalising, enriching feasts of my life. Watching Chet cook felt to me like being in the presence of a wise sculptor revealing what only he could see from the living material in his hands. Every dish another milestone, cocktails to blow your mind, the wine pairings pitch perfect. Chet and his team could not be more serious-minded in their approach to making the rest of us all feel great. For that, our thanks should be innumerable.

Brett Graham

BiBi is an exceptional restaurant and Chet is an exceptional chef. His dedication to the craft and his passion for the most incredible produce from India and the UK are what help make this such a special restaurant. Chet worked at The Ledbury some time ago and I've watched his story unfold. I really admire people who run their own restaurants and I know the years of cooking, research and commitment it has taken Chet to get BiBi to where it is today and create a restaurant that stands out from the rest. The food is special, handcrafted and made with so much passion. I can't wait for my next visit.

Andoni Aduriz

At BiBi, Chet reconciles memories and experiences and the legacy of generations of his forebears with the flavours and textures that shaped them, protecting their essence and the stories that give them their soul. Chet passed through Mugaritz a decade ago. He remembers it (and expresses it) as an experience that changed his life and shaped his journey. Today, he triumphs in London, cooking the landscapes – real and figurative – of exquisite and sophisticated India. Chet, thank you for matching your talent with flair at BiBi.

Mark Birchall

I've known Chet for 15 years. He is a very close friend, an absolutely brilliant chef – super intelligent, really creative, and a really, really nice person. His dedication and precision in the kitchen is always outstanding. At BiBi, he's created something truly special: his food is bold, refined, and deeply personal. I couldn't be prouder of him.

Henrietta Lovell & Richard Hart

The first time we ate Chet's food we knew we were eating something very special. And it wouldn't be the last time. Far from it. There is a very good reason that BiBi is the very first place we head for when we arrive back in London. It's fucking delicious. The menu is mind-bending without twee-zers or drama. BiBi is elegant without being pompous or serious. Chet has so much creativity, but his food is very much about deliciousness above any other consideration. He's not trying to look clever. He just is. He can't help it. Even though you've never tasted anything like the food at BiBi, you are very much aware that this is Indian cuisine and based on love, family and tradition. You can also see what a lovely human Chet is in his kitchen. We love the bar seats best. There is no hiding how happy he looks doing what he loves. Nor how relaxed the team are as they make world-class food right in front of you. That's no easy feat in the pursuit of excellence. And BiBi is truly excellent.

Introduction

BiBi was an accident.

Let me explain. In 2017, I had just helped Mark Birchall open Moor Hall – two years after he first shared the blueprints of a Tudor manor located somewhere called 'Ormskirk' – and was considering whether this time I was truly 'done' with London. I had spent the first 20 years of my life in and around the city followed by a seven-year sojourn that saw me through Oxford, San Sebastián, Copenhagen, Cartmel and Bray, before a brief return to London that ended when Mark convinced me to pack up and head back north again.

Then, Karam Sethi called. Anybody who knows him knows he is not a man that 'calls'. You can barely tie him to a post-pandemic Zoom call. Karam sends WhatsApp messages. Never SMS, never emails and never, ever calls.

We had met briefly about some consultancy work a few years earlier and it's a meeting I'll never forget. I had eaten at Gymkhana – then, as it is now, the pre-eminent classical Indian restaurant in Mayfair – and when I walked in and was greeted by the reception team, nothing seemed out of the ordinary. I was escorted down to one of the private dining rooms (the 'vaults', as they are still known) where Karam was sitting, Maharaja-like, in front of a spread of polished brass and silver serviceware full of foods that smelled of my child-hood. Karam went about tasting a spoonful of each dish, while a chef stood nearby eagerly awaiting feedback. 'Needs more *bhuna zeera*', he said, in his polished British-Hindi. 'Have you toasted the *kasoori methi*?', 'biryani needs more *kewra*, and to be a bit more *masaledaar*'. Now, as a chef with a European background, receiving feedback from your exec chef / owner is normal. Hearing words that my grandmother would have used was new.

Without hesitation, Karam called a commis to clear the dishes away. 'So, you're the doctor chef?', he said, in his first acknowledgement of my presence. 'Ben [Chapman from Smoking Goat and Kiln] said you're helping him with a duck noodle dish. Are you sure you wouldn't rather make kebabs?'

We talked for an hour or so, essentially with no end point in sight, and I had to get to another meeting, so I excused my-self, shook hands and – despite emailing Karam a few times to follow up – didn't hear from him for the next 27 months. (Not that I was counting.)

And then he called. It was May 2017, and I was two months into the opening of Moor Hall; my contract was due to expire in September, and with my wedding fast approaching, I needed to start thinking about the next project. 'Fancy a coffee next time you're in London?' (Karam doesn't drink tea or coffee, one of many red flags that indicates that his brain already works more quicky and effortlessly than any of us mortals). JKS was at the time the most exciting restaurant

group in the country. Everything it touched turned to gold. Trishna (one Michelin star), Kitchen Table (one – now two – Michelin stars), Gymkhana (one – now two – Michelin stars), Lyle's (one Michelin star – seeing a pattern?), Bao, Hoppers … all were all huge successes and there were more restaurants in the pipeline. If ever a group needed a geeky development chef, it was JKS in 2017. So, I went into it with a fairly good CV and the confidence that I could at the very least secure some work from the ever-growing group.

'When are you going to stop being a coward and open your own restaurant?', Karam asked. This was definitely not where I thought our conversation would go. I had just spent two years with Mark seeing him tear his hair out, go grey over selecting taps for the guest bedrooms and generally mill about a crumbling building site trying to get his dream restaurant off the ground. I knew the toll it took on him personally, how he missed spending time with his wife and son, and how at the end of all that hard work, we still had the occasional weekday lunches with fewer than ten guests booked in[1] (see page 19). Opening a restaurant really wasn't in the cards. I wanted intellectual stimulation, to keep opening and operating restaurants for other people – all the stress / fun, none of the actual responsibility, plus the security of a pay cheque at the end of it. Different restaurants, different food, different parts of the world … but then there is that niggling bit that all creatives have: 'what if I could tell a story with my food that hasn't been told before?' And so, on the spot, I pitched three ideas:

1. A scalable Middle Eastern concept (not sure why)
2. A farm-to-table tasting menu restaurant in the country-side (I'm pretty sure Karam actually yawned at that one)
3. An Indian chef's table. Indian spices and stories, British produce, cooked for a wanky chef's table for 12–20 guests a night.

We arranged a tasting to be held a few months later at a flat I had bought in Slough. I did most of the prep up at Moor Hall on a Sunday / Monday, drove down in the evening and held the tasting at the flat on a Tuesday lunchtime. Jyotin Sethi – Karam's older brother and the CEO of JKS – and Karam made the trip out to 'past Southall' (as Jyo still describes it) and sat down for lunch in my small one-bedroom flat, on a hot July day where the temperature inside was over 30 deg-rees centigrade. As soon as they sat down I offered them a drink, as is customary in an Indian household. Straight away, Karam asked for a savoury lassi. Okay, great, I thought. As a young but experienced chef, back then I worked religiously off mise-en-place sheets. Everything I cooked would have a list of pre-prepared items, which have been tested, tasted and re-formulated to be the best I can put forward. 'Cooking from the hip' is just something you can't do at the Moor Halls and L'Enclumes of this world. I had never made a savoury lassi in my life. But I winged it. Tasted it, adjusted it with black salt, then poured it into a glass and served it. It doesn't sound like a big deal – and this is a drink that my grandmothers would make daily just off instinct, which is what I relied on here for the first time as a chef, too – but when Karam took his first sip, he said 'Fucking good. Why can't we do this in our restaurants?'

Despite this, in my eyes, that lunch was still a disaster. I can still tell you what was wrong (sadly an indication of how my mind works rather than looking at the positives), and I'll never forget the mistakes: the keema in the bun was underwhelming, the raw scallops were from the supermarket (and tasted like it), the kohlrabi on the fish course was over-pickled, the duck sauce was too thin, the toasted-rice-milk ice cream melted so quickly it basically became a soup ... But they liked something about that day enough that they brought me on board with the idea that we would open a restaurant together in the future. When that would be was unclear because – as ever – JKS had plans to open a handful of restaurants the following year, so I would support the new openings in the pipeline, until we nailed down the concept and location of what was then termed internally as 'Project two star, CS'.

I spent the next three years under Karam's wing, reeducating my Indian palate to understand what had made the current JKS Indian restaurants so successful. This involved opening Brigadiers, as well as supporting any practical needs for development across the JKS group. In many ways, I became Karam's right-hand man through this time, his loyal lieutenant who tried to satisfy his operational needs while also supporting the creative drive with new dishes, sweet or savoury, across the brands. Karam needed me to do the dirty work so he could remove himself from service and think more 'big picture'.

The only downside was, I couldn't think 'big picture' about what I wanted my restaurant to be.

42 North Audley Street

At the beginning of 2019, fresh from getting married, I convinced the team at JKS that I needed to get out of day-to-day restaurant operations, and I embarked on a series of journeys that took me across India and lasted a total of nine months. There will be separate stories and pages dedicated to these trips, as it was probably the most influential time for me, as I shaped the BiBi identity and my voice as a chef, too.

One trip ended with a few days in Kolkata and, just as I was getting ready to board the 3:05 am flight back to London Heathrow, via a pit stop in Muscat, Billy messaged me to call him urgently. Billy Hookway, for many, was the fourth Sethi sibling whose name didn't make it into the initials of the company. A colleague of Jyo's from their time together at Barclays, Billy was an early investor in the JKS structure, and joined full-time as the Commercial Director to be the steady hands that steered the company in its future direction.

Billy had been in touch with the Crown Estate and had been made aware that a new property on Heddon Street was coming to the market. JKS were in a great position to snap this up, having opened Sabor on the same street with Nieves Barragán just over a year earlier, with *massive* success. The only drawback was, I needed to be at Heddon Street the following morning. After an overnight 13-hour flight. Oh, and I probably should mention that I needed a concept to pitch in there because 'Project two star, CS' – now named *Loha* – probably wouldn't be a good fit there.[2] It would need to be something more casual. I spent the flight thinking through myriads of dishes, ingredients, people and stories I had encountered in my travels; how, despite trying tasting menus in the best restaurants in India, every truly great meal was cooked with the love and warmth of home cooks, usually older ladies, who would enjoy the intrigue of a curious young chef from London and so divulge their secrets to me[3].

Why was it that every delicious thing I ate in India came from the hands of these 'ladies of the house' or *Bibis*? And so, the pitch for Heddon Street was titled 'BiBi: not what your grandmother made'. Because I wanted to pay homage to all of these delicious dishes, but still show that the touch of a chef can make *authentic* food that is still *unique*.

After a few viewings, we decided that the site at Heddon Street wasn't right for the project. It was a strange space where there were too many concerns over the extract and existing back-of-house equipment. But the seed had been sown with Billy and Karam; now it was just a matter of time before we convinced Jyo that BiBi was a concept worth exploring.

Fast forward a few months and Billy had started conversations with Grosvenor Estates about a site on North Audley Street, for a 'casual all-day Indian brand'. Karam had been talking for years about a Brigadiers Canteen, a more laid-back and smaller setting for Brigadiers, specialising in biryanis, kebabs and the less boisterous elements of the original. He still maintains that a pool table would have worked where our pastry section is. As a senior kitchen presence, Billy, Jyo and Karam took me along for a site visit to 42 North Audley Street.

It couldn't be more different to the Heddon Street site. On this busy, leafy throughway between the posh end of Oxford Street, leading to Grosvenor Square, number 42 is a narrow corner unit which sits a little uneasy next to its more modern neighbours, with its grand doors, high-vaulted ceilings and galley-like feel.

While Jyo and Karam talked about how the biryanis would make it from a basement kitchen to the dining room, Billy led me down the temporary staircase to the lower-ground fire exit. 'What if we put Loha down here?' he said. Confused, I asked what that meant for Brigadiers Canteen and their basement kitchen. 'No, you don't get it', Billy continued, 'this isn't for Brig canteen. BiBi *has* to be upstairs'.

I loved it. The site, the idea of two restaurants rolled into a single space. Something casual upstairs, then – hidden in the depths – a unique dining experience around a chef's table. James Knappett had done something similar with Kitchen Table and Bubbledogs. Plus, it felt like a much more natural fit for me as I wasn't keen to be compared to the other Mayfair Indian restaurants, and wanted to do something more progressive. Something extraordinary. Two sites in one was the answer. The casual brand feeds the ambitious project; one makes money, one wins awards.

We were due to break ground on BiBi / Loha in April 2020, with upstairs opening in June, and downstairs opening in September: 38 seats on the ground floor, 12 in the basement. I had started building my team and wanted them to see the site. Keiran Mustafa was going to be the head chef of BiBi while Ben Watson, fresh off six years working under Clare Smyth, was going to be my sous down at Loha. I took them to see the site and have a coffee next door at North Audley Canteen (NAC).

It was an odd time on a Monday afternoon, around 5.30pm. NAC was empty, but we didn't think much of it. The waiter clearly heard us talking about the site next door, so realised we were in the trusted hospitality inner circle. He said the weekend before had been the quietest weekend they had ever had, and that they had no bookings for the evening so were shutting around 7pm. I had noticed as much – bookings were dropping across the JKS sites, too, with fear of this new virus from China taking hold.

Then the Prime Minister, Boris Johnson, held an emergency press conference and pleaded with the public to stop going out to bars and restaurants. Almost like a light-switch being flicked off, London emptied. As we walked up to the tube station at Marble Arch, we noticed Roka had just one table occupied. I stopped to ask the reception how business was looking and they said they had four reservations for the whole week. That evening, around midnight, Jyo Sethi called me: 'Don't come into the office tomorrow, it's not going to be a great environment. We're turning off the lights and don't know if we'll ever switch them back on'.

The pandemic was a difficult period for everyone; many lost loved ones, many lost jobs, all of us lost time. But I only realise looking back now just how unusual it was to not work for a whole month. Every day, I'd get up, work-out in the garden, shower and then ... nothing. I sharpened my knives, made sourdough (of course), did puzzles, read, wrote menus, threw the menus in the bin, made my wife lunch, milled around a bit, opened a bottle of wine, made dinner. Maybe made a digestif (finally, my Armageddon-ready store-cupboard of alcohol and preserves was coming into use). But for a chef to have nowhere to cook, and no dining room to feed ... I was lost.

We spent evenings talking about what the point of restaurants was. The root of the word restaurant means 'to restore', and the first Parisian restaurants just served a rich soup, a meal in a bowl[5]. One day my wife and I drew up a 'word cloud' of all the words we could come up with to do with the best

meals we've had – my wife and I built the basis of our relationship on our mutual love of restaurants. Interestingly, the fourteenth word was 'food'. Instead, the first thirteen words that came to mind were all centred around the art of hospitality: looking after people, taking care of them and making their lives a bit easier.

As a chef with a giant ego, the pandemic was a revelatory period in my life: I realised the fact that the dishes are being washed by someone else is more important to a guest than if the onion in the mignonette was a textbook-perfect brunoise. Chefs are often (myself included, sometimes) too driven to give the guest what they want to serve, rather than what they would want to be served if the roles were reversed.

Soigné is a word that gets used constantly in the best restaurants around the world. It means 'well-dressed' (i.e. 'make it look good'). We sometimes slip into using that word, occasionally ironically, in the restaurant, but I learned during the pandemic that guests, deep down, couldn't care less if the food is soigné. They want delicious. The two aren't mutually exclusive, but on the Venn diagram of food, 'soigné' and 'delicious' intersect surprisingly rarely.

As the pandemic continued, I had time to speak to chefs from other kitchens I had been in – we even managed a mini-Mugaritz reunion Zoom call eight years since I'd left – and I started thinking more about what I wanted my restaurant to represent, not just for guests, but also for our team. Much is often made about the back of house / front of house divide in high-end restaurants. As much as anybody, I had been guilty of engendering the spirit of kitchen versus service. I had always gravitated towards working in places led by chef-patrons, like Simon Rogan, Mark Birchall, Brett Graham, Giorgio Locatelli, Andoni Luis Aduriz. And in those restaurants, if there was a dispute, the kitchen invariably won. But by not working at all during the early stages of the pandemic, I latently concluded that we are supposed to be on the same team. Of course, a bit of sibling rivalry is healthy, but in the end we're all there to make a guest's experience at the restaurant that little bit better. And most struggles just came from poor communication. So, I wanted to make sure that at BiBi, chefs have to serve some of the food, and that the front of house spends time with us in the kitchen prepping herbs, vegetables and our 'family meal'.

And I wanted my restaurant to be a nice place to work. It sounds like a basic concept, but if I'm honest, I'd never thought it was *that* important. Back then, it just wasn't the main priority of leading a team, which shows how far the industry has come since then. Me not working in a restaurant was, in many ways, what helped make BiBi such a special one. Before Covid, I wanted a restaurant. I wanted Michelin stars, I wanted praise, I wanted the awards. Before Covid, I knew *how* to cook. After Covid, I remembered *why* I cooked.

We went back to the drawing board and tore up the plans for North Audley Street. Gone was the admittedly self-serving chef's table downstairs, and along with it, we opened up the space for staff welfare. Proper lockers you could actually

fit things inside (anyone who has worked in a restaurant in a big city knows how rare this is), air conditioning through the prep kitchen, even a second filtered water font so the team could get still and sparkling water during long prep days.

These were all small points, in hindsight, as the whole world seemingly moved towards a better work-life balance and better welfare post pandemic. But at the time it was hard to justify. Losing a chef's table like that, in an area as expensive as Mayfair, took the total cover count from 50 down to just 31. Suddenly, each seat in the restaurant now had to generate a third more revenue than before. For a casual restaurant, that means more turns; in fine-dining, higher prices. The BiBi that emerged post pandemic was neither and both at the same time. 'Fine-casual' is a term I hate but have found myself adopting more and more over time, as pinpointing what BiBi is can be extremely tricky.

Like *Bibi*, like *Beta*

I am the youngest of my late grandmother's four grandchildren. And the second youngest of an army of 11 Sharma boys who grew up in and around Slough - all of us born between 1983 and 1990. We were known in our area for good and bad reasons, but mainly for our sporting ability. We famously had a cricket team of 10 Sharmas and one unfortunate tagalong. While we had different grandparents, we were all close with our grandmothers. There is an obvious cultural link but also a generational pattern. In the vast majority, the grandmothers didn't work, the grandfathers did. As homemakers, they naturally became the focal point of the family dynamic. All of our parents worked, so we were invariably raised by our grandmothers.

Ranjana, my *dadima* (my dad's mum), was a powerhouse of a woman. She was married at fifteen - maybe fourteen - widowed at eighteen and by twenty-seven was building a new life for herself and her two sons in Chalvey, Slough. According to my uncles and aunties, she was always a larger-than-life personality. That's the interesting thing about grandparents - as grandchildren, we tend to see the mellowed, relaxed version of them rather than their more authentic younger selves that our parents would have had to contend with. Don't get me wrong, my dad and his brother got in enough trouble to make any single parent turn grey. My uncle famously stole the neighbour's Mini Cooper in the 1970s and got brought back in a police car, a family trait that one of my cousins repeated 20 years later.

Ranjana was an incredibly honest person, hard-working and warm, and had a way of looking at life that hinted at a wisdom that someone with a relatively comfortable life like mine may never fully understand. When she came to Britain, just after the 1966 World Cup win, she had no education, no money, two hungry, growing boys and had never seen snowfall. How she managed to convince the Mars factory managers to let her loose with power tools to fix vending machines is beyond me. But that was her; she wasn't going

to let something as small as having no idea what she was doing stop her from doing whatever she needed to do to look after her family.

After retiring, every morning until the day she passed, she woke up and had a cup of tea with two Marks & Spencers digestive biscuits, showered, did her prayers, had her porridge, cleaned the kitchen and only then went about starting the rest of the day. People who didn't know her wonder where my OCD tendencies came from; why I have an insatiable need for order, symmetry and for everything to be at the correct angle. And why running late drives me mad. It is all from her. As a child, I remember setting my watch by the time she woke up. She even counted the number of times she brushed her hair in the morning.

This was all juxtaposed by her desire to have a good time. She had had a difficult life but never have I met someone who willed laughter out of people like my dadima. Punjabi people are often comically portrayed in Indian media as uncultured, uneducated farmers with famous appetites for food, drink and *bhangra*. While she only occasionally enjoyed a glass of red wine - doctors told her it would be good for her handful of cardiac issues - Ranjana really did fill every one of the Punjabi stereotypes. She was never happier than when her disobedient grandsons were causing mayhem around her, living out a kind of carefree life that she wasn't able to have.

Aside from all of this, she was an incredible cook. I've been doing this job professionally for twenty years. Still, I don't have the resourceful, instinctive ability she has to make something mundane and simple taste delicious. And the fact that she did this while also being a strict vegetarian makes it all the more impressive. All chefs know that adding a little bacon to a sauce, some chicken stock to a stew or frying something in tallow is a cheat code for flavour. But how she took butternut squash peels - yes, the peels - and transformed them into something moreish is a skill I'm yet to learn. It's been over 10 years since she passed, and I'm still trying to figure out how she made her famous 'pizza bread'.

My other grandmother, Kamal - my *nanima* - was an equally talented, pure vegetarian cook from a diligent and religious family in India. Growing up on a farmhouse in Haryana and eventually settling in Mumbai, she was a woman of incredibly restrained tastes. While Ranjana was loud and boisterous, Kamal was quieter, studious and devout. My fondest memories with her were getting up at the crack of dawn, having a cup of chai with Parle-G biscuits, then heading out to collect flowers for the morning *puja* (prayers). On returning, after completing our morning prayers, we would head into the kitchen where fresh buffalo milk would be churned into *makhan* (white butter) and the buttermilk would be whisked into *dahi* (yoghurt) to make a proper salty lassi. Not a mango in sight. If she were here to see it, I'm sure she would chuckle at the idea that churning your own butter or making your own yoghurt was something that waiters would talk about so proudly at the table of a high-end London restaurant.

Where Ranjana learnt resourcefulness through necessity, Kamal had the luxury of living in a middle-class family in Mumbai. My first introduction to the importance of ingredients came from her. As a reserved woman, she rarely got overly excited, but I'll always remember her beaming smile when she had a stone mill installed in our Mumbai home. Whenever I smell our roomali roti dough – which contains her beloved, nutty *paigambri* wheat variety – as it toasts on the cast-iron *ulta tawa*, I'm transported back to that house as an eight-year-old, sitting in front of the TV watching Doordarshan news as dinner was being finished in the adjacent kitchen.

One day we were walking through the market, and she knew she needed some aubergines for a dish that evening. Well, I say market ... it was a series of sheets with vegetables and produce strewn across them, lining each side of a small but busy street. As her eager assistant, I ran to the first man I could find with produce and started to negotiate the price for one kilogram of aubergines. Nanima barely broke stride as she took a momentary glance at the aubergines and called me to follow in line. I asked what was wrong; she pointed to the sky and said the sun is too intense in this corner of the market at this time, let's come back when the next delivery comes in at dusk. I remember coming back from that trip and annoying my mum in a British supermarket, trying to understand why we only had one type of aubergine in England, and why all of them looked so perfect but tasted of nothing.

How to use this book

Emilia Terragni, a pretty accomplished writer in her own right, has been given the moniker 'the queen of cookbooks' by *The Wall Street Journal*. She worked with Ferran Adrià, Massimo Bottura, René Redzepi, Corey Lee, Clare Smyth and Andoni Luis Aduriz on all their debut cookbooks. So, you can imagine my surprise when, booked under another name, after her first meal at BiBi, she handed me her business card and said, 'We would love to bring your restaurant to paper. When you want to write a book, please give my office a call.'

This was September 2022, barely a year after we opened the restaurant, when I was still there for every minute of every day. We had just lost our head chef from the opening year, and didn't have a general manager, so I really was doing everything I could to hold the restaurant together as we continued to grow every week. I've always loved books, not just cookbooks, and often keep my very young and very energetic nephews occupied by getting to count the thousand-plus books in our collection at home. But the idea of writing a book at that stage was overwhelming, to say the least.

I spent so many years as a development chef, trying to execute dishes to suit the limitless creativity of my former mentors. And for that reason, BiBi really is a restaurant of systems, gram-specific recipes and extreme detail in communication. Each dish at BiBi can have anywhere up to fifteen individual preparations, some of which contain twenty-plus

ingredients each. Who in their right mind would try to cook these recipes outside of the meticulously designed kitchen and specialist equipment of BiBi? Well, if you're still reading, maybe you.

BiBi is an ingredient-led restaurant, so almost none of the recipes in this book are still served in the restaurant, besides the Essentials and the Sharmaji's Chicken. Proteins, garnishes, sauces – they all change more or less weekly depending on what is best in the market. For example, you'll find a recipe for a raw bream and truffle nimbu pani, but for six-plus months of the year, we serve scallop nimbu pani instead. Sometimes it has blood orange in it, sometimes white peaches. As the protein and garnish changes, we use our intuition to modify recipes. Sweeter shellfish and ripe peaches? We make the dressing sourer. Lean and neutral fish like wild bass? Maybe we emulsify a little more oil into the dressing and add a little less coconut water.

At a basic level, onions, chillies, ginger and garlic are available all year, but their characteristics change massively. The recipes in this book are a snapshot, but nothing in this book is verbatim, it's not going to be an exact science when you are working with ingredients you've sourced yourself in another season, another year, so all I can ask is, taste, taste, taste and adjust the dishes as your palate feels appropriate. And don't feel like you can't improvise with what you have. You probably won't find *chamba chukh* chillies from the hills of Himachal Pradesh. Even Amazon isn't that good. But do spend the maximum your budget will allow on cupboard staples such as ghee, spices and salt.

Iodised salt is the antithesis for a BiBi chef. Mass-produced ghee isn't always terrible, but a 900g jar of an organic, grass-fed butter ghee lasts our household for the best part of a year. And when you want a warming bowl of *kichdi*, or proper *daal*, there is no substitute for the best ghee. It's not cheap but it goes a long, long way.

On spices: please don't buy pre-ground spices. They are *never* good. I have a little pestle and mortar next to the stove at home, and my grandmother Ranjana's marble one sits by the pass at the restaurant. It takes seconds to grind spices, and the result is truly transformative. With spice mixes, try to make the mother mixes maximum once a month, garam masala especially. Failing the manual method, buy a £20 coffee grinder and use it to grind spices as you need them (just don't grind your coffee beans in them after).

Science in the kitchen vs cooking in a lab

It's time we address the elephant in the room. Most guests, especially South Asian ones, ask me, 'You were a doctor of physics and now you are a chef ... how did your parents feel about that move?'

In all honesty, much of what we do at the restaurant is intentional. Becoming a chef wasn't. I was a middling

academic, coasting on a stellar memory and fortuitous timing. I stumbled from degree to degree with no real direction, just curiosity. But I much preferred my time in kitchens during my studies than my time in the lab. And for the record, to borrow a line from Ross Geller, I am still technically a doctor!

The second question I get asked: 'does your scientific background help you to come up with dishes? And which ones on the menu?'

My stock line is: 'understanding the intricacies of string theory doesn't really help when my onions are burnt'. A bit tongue-in-cheek because, of course, understanding the concept of a multiverse, I can take some pleasure in knowing that there is a version of me who cooked those onions perfectly. The true answer is *of course!'* Nobody spends eight years in academia to throw it all down the drain and follow the dogmatic systems put in place by angry French chefs hundreds of years ago. But years of poor renditions of foams and espumas, 'textures of foie gras' and a lack of understanding of what the pioneers of molecular gastronomy actually wanted to achieve, means that to be labelled a modernist chef is almost as offensive as being accused of serving 'fusion cuisine'.[5] I want my own legacy to be as a high-calibre chef who understood the science, rather than a scientist who knew his way around a barbecue.

I was fortunate enough to study in the Physics department where Nicholas Kurti, widely considered to be the co-father of molecular gastronomy, ran his laboratory and famously said, 'We know more about what's happening in the centre of our sun than we do in the centre of a soufflé'. Unfortunately, the great man had passed before my time, but conversations with his disciples, as well as his inimitable partner-in-crime, Hervé This, meant that while I was supposed to be looking into the electrophysiology of nerve conduction, I was also developing my own understanding of the science of food. Very different to food science, just for the record.

Another great claim to fame: I once kicked a football so far off-target that I broke a window of Professor Charles Spence's office. His groundbreaking work with Heston Blumenthal paved the way for chefs to start understanding, as he calls it, 'neurogastronomy'. Most chefs turn a blind eye to it as if it's witchcraft but follow the principles unknowingly. Every time you consider the texture of a plate, or the temperature of the cutlery, or the music, the aroma of the dining room, even the colour of the paint on the walls, that is neurogastronomy. Even when you craft the menu introduction or instruct how the waiter should stand at the table – and where they hold a wine bottle while describing it to a guest – that is science first and hospitality second. Or at least it should be; without that care and attention to detail, there cannot be any progression or evolution in dining out.

Lots of negative things can be said about BiBi. The historic facade of the building means we're poorly insulated in the winter, and the room heats up too much in the summer. The room is too narrow and small. The loos are downstairs and separated only by a thin wall from the kitchen porter's pot-wash area. The crockery is chipped (intentionally). The food is sometimes a little odd. The chef is an egotistical narcissist and spends too long on his hair every day. But what nobody can ever say is that what we do isn't considered.

Our team, my second family

Let's cut all the BS. What we do is just a job. We cook food, put it on plates and serve paying guests. Sometimes we open some wine, or pour them a cocktail. It's neither brain surgery nor astrophysics. I'm pretty sure, as a person with a restaurant alongside degrees in both Neurology and Physics, there is nobody better placed to make that statement than me.

Big caveat – you would have to be pretty maladjusted to do what we do at BiBi if you didn't absolutely love it. The hours are long, the nature of the work ranges from incredibly mundane prep to high-octane and adrenalin-fuelled services. Working in any restaurant is antisocial. When you're out with your friends, enjoying a meal or some drinks in a nice bar, we're the ones working behind the scenes. For fifteen years, I missed birthdays, anniversaries, weddings (sorry Dan, but your dad was a chef so if anybody understands it should be you). Even now, best-case scenario I'm at the restaurant before 10am and leaving around 11pm. Five, six days a week.

All of which is why we needed to change the narrative at BiBi.

This is probably the part of the book that many old-school chefs flick through to reach the recipes and photos. Don't feel ashamed, every one of us does it. I have eight hundred-plus cookbooks and can't claim I've read every inch of each one.

This is also probably the part of the book that I wish my old self read back in 2020 when we were desperately sketching out version 1-22 of the BiBi design. Because if the old me had read it, I would have done things so differently. Firstly, I would have made sure I had a proper office to work from, instead of scribbling notes for this book while sitting at the pass, or on table one before lunch or table five after. I would have also made sure that the 'changing room' at BiBi was more than a loose interpretation of the term. Our changing room currently contains staff lockers, chipped plates, back-up wine glasses, five hundred BiBi chocolate bars, a wall-mounted TV screen, a desk, a comms cupboard, an oversized printer and a disgruntled member of the team trying to place orders for tomorrow's menu.

The need to invest in staff infrastructure is evident now as we come into a new age of restaurants. However, coming through the ranks of Michelin-starred kitchens with hard-nosed chefs and belt-tightening owners, especially in a cramped and expensive city like London, meant I rarely saw the kind of facilities that any other world-class organisation would have for their teams. I'm not saying restaurants should try to replicate the Google sleep pods, or the Xbox playrooms at Microsoft. But somewhere to sit for 15 minutes? A decent staff coffee machine? Even just taking briefings outside so the team gets to experience daylight (!). Small touches to make the team feel more appreciated, more human.

I would have also told the old me to take my father's advice. In the early days of the restaurant, he said 'don't hire any arseholes - if you can't go for a drink with them after work, you're probably not going to want to work with them'. Okay, Dad, you were right. In my defense, you've been working for at least 35 years longer than I have so maybe I would have come to the same conclusion myself. It sounds simple, but that's the best advice I would pass on to any small-business owner or restaurateur. As a leader, you have to keep some distance from everyone you work with - you'll have to conduct their probation reviews, appraisals and, in extreme cases, termination consultation - but, especially as a chef, you'll be with these people for 14-16 hours a day, five or more days a week. If you don't hold a mutual respect (as a minimum) and share some comradery with them too, those days will feel even longer. Moreover, how can you all pull in the same direction as a team, if you aren't able to stand side-by-side and support each other?

I'm not the perfect leader. I make mistakes nearly every single day. But I have the ambition to improve myself and become a better boss. It doesn't really make sense not to - why would you spend weeks, months, or even years, training a chef or waiter, only for them to leave because they weren't managed better?

This misnomer about the alpha in the pack has always struck me. Through bad marketing it's come to mean the wolf at the front; the strongest, the fastest, the loudest. And the term 'alpha male' is now attached to a toxic masculinity which has long been associated with kitchen brigades. But when Rudolph Schenkel first described the 'alpha wolf' back in the 1940s, he was actually referring to an entirely different character within a team: the true alpha is actually at the rear of the pack, pushing the others forward. The true alpha

doesn't run ahead to set the pace, but instead makes sure nobody gets left behind.

For me, leadership is more about looking internally than externally. Yes, you build a team with the right mentality, surround yourself with hungry, ambitious people. But your role as a leader is to feed that hunger (sometimes quite literally - doughnuts have always been a good incentive on a Saturday morning) and build the skills in those around you. In the end, we're just temporary stewards of this industry and we have to do our part to give back to the next generation.

1 Spoiler alert: Mark is doing a bit better than okay. Three kids with Jen, three Michelin stars, and Moor Hall has twice won top spot in the National Restaurant Awards.

2 The fact that JKS have now opened a completely different restaurant on Heddon Street as a more accessible all-day dining operation in a site five times the size of the one we first saw is one of life's unpredictable coincidences. Guess Billy was right about that street all along.

3 Many of these ladies still keep in touch now, and while none have actually made it to the restaurant, they still message me every year on my birthday to send their wishes.

4 It is why we still open the menu at BiBi with a *shorba* - an Indian broth or consommé - to warm or cool guests, depending on the season, as soon as they arrive at the restaurant.

5 Guess what - fusion food is made every day, in every restaurant and probably every home, too. The tandoor was introduced to India by the armies of Alexander the Great, who themselves 'borrowed' the technology from the Persians. Chillies and tomatoes were only brought to India in the 17th century by Vasco da Gama after plundering the Americas. Chicken wasn't a widely consumed protein in India until the British East India Company enforced it for the Sepoys in the late 18th century to help build their strength. Good luck making North India's favourite 'authentic' dish, butter chicken, without any of those components. Oh, and butter chicken was invented in the 1950s.

The ten BiBi non-negotiables

Defining the culture of any business is tough. Any book on leadership will tell you that culture starts from the top. Here's the challenge – I was fortunate to work in some of the best restaurants in the world under amazing, inspiring leaders, but I didn't really know what the culture of *my* restaurant should be. I was 31 when we signed the lease and, while I felt like a fully-formed adult, I had (and still have) so much to learn.

When we started to build the team, we realised we urgently needed to develop a training plan and onboarding documents. Some of these are fairly cookie-cutter pieces taken from other restaurants I've worked in, or from our food safety consultants, but it came to define the goals of our small space on North Audley Street. In mid-2021 the BiBi ten commandments – a kind of mission statement – were scribbled on the back of an envelope and they've remained unchanged since day one.

1. Always ask: what would BiBi do?
Before you carry out any action, remember that not only are you representing yourself, but you're also representing your colleagues, friends, managers and the company.

2. Hacks are good, shortcuts are not.
If there is a quicker way to get to the same or better result, great. If not, there is method to our madness.

3. Taste trumps authenticity.
We have access to world-class produce in the heart of London from around all over the British Isles and so should be able to serve it *within* the constraints of our identity. Local doesn't always mean better, but it usually does.

4. Collaborate.
In all ways we can: to build our skills, grow our networks and create opportunities for the restaurant and our team.

5. Work lean, work sustainably.
The menu at BiBi will be low waste and champion less-desired offcuts alongside the most prized produce.

6. We believe that our quality is in the detail.
We are as attentive to the temperature of the room, to the volume of the music, the texture of the cutlery, as we are to our produce.

7. We source with pride.
We will only ever use free-range meat, eggs and sustainably sourced seafood in all our cooking. Vegetables need not be certified organic but must be free of any chemical intervention.

8. Don't be pretentious.
Eating should be convivial and dining out should be enjoyed. We could wear white gloves and have fancy linens – there is a place for that – but that isn't us.

9. Serve produce at its very best.
We are dictated to by the seasons, not our appetite. Nobody really wants a Peruvian fridge tomato in January.

10. Embrace Hospitality.
We're here to help our guests have a good evening. Dining out is about building experiences, laced with conviviality and generosity. Not to chase awards, not to chase cash. We cannot forget that.

The Streets
Shuraat

The importance of the beginning of a meal

The importance of how you begin a meal mustn't be underestimated. Picture it: you arrive at BiBi, walking in from a rainy London evening, probably running late due to tube strikes or a lack of taxis. Or maybe your day at work carried over a little and you lost track of time. If you're like me, it's probably a combination of all of the above. And – if you're also like me – this probably means the person you're meeting will have been waiting at the table for at least ten minutes.

As a restaurant, we have a very short window of time to fix your day. I always stress to my team that people only eat out to be looked after, and to leave the restaurant feeling slightly better than when they came in. It is said that consumers can decide if they're really into a product within ten seconds. And we can walk into an establishment believing that we are going to have a great time, consciously, but something hidden can get in the way. The admirable Professor Barry Gordon wrote, 'We are aware of a tiny fraction of the thinking that goes on in our minds, and we can control only a tiny part of our conscious thoughts'.[1]

When you walk into BiBi, the first thing you see is a reception desk at an angle. While it troubles my OCD immeasurably, the last thing I want a guest to face when they come in is a barrier, so the angle softens the approach. We always have air conditioning units above the front door to ensure guests are warmed or cooled (sometimes even misted) as they walk in. We burn sandalwood incense before every sitting at the restaurant so that guests can be transported either into somewhere exotic or somewhere familiar. Funny how that works. The smell is so nostalgic for anybody who grew up in an Indian household. The first time my brother walked into BiBi, he said 'this smells like Mum'.

And then, the music. Ah, the music. At BiBi, you're likely to be met with the deep baseline of 1980s hip hop. It's a love-it-or-hate-it moment. And that's fine. We soften everything until that point, so we need something that lets you know this isn't a meal at your grand-mother's house. And, it's also the music my cousins and I would listen to at my grandmo-ther's house (hardcore hip hop was banned by our parents, but my grandmother didn't understand enough English to be offended by tracks like N.W.A's 'Fuck the Police' or Snoop Dogg's 'Doggystyle').

As you're guided to the table, maybe you notice the unusual shape of the room, the fully exposed kitchen, the language being used – no 'sir's or 'madam's – or the abstract art on the walls. All of these cues intentionally remove the comfort we so quickly build when you're greeted at the door. It's abrasive, but inoffensive. It's there to remove all preconceptions of a traditional Indian meal.

We start the meal with a broth, hot or cold depending on the weather, as a nod to France's first pre-Revolution restaurants – adopting their original intention to restore – quickly followed with a temperature-appropriate flannel to refresh yourself.

Finally, we start with the food. Some *poppadoms*. How can we keep saying we're not a curry house but then start the meal with a poppadom? Well, that's kind of the point. They are *papads* (let's stick to north Indian nomenclature when possible) and they're served with our take on the same holy trinity of condiments all Indian restaurants serve: yoghurt and mint, chopped onions and chilli and mango chutney. The difference is everything we serve is made in house. And we spike our papads with Wookey Hole cheddar cheese. And when we feel particularly boujis, we add a layer of caviar to the chutney, too.

Familiar but different. Definitely our vibe.

1 If you have time, read any of Professor Gordon's publications. As the Professor of Neurology and Cognitive Science at the Johns Hopkins University School of Medicine, chances are he knows more about what you're thinking than you do.

Passage to India

I have and will talk a lot about how the women in my life have influenced the food at BiBi. But as with Sharmaji's Lahori Chicken (which is named after my grandfather and explored in a later chapter), the *papad* chutney was inspired by my dad scolding me whenever we visited our favourite Indian restaurant growing up, Passage to India in Heston, Middlesex. We eagerly anticipated the beginning of the meal when a basket of *urad dal papad* would hit the table, so distinctly different to the roasted black pepper ones we had at home.

There is a lot in those early dining experiences that I circle back to at BiBi. Sometimes it's a small thing, like the sound of a ticket machine in the kitchen as orders were being placed. Or the smell of deeply roasted kasoori methi [dried fenugreek] that inevitably wrapped throughout the dining room as the extraction was never quite strong enough. And the almost sharp sizzle of the paneer and dressed onions hitting the cast-iron platters as they were being carried out in the kitchen, engulfing us all in a thick smoke. More than anything, I just used to love watching everyone else eat. A voyeur for all the mistakes they would make as they tried to navigate the menu.

My brother would make a kind of pizza with his papad, which was quite unintelligible as it would get soggy and fall apart; good thing he stuck it out with being a lawyer while I focused on the food. My mum, weirdly, just ate it plain. And then there is my dad: from what I understand, his mum was very strict, which really affected his eating habits. He was a big, sporty, hot-blooded Punjabi man in his youth, but would eat demurely. Even to this day he eats his daal with a teaspoon. When it came to selecting his papads, he would take a small piece and a tiny amount of a single condiment – he would eat the mint chutney first, then the mango chutney, and then a dry papad with just the onions and chillies.

I would observe this until the very last minute, when the hot starters arrived, then I would place the chutneys one by one on my plate, just touching but not overlapping. I'd take the papad and wipe from right to left to ripple all the condiments together, so that you could take in all the flavours separately, but ended with the rounded flavour of all three. And, almost like clockwork, my dad would tell me to stop making such a mess on the plate and stop eating 'like a *bhandar* [monkey]'. But the scolding was worth it. The ritual of watching everyone else get it wrong, intentionally building my own appetite, the smug satisfaction of knowing my bite tasted better than everyone else's.

Wookey Hole Chilli Cheese Papad

'Curry house Quavers'. This is probably about as accurate and derogatory a description as you can come up with for this dish. The irony is, this is a Moor Hall recipe, which before that was a L'Enclume recipe and probably before that came from a cookbook that Simon Rogan read. Both of those restaurants are three-Michelin-starred and as far from 'curry house' as you can get.

The recipe starts with a thick, tapioca-based cheese paste. This is steamed in a loaf tin, chilled, rested, sliced, dehydrated, rested again, then deep fried. Of course, this sounds very technical – I've even seen experienced chefs at those three-star restaurants struggle to get it right – but this is exactly the same way papads have been made for thousands of years in India, where they are sun-dried rather than dehydrated (they are also more likely to use the same cast-iron *kadai* [wok] for all the cooking rather than combination ovens and programmed deep-fat fryers). In principle, this is classical Indian cookery, just not how you would expect it.

Then there's the dip. It's the recipe that people most often ask for, because it appears deceptively simple. Of course, you can buy crème fraîche and mango chutney, but the magic is in the chutney. We make it fresh every day, often twice a day to make sure it's fresh for each service. You want to catch the herbs at their peak; and for all the freshness of the onion, ginger and garlic not to be softened by prolonged exposure to the salt and acid. It might seem excessive, but with something so simple, there really is nowhere to hide.

Serves 4

For the papads
28g Green Chilli Pickle (page 224)
400g tapioca flour
200g cave-aged Wookey Hole cheddar
    cheese, finely grated
15g kosher salt
265g filtered water
neutral vegetable oil, for deep frying

For the layered dip
80g Cultured Cream (page 209)
4g green bird's eye chilli, finely chopped
4g Indian onion, finely diced
40g Mango Chutney (page 219)
60g Green Chutney (page 218)

To serve
2-3 dehydrated papads per person
layered dip

Papads

Set up a steamer, or a combination oven, on full steam to 100°C. Grease a 900g loaf tin and line it with parchment paper.

Blend the green chilli pickle to a fine paste in a high-speed blender or Vitamix. Blend the tapioca flour, cheese, green chilli pickle paste and salt in Thermomix or food processor, then add the water slowly while the machine is running, until the mixture forms a homogenous paste. Transfer the tapioca mix into the greased and lined loaf tin. Steam for 1½–2 hours until a thermal probe reads 98°C, then remove from the steamer or oven and leave to cool and set in a refrigerator for at least 24 hours. Using a deli slicer, shave the blocks to a thickness of 1.4–1.6mm, then dehydrate at 65°C for 45 minutes. Turn the slices and dehydrate for a further 45 minutes. Leave the sliced papads to cool down on a tray before storing in an airtight box at room temperature for up to 3 months.

Heat enough neutral vegetable oil for deep frying to 190°C in a deep fat fryer (two-thirds to three-quarters full). Add one papad at a time to the oil, using the back of two slotted spoons to press the papads relatively flat and keep them submerged in the oil until puffed. This usually takes 5–10 seconds, but the papads benefit from a further 10 seconds in the oil after they puff (without being pressed by spoons) to ensure the best results. Carefully drain the excess oil in kitchen paper and keep the papads on a rack under heat lamps while you fry the remaining papads. Once fried, the papads are best eaten within 2 hours.

Layered dip

Put the cultured cream at the bottom of 2 ramekins and spread the chopped chilli and onion over the cream. Cover with mango chutney and tap the ramekin to get rid of any air pockets and flatten the mixture, then cover the dip with green chutney.

Serve

Serve the layered dip alongside the papads.

Sweetcorn Kurkure

Rishi Singh is a new-age Mayfair legend. He stalks Mount Street and its tributaries in almost statesman-like fashion. If you don't know Rishi, you don't really know Mayfair. When BiBi first opened in September 2021, he was one of the first guests through the door and has been coming back every couple of months since. His first question is always the same: 'When's the sweetcorn back on?' (His second question is routinely 'can I get an Old Fashioned?')

Kurkure, for the uninitiated, are India's answer to the Nik Nak, a crispy, extruded corn snack that is enjoyed all over the country, and that my cousin Nanu would smuggle into our home in Bombay whenever she came back from school. When on the menu, we serve it as one of the early snacks, occasionally garnishing it with raw Mylor prawns or the final shavings of Australian winter black truffle, always generously bathing it in our kurkure masala mix. The secret is only use peak-season fresh British sweetcorn, which makes our version a true labour of love; a dish that involves such a great workload that every chef in the kitchen dreads the moment whenever we reach late summer and sweetcorn is at its best.

But, at least it keeps Rishi coming back.

Serves 12

For the yellow chilli emulsion
23g garlic cloves
1 tablespoon neutral vegetable oil
3g kosher salt
17g lemon juice
55g aji amarillo paste
28g egg yolk
2g Kashmiri yellow chilli powder
10g Pre-Hy (page 212)
200g corn oil

For the tempura flour mix
70g plain flour (T26)
275g potato starch
5g kosher salt

For the corn fritters
220g fresh corn kernels (keep the cobs
　for the Sweetcorn Shorba, page 58)
95g cool water
75g tempura flour mix
neutral vegetable oil, for deep frying

To fry again and serve
12 corn fritters
neutral vegetable oil, for deep frying
Kurkure Masala (page 214)
kosher salt
100g Jalapeño Emulsion (page 218)
100g yellow chilli emulsion
cornflowers, to garnish
apple marigold leaves, to garnish

Yellow chilli emulsion
Preheat the oven to 160°C. Wrap the whole peeled garlic cloves and neutral oil in foil and roast in the oven for 1 hour, or until the garlic is completely cooked through and lightly coloured. Blend the salt, roasted garlic, lemon juice, aji amarillo paste, egg yolk, chilli powder and pre-hy together in a food processor. Slowly add the corn oil in a steady stream, while the blade is turning, until the mixture is fully emulsified. Transfer to a fine-tip squeezy bottle and store in the refrigerator for up to 3 days.

Tempura flour mix
Mix all the ingredients together in a bowl until thoroughly combined.

Corn fritters
Make the dry mix by tossing the corn kernels with 15g of the tempura flour mix and set aside. Make the slurry by thoroughly whisking the water in a bowl with the remaining tempura flour mix. Fold the dry mix in the slurry. Place in a container, cover and leave to rest in the refrigerator for 1 hour.

Fry the fritters by heating enough neutral vegetable oil for deep frying to 180°C in a deep fat fryer (two-thirds to three-quarters full). Use a medium ice cream scoop to portion the fritter mix and fry the fritters in batches for 1½ minutes per batch until crispy, turning them once – after 45 seconds – with a spider as they fry. Remove with the spider and drain on kitchen paper to absorb excess oil, season and leave to cool. The fritters can be frozen for up to 1 month; to cook from frozen, fry at 170°C for 2½ minutes.

Fry and serve
Heat enough neutral vegetable oil for deep frying to 180°C in a deep fat fryer (two-thirds to three-quarters full). Once the oil is hot, fry the fritters in batches for a second time for 2 minutes. Remove with a spider and drain on kitchen paper to absorb excess oil, and season liberally with kurkure masala until completely coated, adjusting salt if needed. Make three dots of jalapeño emulsion and yellow chilli emulsion on each of the seasoned corn fritters. Garnish with cornflowers and apple marigold leaves.

Langoustine Ghee Roast

Some of the dishes on the BiBi menu take months, even years, to develop. Others are really forced on us – well, on the team – in minutes or hours. This is not due to my desire to constantly tinker, but by the sudden and unexpected appearance of a temporal ingredient of undoubted beauty. A fleeting moment of pure, natural excellence that we have to shoehorn into the menu. It's one of the reasons we ditched an à la carte menu, so that we can use more ingredients for (sometimes) a few days at a time.

The langoustine ghee roast started life because one of our fishermen mentioned he had Cardigan Bay prawns – these are available at most for a few weeks of the year, so we had to find a way to use them. A few years earlier I had eaten the Chinese dim sum *cheung fung* and noticed a similarity in slippery texture to the *neer dosai* from Bangalore, which are also best served with prawn ghee roast. Well, the Cardigan Bay prawns ran out pretty quickly, but the dish was so perfect we subbed in langoustines, which made it even better.

Serves 4

For the Mangalori sauce
Base
12g coconut oil
5g chana dal
7.5g urad dal
4g cumin seeds
5g coriander seeds
5g white sesame seeds
3g dried gundu chilli
200g coconut milk
2g kosher salt
10g Tamarind Paste (page 208)
5g jaggery

Tempering
25g coconut oil
2.5g black mustard seeds
6 curry leaves
7.5g deggi mirch

For the neer dosa
110g Dosa Batter (page 212)
oil spray

For the ghee roast dressing
20g ghee
20g green bird's eye chilli, cut into fine 3mm brunoise
20g Indian onion, cut into fine 3mm brunoise

For the steamed langoustine
4 langoustines, heads and claws removed (reserve these for another recipe, such as a bisque)
bamboo skewers

To serve
4 steamed langoustines
4 neer dosa strips
20g ghee roast dressing
60g Mangalori sauce
2 lightly toasted curry leaves, cut into a chiffonade

Mangalori sauce
For the base, heat the oil in a frying pan over a medium-high heat. Once hot, add the dals and fry for 1–2 minutes until the edges start to turn golden. Add the cumin, coriander and sesame seeds and fry until the cumin cracks and the mixture is fragrant. Take the pan of tempered spices off the heat, add the gundu chilli, mix it through the oil and allow to infuse for 5 minutes.

Place the masala in a high-speed blender or Vitamix with the coconut milk, salt, tamarind paste and jaggery and blend until smooth. Set aside. To make the finishing tempering, heat the coconut oil in a frying pan over a medium-high heat, add the black mustard seeds and cook until they crack, then add the curry leaves and mix until they splutter. Take the pan off the heat and add the deggi mirch. Fold the tempering through the blended base to finish the sauce.

Neer dosa
Set up a steamer, or a combination oven, on full steam to 100°C. Coat the surface of a 60 x 40cm tray with oil spray. Ladle the dosa batter into the middle of the tray, then spread the batter into a thin layer using an offset spatula, aiming to cover the whole surface of the tray. Place in the steamer and cook for 15 minutes. Take out of the steamer and, while hot, carefully remove the dosa sheet and place it on a chopping board. Trim off the edges to give it a rectangle shape. With the help of a dough wheel cutter (bicyclette), or a knife and a ruler, cut the sheet across the longest side of the rectangle into 6cm-thick strips. You may have to cut them shorter, depending on the size of your langoustines. Roll the strips into themselves. Store in the refrigerator until needed (discard at the end of the day if not used).

Ghee roast dressing
Heat the ghee in a frying pan over a medium-high heat. Once hot, add the chilli and onion and fry for 30 seconds until fragrant and the onion starts to become translucent, then remove from the heat.

Langoustine
Place 2 bamboo skewers through each of the langoustine tails to avoid them from curling when cooking them. Set up a steamer, or a combination oven, on full steam to 100°C. Steam the langoustine tails for 2 minutes. Take out of the steamer and remove the shells while they are still warm. Portion into 6cm pieces, cool down and keep in the refrigerator until ready to serve.

Steam and serve

Set up a bamboo steamer over a boiling pot of water. Season a langoustine piece with kosher salt and roll it in a neer dosa strip. Place the roll in the steamer for 2 minutes, until it is warmed through. Warm the Mangalori sauce in a pan. In a separate pan, warm up the ghee roast dressing. Place ½ tablespoon of warm Mangalori sauce on a plate. Put the langoustine dosa roll next to the sauce. Dress the roll with ghee roast dressing and garnish with chiffonade curry leaves.

Pictured on p.34

The Streets

Hay-roasted Carrot and Passion Fruit Gol Gappa

At BiBi, we occasionally serve *gol gappay* (literally 'round mouthfuls') early in the menu. Sorry Gujratis and Bengalis, these are neither *pani puri* nor *puchke*. A proper Panjabi *gol gappa* is only as good as the *jal jeera* (cumin water) it is served with. The Sharmas are such lovers of *jal jeera* that we drink it chilled, by the glass, in the heat of the Indian summer. We have many variations in the restaurant; pear *jal jeera* is probably the longest serving on the menu, but practically any juice can be modified to hit the same flavour notes of this quintessential *chaat* ingredient. When spiked with tamarind, *chaat masala*, chilli powder, spearmint and dark-roasted cumin, most juice bases can be transformed into something that immediately transports me to Saturday afternoons at my grandmother's house. After hours of rolling, cutting and frying the *puriyan*, boiling, peeling and dicing potatoes and mixing them with black chickpeas cooked the night before, my cousins and I would gorge ourselves on anywhere up to 40 of the classic gol gappa each.

For a restaurant named BiBi, there are really very few dishes that I think my own grandmother would recognise as directly inspired by her own cooking. The gol gappa has always been an exception.

Serves 4

For the hay-roasted carrots
30g hay
200g sand carrots
4g kosher salt, plus extra for covering
20g grapeseed oil

For the toasted hay oil
50g hay
500g grapeseed oil

For the mango ginger buttermilk dressing
30g mango ginger
100g buttermilk
1g kosher salt, or to taste

For the carrot and yellow chilli purée
350g carrots, peeled
5g kosher salt, or to taste
50g toasted hay oil
35g aji amarillo paste
25g orange juice

For the carrot gol gappa mix
60g hay-roasted carrots, diced
16g trout roe
20g ghee roast dressing (page 32)
4g kosher salt
3g Indian green chillies, finely chopped

For the passion fruit and sea buckthorn jal jeera
70g passion fruit purée
10g sea buckthorn purée or juice
20g orange juice
50g water
25g caster sugar
1g roasted ground cumin
0.8g Jeera Chaat Masala (page 214)
1.2g BiBi Chaat Masala (page 213)
0.6g deggi mirch
0.8g black salt
0.8g kosher salt
3.5g Pre-Hy (page 212)

Hay-roasted carrots

Put the hay in a large heavy-based saucepan or pot and place over a high heat. Stir the hay until it starts to emit a sweet smell and turns a deep golden brown. Preheat the oven to 160°C. Put the toasted hay on a baking tray, place the carrots on top of the hay. Roast in the oven for 15 minutes, then remove the tray from the oven. Wrap the hay around the carrots, add the salt and grapeseed oil and seal in a vacuum pouch. Set up a steamer, or a combination oven, on full steam to 100°C. Place the vac-packed carrots on a steamer tray and cook for 20–25 minutes, or until tender. Cool the pack of carrots in iced water to stop them from cooking further. Once cold, remove the carrots from the bag, peel them and cut them into 1cm dice. Reserve in the refrigerator for up to 2 days.

Toasted hay oil

Put the hay in a large heavy-based saucepan or pot and place over a high heat. Stir the hay until it starts to emit a sweet smell and turns a deep golden brown. Set up a dehydrator or an oven to 70°C. Put the toasted hay and grapeseed oil in a vacuum pouch and seal. Put the pouch inside the dehydrator and allow to infuse for at least 12 hours. Pass the mixture through a fine chinois, then discard the hay. Keep the oil in an airtight container in the refrigerator for up to 3 months.

Mango ginger buttermilk dressing

Peel the mango ginger and juice it with a centrifugal juicer. Mix all the ingredients together and adjust seasoning if needed.

Carrot and yellow chilli purée

Set up a steamer, or a combination oven, on full steam to 100°C. Put the carrots, salt and toasted hay oil in a vacuum pouch and seal. Steam the mixture for 40 minutes, or until the carrots are completely soft. Once cooked, strain the carrots. Blend the carrots and the chilli paste and orange juice to a smooth purée in a high-speed blender or Vitamix. Store in a fine-tip squeezy bottle in the refrigerator for up to 2 days.

Carrot gol gappa mix

Mix all the ingredients in a bowl just before serving.

To serve
4 Gol Gappa (page 229)
100g carrot gol gappa mix
20g mango ginger buttermilk dressing
20g carrot and yellow chilli purée
80g passion fruit and sea buckthorn jal jeera
dianthus flowers

Passion fruit and sea buckthorn jal jeera

Blend all the ingredients together in a high-speed blender or Vitamix on full speed for 1 minute. Pass the mixture through a fine chinois lined with muslin cloth. Keep in an airtight container for up to 3 days in the refrigerator.

Assemble and serve

Just before serving, season the chilled carrots with kosher salt and the ghee roast dressing. Open the top of a gol gappa by gently hitting it with the back of a spoon, trying to get a perfect circle. Place 25g of the carrot gol gappa mix at the bottom of the gol gappa and cover it with a teaspoon of the buttermilk dressing. Make 3 small dots of the carrot and yellow chilli purée on top of the carrot mix and around the edge of the hole. Garnish with dianthus flowers. Pour 20ml of the passion fruit and sea buckthorn jal jeera inside the gol gappa and eat right away.

Pictured on p.35

The Streets

Cod Shammi Kebab

When we opened, we used to have a dish called Khatti Meethi Cod on the menu. It was a pain in the arse: we filleted and prepped the cod, wrapped it in a ton of cling film (now a BiBi no-no, as we avoid single-use plastics) and ballotined and portioned it to 100g. For 500g of cleaned cod – a figure you can double if you consider carcass weight – we would get, at best, six usable portions. Which meant for 50 portions, we were getting through close to 9kg of line-caught cod just for a dinner service. We would be left with about 1.5kg of cod trim every day, so we needed to find something to do with it.

I loved the period of my life spent in San Sebastián, and for anybody who has spent any duration of time in the northern Iberian Peninsula, you'll know that they have a special connection with salt cod. A favourite for the team at Mugaritz after a shift (always with a cold beer) were *buñuelos de bacalao*. There is no hiding from it, this shammi kebab is a reimagined version of those late-night snacks, pimped with caviar and best enjoyed with a cold glass of something fizzy.

Serves 12

For the passion fruit and sea buckthorn jal jeera fluid gel
100g passion fruit purée
50g water
25g caster sugar
1g roasted ground cumin
0.8g Jeera Chaat Masala (page 214)
1.2g BiBi Chaat Masala (page 213)
0.6g deggi mirch
0.8g black salt
0.8g kosher salt
3.5g Pre-Hy (page 212)
2.5g agar agar

For the cod shammi kebab
Cod trim mix
150g cod trim
4.5g kosher salt
0.6g ground turmeric
0.3g ajwain seeds
30g neutral vegetable oil

Chana dal mix
60g chana dal, rinsed
22g Indian onion, sliced
3g garlic, chopped
1.2g roasted cumin seeds
3.6g kosher salt
0.6g black peppercorns
1.2g cloves
0.3g whole black cardamom
0.3g cinnamon stick
0.6g turmeric
filtered water, to cover

Shammi mix
6g coriander stems, chopped
1g mint, chopped
3g hot green chillies, chopped
20g Indian onion, grated
3g fresh peeled ginger, grated
22g gluten-free panko breadcrumbs
20g Roasted Besan Flour (page 212)

neutral vegetable oil, for deep frying

Passion fruit and sea buckthorn jal jeera fluid gel
Blend all the ingredients, except the agar agar, together in a high-speed blender or Vitamix. Pass the mixture through a fine chinois lined with muslin cloth, then bring it to the boil in a large saucepan and blend in the agar agar. Remove from the heat and cool down in a container over ice or in the refrigerator for 15–30 minutes until set. Once solid, blend to a smooth, shiny texture in a high-speed blender or Vitamix. Pass through a sieve, place in a container and remove the air in a vacuum machine. Store in a fine-tip squeezy bottle in the refrigerator for up to 3 days.

Cod shammi kebab
Set up a steamer, or combination oven, on full steam to 100°C. Place the cod trim mix ingredients in a vacuum pouch, seal and place in the steamer for 15 minutes. Open the pouch, strain and keep both the juices and cod trim.

Cook the chana dal mix ingredients in a pressure cooker at high pressure, with enough water to cover, for about 40 minutes. Strain the juices and reserve the solid mixture. Blend the solid mixture in a high-speed blender or Vitamix until smooth.

Add the cod trim mix and the shammi mix ingredients to the food processor and blend until a smooth, dry paste is formed. Adjust the seasoning with salt and lemon juice if required.

Heat enough neutral vegetable oil for deep frying to 180°C in a deep fat fryer (two-thirds to three-quarters full).

Portion the kebab mix into 12 x 20g balls. Gently place the balls in the hot oil and fry for 1½–2 minutes until golden brown. Once ready, transfer to a tray lined with kitchen paper to drain any excess oil.

To serve
20g crème fraîche
10g passion fruit and sea buckthorn
    jal jeera gel
4 x 20g shammi kebab
20g N25 Schrenckii caviar

Serve

Put crème fraîche on a plate, then place a dot of the passion fruit gel in the middle. Sit the kebab on top of the gel and crème fraîche and top with a quenelle of Schrenckii caviar.

Pictured on p.44

Bhaiya mama's Malai Kofta

Paradoxically, for anybody who speaks Hindi, *bhaiya mama* translates as 'brother uncle'. Bhaiya wasn't my uncle's birth name, but through some slightly nefarious connections, he was known throughout Gurgaon as 'Bhaiya' by everyone, as a sign of respect. To illustrate why he commanded such respect, let me tell you a story: when my mum first enrolled at the university in Delhi, Bhaiya and his henchman drove motorcycles into the student dormitory and wielded their Colt 1911 pistols (in tribute to Tom Selleck's Magnum, P.I. – they had the trademark moustaches, too) just to make it clear that if anybody crossed my mum, they would have to answer to him. Coincidentally, three weeks later, Mum won the Miss Delhi University beauty pageant, despite not even entering.

Bhaiya mama was a larger-than-life character, and though our time with him was short, it was hugely impactful on my cooking. He was the one who took us to the farmlands in outer Haryana and taught me about how cow dung patties were dried on the roof to be used as fuel. He was the first person to show me how to use a *choola*, a traditional earthenware stove, and teach me how to regulate the heat for different dishes. He had a tandoor in the central courtyard of his home, and we would have the best tandoori rotis I've ever eaten whenever we visited him.

On one trip to see him, we caught a late-night flight from Bombay to Delhi, then had a two-hour drive to his farmhouse. I was seven or eight years old, exhausted, grumpy, and in desperate need of a proper night's sleep. At the front door, bhaiya mama greeted us, along with the armed policeman who doubled up as his private security, and forced us to sit with him and have dinner. Many of my regrets in life are down to my inability to keep a diary. With no official record, I can't remember everything that was on the table, but there was a spread of chutneys, achaars and various vegetable-based north Indian dishes. Yet the memory of watching the cooks bring in a scorchingly hot *tandoori rotiyan* from the courtyard, charred and blackened with the smoke of tamarind wood, and the deepest depth of the *malai kofta kebab* will never leave me. If I close my eyes and still my mind, to this day I can still taste the *jaivitri-elaichi* masala from that meal eaten in the twilight of the dawn in Haryana.

As with all recipes handed down within Indian families, he willingly divulged 80 per cent of the recipe to one of his few remaining bloodline relatives, but also left out just enough to know a lifetime of attempts would only get me so close to the original result. I know that the raisins and cashew nuts inside the *koftay* were fried in ghee, from cold to hot, until the raisins swell. And I know part of the secret was to slowly simmer the cashew and tomato sauce for six to eight hours before smoking it using the classic *dhungar* method – placing a piece of white hot charcoal in a bowl, on top of the sauce, then dressing it with ghee, cardamom and cloves, before sealing the top airtight with a wholewheat *atta* lid. But beyond that, I'm left with no quantities and no temperatures and mostly left to rely on my own experience to recreate inarguably one of the single greatest mouthfuls of food I've ever eaten.

Malai Kofta Kebab

This is a classic example of a dish that snuck onto the menu as a way to use up excess hung yoghurt and paneer trim, but became so popular that we were hanging yoghurt and using portioned paneer just to make the dish. This seldom makes it on the menu these days. While undeniably delicious, it's also quite heavy, and maybe not the most refined way to open a long tasting experience. That said, it's a great canapé for events – it has become a staple for the annual Condé Nast Traveller and Cartier Diwali party we cater – and can be made in fairly large quantities and frozen for use at home.

The mix needs to be as runny as possible. It's going to feel counterintuitive, but the *besan* in the recipe really sets the mix up, especially if you can leave it overnight. Ideally, the cooked kebabs can just about hold their shape but ooze a little when cut into.

Makes 12

For the burnt tomato chutney
500g whole San Marzano tomatoes
100g Indian onion
15g mustard oil
60g rapeseed oil
2.5g black mustard seeds
1g asafoetida
1.5g nigella seeds
2.5g cumin seeds
25g fresh peeled ginger, chopped
12.5g garlic, chopped
15g bird's eye chilli, chopped
10g white caster sugar
7g black salt
7g kosher salt
40g coriander stems
20g Pre-Hy (page 212)
12.5g lemon juice, plus extra if needed

For the malai kofta kebab
Kofta masala
12g black salt
10g fennel seeds
10g cumin seeds
10g royal cumin seeds
10g white peppercorns
2g freshly grated nutmeg

Kebab
100g Buffalo Milk Paneer trim (page 70)
20g Roasted Besan Flour (page 212)
25g Fried Onions (page 225)
12.5g ghee
15g green chilli
10g ginger
10g coriander stems
1g black salt, if needed
1g kosher salt, if needed
6g kofta masala
175g Hung Yoghurt (page 209)
100–150g gluten-free panko breadcrumbs
neutral vegetable oil, for deep frying

To serve
4 x 25g malai kofta kebabs
40g burnt tomato chutney

Burnt tomato chutney
Set up a charcoal grill. Once the charcoal is ready, cook the whole tomatoes and onion over the charcoal, turning them so they char all over. Heat the mustard and rapeseed oils in a saucepan over a medium-high heat, then add the mustard seeds and fry until they crack. Add the rest of the spices, ginger, garlic and chilli and fry for 1–2 minutes until the garlic and ginger are fragrant. Blend the tempering, charred tomatoes and onion, along with the remaining ingredients, in a high-speed blender or Vitamix until smooth. Season with black salt, kosher salt and lemon juice.

Malai kofta kebab
Mix all the kofta masala spices and grind them to a fine powder.

Mix and process all the kebab ingredients except the yoghurt, panko and oil in a Thermomix or food processor to a coarse paste. Mix in the hung yoghurt by hand. Season to taste, if needed, with 50/50 kosher salt/black salt. Using a medium ice cream scoop, divide the mix into 30g portions and finish shaping the koftas by rolling them between your hands to form smooth spheres. Roll in the gluten-free panko.

Heat enough neutral vegetable oil for deep frying to 180°C in a deep fat fryer (two-thirds to three-quarters full). Gently place the koftas in the hot oil and fry for 1½ minutes until golden brown. Once ready, transfer to a tray lined with kitchen paper to drain any excess oil.

Serve
Serve each kofta with burnt tomato chutney on the side.

Pictured on p.45

Truffle and Mooli Dokhla

Many people in my life – my team, my friends and family – often claim I have a non-linear mind; that I start sentences and skip onto the next one halfway through. In my defence, anybody who has met my mother will understand where this comes from. I often start stories and move on before their conclusion because the conclusion becomes clear enough in my own head that discussing it further seems a moot point. Much to my wife's chagrin, I also do this with movies or TV shows, because what's the point in seeing out the journey if you've already reached the destination?

One night, before BiBi opened, I got home late and was starving. My wife had eaten a jacket potato with tuna mayo. We had an avocado, and some dokhla – the quintessential Gujrati semi-sweet-savoury sponge – tucked away at the back of the fridge, along with the leftover tuna mayo. To this day I'm not sure why I did it, but alongside some pickled chillies, I mixed everything together and devoured the lot. Having learnt that tuna mayo and dokhla was apparently 'a thing', I then decided the next step would be to take some crab mayo and do the same. It was even better. Now we top the dokhla – this considered accident of a dish – with a spicy dokhla chutney, truffle mayo to mimic the richness of that original tuna mayo combination, exactly 13 rondels of chives (14 is overkill) and some shaved fresh black truffle.

Serves 12

For the dokhla tempering
50g rapeseed oil
3g black mustard seeds
12g freshly grated coconut
4g white sesame seeds
3g dried red chilli
2g kosher salt
6g coconut water

For the dokhla chutney
25g green chilli
25g Roasted Besan Flour (page 212)
12.5g garlic
60g freshly grated coconut
7.5g roasted ground cumin
25g caster sugar
38g lemon juice
15g kosher salt
125g coriander leaves

For the dokhla
125g besan flour
10g fine semolina
0.8g ground turmeric
4g white caster sugar
2g kosher salt
1.5g citric acid
100g room-temperature water
15g grapeseed oil
1.7g ENO unflavoured fruit salt
oil spray

For the confit mooli
500g mooli
5g kosher salt
100g dokhla tempering
1.5g ajwain seeds

Dokhla tempering
Heat the rapeseed oil in a frying pan over a medium-high heat, then add the mustard seeds and fry until they crack. Add the grated coconut and sesame seeds and cook for 2–3 minutes until light golden. Add the dried chilli and remove from the heat. Allow the mixture to cool. Once cool, add the salt and coconut water. Remove the chilli from the mixture and stir thoroughly. Keep in an airtight container in the refrigerator for up to 5 days.

Dokhla chutney
Put all the ingredients except the coriander in a high-speed blender or Vitamix and blend to a paste. Once the paste is formed, add the coriander and blend until homogeneous and smooth. Store in a fine-tip squeezy bottle in the refrigerator for up to 3 days.

Dokhla
Set up a steamer, or a combination oven, on full steam to 100°C. Spray the mould for the dokhla with the oil spray. At the restaurant, we use 40mm wide, 20mm deep silicone mini muffin moulds, however moulds of other sizes can be used as the dokhla can be portioned once cold.

Put all the dry ingredients except the ENO on a tamis and pass to break any lumps. Add the dry mix to a bowl and slowly whisk in the water and the oil, making sure no lumps form. Allow the batter to rest for 10 minutes at room temperature. The next step needs to be done very fast, as the fruit salts react very quickly: sprinkle the ENO salt on top of the rested batter and whisk vigorously – the batter will start to become lighter in colour and bubbly. Transfer to the greased mould and immediately put inside the steamer. Steam for 12–20 minutes, depending on the size of the mould. The dokhla is ready when you insert a cake tester and it comes out clean. Once the dokhla is ready, remove from the steamer and brush liberally with dokhla tempering. Allow the dokhla to cool at room temperature. Store in an airtight container for 1 day.

For the truffle mayo
20g egg yolk
35g Truffle Paste (page 208)
10g moscatel vinegar
5g lemon juice, plus extra if needed
4g kosher salt, plus extra if needed
7g Pre-Hy (page 212)
165g grapeseed oil

To serve
4 x dokhla
20g dokhla chutney
20g truffle mayo
60g confit mooli
shaved black truffle, to garnish

Confit mooli

Grate the mooli using the fine side of a box grater. Mix the mooli with the salt in a bowl and let it sit in the refrigerator for 30 minutes, then remove the mooli from the bowl in small amounts at a time and squeeze all the water out of it. Place the grated and drained mooli in a vacuum pouch along with the dokhla tempering and ajwain seeds, then seal it. Set up a steamer, or a combination oven, on full steam to 100°C. Place the pouch in the steamer and cook for 30 minutes. The mooli should be soft with a bit of a bite. Cool down and keep the pouch in an airtight container for up to 5 days until ready to serve (let it come to room temperature before serving).

Truffle mayo

Place all the ingredients except the oil in a Thermomix or food processor and blend until fully combined. Slowly add the oil to the mixture while blending until emulsified. Adjust seasoning if needed with salt and lemon juice. Keep in a fine-tip squeezy bottle in the refrigerator for up to 3 days.

Assemble and serve

Set up a steamer, or a combination oven, on full steam to 100°C. Warm up the dokhla in the steamer for 2 minutes. Using the squeezy bottle, stuff the dokhla with the dokhla chutney until it starts to come out of the surface. Place a large dot of truffle mayo on top of the dokhla. Place a tablespoon of confit mooli on top of the truffle mayo and cover it with shaved black truffle.

The dokhla is best eaten while still warm.

C***nation Lobster Pao

Imagine the scene – a 26-year-old Londoner gets a job offer to work with one of the most inspirational chefs in Britain as his Director of R&D. The only caveat: the job is in the depths of Cumbria, where, at the end of his first week, said Londoner is greeted at the local pub as 'the new Asian fella in the village'. My time in the Lakes was formative in so many ways, but the absence of any ethnic food really hit me. I didn't realise how much I had always turned to nostalgic Indian comfort dishes until I was so far removed from Asian ingredients that I could never get a taste of home. At least not without driving an hour each way to Manchester.

One small respite: the Coronation chicken bap at the Cartmel village shop. While in no way Indian, the filling at least had curry powder and mango chutney (also, for reference, ingredients you just don't see in India) to loosely nod at some semblance of the flavours of my childhood. Now, a dish that is so clearly rooted in colonial history, and celebrates the installation of yet another British monarch, really does nothing for me. But, based purely on my personal memories from L'Enclume, I'm happy to celebrate our version at the restaurant whenever we can.

Serves 12

For the crispy chicken skin
200g chicken skin
neutral vegetable oil, for deep frying
kosher salt
Kurkure Masala (page 214)
MSG

For the brown crab mayo
16g egg yolk
40g brown crab meat
24g Mango Chutney (page 219)
10g lemon juice, plus extra if needed
2g kosher salt, plus extra if needed
120g rapeseed oil

For the lobster pao mix
180g picked lobster claw
30g Awadhi Marinade (page 215)
200g brown crab mayo
60g Indian onion, finely chopped
16g green chilli, finely chopped
4g BiBi Chaat Masala (page 213)
kosher salt

To serve
4 x 25–30g Sourdough Pao (page 231)
100g lobster pao mix
12g crispy chicken skin
melted butter, for brushing
chopped chives, to garnish

Crispy chicken skin
Place the chicken skin in a saucepan and cover with water. Bring to the boil and cook for 20 minutes until tender, then drain. Lay out the skin on dehydrator trays and leave to dehydrate overnight at 60°C.

Heat enough neutral vegetable oil for deep frying to 180°C in a deep fat fryer (two-thirds to three-quarters full). Fry the skins in the oil until golden brown and crispy. Remove from the oil, drain on kitchen paper, then season with kosher salt and allow to cool before cutting into a large crumb. Dust generously with kurkure masala and season with salt and MSG. Store in an airtight container at room temperature for up to a week.

Brown crab mayo
Put all the ingredients except the oil in a Thermomix or food processor and blend until fully combined and the mango chutney is fully smooth. Slowly add the rapeseed oil to the mixture, while blending, until emulsified. Adjust seasoning with extra salt and lemon juice, if needed. Store in a fine-tip squeezy bottle in the refrigerator for up to 3 days (the lobster pao and mayo together will keep for a maximum of 3 days).

Lobster pao mix
Set up a charcoal grill. In a bowl, mix the picked lobster claw with the Awadhi marinade. When the charcoal is ready, put the marinated lobster claw in a metal sieve and cook directly over the charcoal. When it is fully cooked, remove from the heat and allow to cool. When the lobster claw is cool, add it to a bowl along with the brown crab mayo, chopped onion, chilli and chaat masala. Mix thoroughly and store in an airtight container in the refrigerator for up to 3 days.

Heat and serve
Set up a combination oven at 160°C 60% humidity steam roast. With the help of a knife, create a pocket in your pao to stuff with the lobster mixture. Warm up the pao in the oven for 3 minutes, then remove and brush the tops with melted butter. Stuff the pocket you made before with the lobster mixture. Garnish with crispy chicken skin and finely chopped chives.

The Garden
Kethi

Child of the land

I was born and raised outside London as the child of two accountants. One of these acc-ountants is from India, the other from Kenya. Each of their parents is from Northern India (75% Punjabi, 25% Haryanvi – which was historically Punjab anyway). One of those four grandparents was from a large city, Lahore, the others were all from farming communities. My parents and both my grandmothers are / were (respectively) vegetarians.

Growing up we were always surrounded by lots of wonderful ingredients. Some would be grown by our family – wet walnuts and greengages fresh off the tree in late summer just hit different – or foraged from the hedgerows behind my uncle's house nearby. This was back in a time where Berkshire was still a grower-friendly area, much of the farmland taken over by cookie-cutter housing developments. Other slightly more exotic produce would make it into our kitchen from speciality Indian shops or be occasionally smuggled in by Mum from a recent trip to India. It's hard to imagine but there was a time when alphonso mangoes, pickles, chikoo fruits and even spices would need to be brought over as contraband hidden in suitcases. She did this with such regularity that we even had – perhaps she still has – ded-icated suitcases for the transport of ingredients to and from India, as once the smell of kasoori methi seeps into the fabric, nothing will take it out.

In addition to the ingredients, there were many practices in my family home that seem nor-mal because of our heritage, but would probably seem quite unusual to non-Indians. Or, in the new world of sourdoughs and kimchis, maybe not? We made pretty much everything ourselves. Our own ghee, yoghurt, bread, achars or pickles, and ferments. Part of this was necessity; you just couldn't buy idli batter in England in the 90s. But this was more to do with the way our family had lived for a very long time. When we went back to India, we would go a step further; whether it was grinding wheat daily to make *rotiyan* or using a wicker *soop* to de-hull lentils with my aunt's grandmother in Haryana (one of my earliest memories).

Hopefully this backstory helps explain why the quality and provenance of ingredients – vegetables first and foremost – are the lifeblood of our cooking. Any chef who has passed through the BiBi kitchen will confirm that the stress we put on the cooking of vegetables is often even higher than that of meat or fish. I often say to chefs as they graduate onto the grill section that it's much easier to make a fillet of fish delicious, only a true chef can do the same to a piece of celeriac.

Western chefs are taught from the moment they can first tie an apron around their waists that fish needs to be cooked to a perfect opaque pearly white, ideally with a rainbow on the cut flesh, to show off the birefringence properties of the protein (for all my fellow physicists). Similarly, we need to cook red meat so that it 'blushes' with a perfect *cuisson* – evenly pink throughout but deep-golden brown outside. But we don't really have any ref-erences for vegetables outside of 'al dente', which literally means 'to the tooth'. Maybe the biggest gift and curse from the Italian kitchen. I love Italian food – I always say I became a chef working for Giorgio at Locanda Locatelli – but the idea that every vegetable should be cooked to retain a bite just doesn't sit well with me. Who honestly wants a squeaky green bean? Or a chickpea that has any remnants of a chalky texture? And in the right setting, isn't an overcooked carrot just a thing of joy?

Early in your career as a chef, you don't necessarily have the confidence to stand up for what you know to be true. The euro-centric way of cooking was so drilled into me that I remember one Christmas I made a huge spread of different traditional dishes, with every vegetable cooked 'restaurant perfect' but when we sat down, they were the saddest brussels sprouts I had ever eaten. It was only through travel that I realised that cultures around the world value braised, slow-cooked vegetables that are on the verge of falling apart.

Every vegetable requires the same respect that you would give a piece of meat. In fact, the artistry behind cooking whole vegetables well is even more challenging than a piece of well butchered meat because nature doesn't believe in consistent shapes and sizes.

Assamese Mushroom Chai

This is the perfect opening to a meal at BiBi - and people never recognise anything about it except the name 'chai'. Before the British came to India and challenged the Chinese monopoly on the burgeoning tea industry, Indians drank a 'chai' based on ayurvedic principles, spiked with liquorice, angelica and lots of warming spices, but definitely without sugar, milk or even what we now recognise as tea leaves. See, *Camellia sinensis* (quite literally 'tea leaves from China') is a Jurassic-era plant that has a documented 5000-year history in Yunnan province. *Camellia assamica* (yep - tea from Assam) is an equally ancient plant, though it has a slightly less storied and refined history in India. This variety is what Indians were using for tea pre-colonialism.

Bibi - by complete coincidence - is a rice farmer in Assam who first offered me a real chai and I was completely taken aback. Just like Bibi made me rethink what Indian gastronomy is, so we aim to do the same at BiBi.

Makes 1 litre

0.8g ajwain seeds
2.3g white peppercorns
1.5g black peppercorns
2g whole dried ginger
0.6g fennel seeds
0.6g cassia bark
5g grapeseed oil
12g garlic, thinly sliced
40g Indian onion, thinly sliced
1.2g dried Gundu chilli
0.6g dried liquorice sticks
0.6g dried angelica root
0.6g green cardamom seeds
50g dried mixed wild mushrooms
10g dried shiitake
5g fresh thyme
75g madeira
1kg cold water
12g kombu
12g gluten-free soy sauce
1g fresh habanero chilli
0.5g star anise
1.5g MSG
kosher salt
sherry vinegar, to taste

To serve
160g mushroom chai
8g MSG Oil (page 221)
4g puffed buckwheat
   (Puffed Grains - page 226)

Preheat the oven to 160°C. Roast the ajwain, white and black peppercorns, dried ginger, fennel seeds and cassia bark on a baking tray in the oven for 4 minutes.

Heat the grapeseed oil in a large saucepan or pot over a medium heat, add the sliced garlic and onion and sweat slowly for 5 minutes until soft and translucent. Add the roasted spices, Gundu chilli, liquorice, angelica and cardamom and cook for 1–2 minutes until fragrant. Add the dried mushrooms and thyme and cook for 15 minutes.

In a separate pan, bring the madeira to the boil and reduce to a glaze consistency, then add it to the mushrooms at the end of their 15-minute cooking time. Add the water, kombu and soy sauce to the mushrooms, bring to the boil, reduce the heat to medium-low and simmer for 3 hours. Alternatively, decant it into a gastro and cook with a lid on in a steam oven at 85°C for 12 hours.

Remove from the heat and add the habanero and star anise. Cover the pan and let it infuse for 1 hour.

Serve
Pass the mix through a fine chinois and season it with the MSG and salt and sherry vinegar to taste. Serve warm in a cup with a few drops of MSG oil and the puffed buckwheat.

Sweetcorn Shorba

Like many of our dishes at the restaurant, this was a last-dash innovation to use an ever-growing pile of food 'waste'. We love the Sweetcorn Kurkure (page 30), but the problem with them is that we just keep ending up with so many stripped cobs of corn.

I wax lyrical about my grandmothers' cooking, but this one I owe to my mum. She used to make a very unusual, very watery sweetcorn curry, often pressure-cooked with potatoes, which we would then mash into the liquor to thicken the broth into something more suited to eating with *rotiyan*. Indians really can't get enough of double carbs, so why not throw in a third for good measure? The memory of taking the stripped cobs, letting them soak in the thickened soup and then sucking them up after is so visceral, and so reminiscent of late summer when the corn is at its very best. Even writing it, I can picture the scent of our cricket whites – such a distinct smell for anybody who has ever worn them – as we sat in the garden as the sky turns dusky, my brother and I slurping away at sweetcorn 'waste'. While I would love to challenge guests to suck on cobs in the same way, this shorba is probably a better approach for Mayfair.

Serves 12

For the sweetcorn broth
12.5g garlic, roughly chopped
50g Indian onion, roughly chopped
60g celery, roughly chopped
500g corn cobs
1kg water
5g black peppercorns
2.5g coriander seeds
5g coriander stems
1g Indian bay or cassia leaves

For the broth seasoning
5g kosher salt
9g Maggi Masala (page 214)
2g Maggi Tastemaker (page 214)
6g Kurkure Masala (page 214)
55g dashi vinegar

To serve
160g sweetcorn shorba
8g Green Curry Oil (page 220)

Sweetcorn broth
Place the chopped vegetables in a large saucepan or pot with the rest of the broth ingredients. Bring to the boil, then reduce the heat and simmer for 2 hours. After 2 hours, pass the broth through a fine chinois. Bring the broth back to a simmer.

Broth seasoning
Add all the ingredients for the broth seasoning except the dashi vinegar and blend with a hand blender until all the spices are fully combined with the broth. Take off the heat and pass the broth through a fine chinois lined with muslin cloth, then add the vinegar.

Serve
Serve the sweetcorn shorba warm in a cup with several drops of green curry oil.

Calixta from Flourish Farm

The biggest compliment I can pay Calixta is that she refused to work with me, for years. So protective is she about her produce that, like an exclusive member's club, you need to be put forward by one of her existing customers. A list of some of those existing customers, for reference, is probably indirectly the second biggest compliment I can pay her: Lyle's, Kol, Ikoyi and Brat. But it's not just Michelin stars or a ranking in The World's 50 Best that gets you on their books. Produce-led casual restaurants, including Anglo Thai, Smoking Goat, Manteca and Noble Rot, all proudly fly the Flourish flag. Basically, everywhere I want to eat on my days off. Even then, the farm is so small and the output so carefully managed that Calixta and her team really don't like taking on new business. And when they do, it's a mad scramble as soon as their list is released for us to all secure whatever passes their strict standard checks.

Why all the hype? Flourish is almost perfectly located on fields just up from the river Granta in South Cambridgeshire and has only been in existence since 2017. Calixta and her two co-founders – working horses Bill and Ben – transformed the land into a regenerative haven, carefully cultivating the soil first, before even thinking about sowing any seeds. For Flourish, the soil is their long-term investment. Their work is all centred around harbouring a vibrant growing medium, while never straying from their biodiverse and organic practices. With time, their practices have built a self-sustaining ecosystem that is conducive to growing world-class produce, without reliance upon intervention and synthetic inputs.

When you visit the farm, you're often greeted by a muddy Calixta and an almost black soil, thriving with life in the form of small insects, field animals and an abundance of the right kinds of microorganisms. From this single farm, we're able to source Heritage April bearded wheat, potatoes, apples, aubergines, cucumbers, pumpkins, strawberries, grapes (!), and every type of brassica and herb you can imagine. And tomatoes. Lots and lots of tomatoes.

While my background in India is agricultural, we didn't grow a great deal here in England. My mother has rediscovered her green thumbs as she's got older, but as children there were very things that we got from our garden, just Victoria plums, walnuts, cherries, wild strawberries and pears, a few cooking apples, and the odd harvest of spinach… Actually, maybe we did grow more than I remember. But I'll never forget the first year we planted tomatoes out in the garden. I was fascinated by the rate at which the plants sprung up. It seemed like it took just weeks from planting them out from the nursery for the plant to reach full maturity. Even flowering that year as early as May. And then, nothing. I waited until the end of September for those pea-sized tomatoes to grow and ripen but they never got there. We would brush past the plants daily as we ran out into the garden to play football or cricket, and the smell off the vine is still something that intrinsically screams 'summer'. Only when I went to my grandmother's friend's house did I see how well tomatoes can grow in the UK, when given the right environment. And that's exactly what Calixta has managed to curate at Flourish.

From around June, we start to see the season unfold through the different tomatoes being harvested at Flourish. First there's Mirabelle Blanche, smallish cherry tomatoes with a pale colour. As an early-season crop they never really develop a great deal of that sun-kissed sweetness you get with European tomatoes, but they're incredibly clean and well balanced. Then, the Indigo Blue beauties; a purple-hued tomato that tells you when it's ready to eat as it turns purple-red at full maturity. These are closely followed by Pineapple tomatoes, so called for their yellow colour and intense fruity aroma, and finally, at the very peak of summer, we start to see the Sungold, Gardener's Delight and Sugardrop tomatoes; all small, intensely sweet tomatoes that really hit their stride in the longest, hottest days of the year, almost cooking on the vine to take on an overt jammy quality. There are only a few weeks of the year where all of these tomatoes overlap; and that's when we serve an old favourite, the Cambridgeshire Tomato Salaad, in the restaurant.

Cambridgeshire Tomato Salaad

It's amazing how a dish can survive the test of time, as everything around it becomes more complex and challenging. Whenever we hit peak tomato season, this salaad makes a cameo. It's also interesting how someone who had absolutely nothing to do with its creation can become forever linked to it. Step forward Joanne Searley, Chief Operating Officer of JKS restaurants.

What you don't really see behind the scenes of a restaurant opening is the gamut of tastings held with investors. And this was a dish that never hit the right note with Jyo or Karam. For all their expertise, they're really just not salad people. And sometimes when you give them an undeniably delicious ingredient, they just shrug. But Joanne happened to be at the table the day we put this dish up for a tasting in mid-summer 2021 and said 'this is exactly the kind of thing I miss whenever I eat at any of our other Indian restaurants. I could smash a whole bowl of that every single time I eat here'. And when it's on the menu, she does.

Now, as the restaurant has moved forward, we sometimes serve this with raw scallops, lightly poached lobster – cooked in tomato-infused oil and served just above room temperature, it's a magical thing – or even lightly cured tuna or gently grilled red mullet. Just nothing that takes too much from something that represents a clean mouthful of summer.

Serves 4

For the pav bhaji oil
115g Pav Bhaji Masala (page 214)
375g Tomato Oil (page 224)

For the tomato dressing
250g Tomato Water (page 209)
75g dashi vinegar
20g mirin
6.75g kosher salt

For the spiced sheep's ricotta
6g nigella seeds
250g sheep's ricotta
25g Yoghurt Whey (page 209)
4g kosher salt
5g dried mint
10g Pre-Hy (page 212)

For the demisec tomatoes
200g datterini tomatoes
2g kosher salt
2g icing sugar
4g Lemon Oil (page 221)

To serve
2–3 medium heritage West Sussex tomatoes
8 demisec tomatoes
5g fresh peeled ginger, brunoised
5g green bird's eye chilli, brunoised
4g Green Curry Oil (page 220)
20g Indian Lemon Dressing (page 216)
Maldon salt, to taste
60g spiced sheep's ricotta
12g Indian onion, thinly sliced
assorted herbs (apple marigold, Thai basil, mint and dill)
assorted edible flowers (calendula and tagetes)
20g pav bhaji oil
60g tomato dressing

Pav bhaji oil
Put the pav bhaji masala and tomato oil in a saucepan and heat the mixture to 100°C over a medium-high heat. Cook for 30 minutes at 100°C, then take off the heat and pass the mixture through a fine chinois lined with a muslin cloth. Store the oil in an airtight container in the refrigerator for up to 1 month.

Tomato dressing
Mix all the ingredients together with a hand blender. Store in a fine-tipped squeezy bottle in the refrigerator for up to 5 days.

Spiced sheep's ricotta
Toast the nigella seeds in a frying pan over a medium-high heat until fragrant. Place the seeds on a tray to cool down. Blend all the ingredients except the nigella seeds in a food processor until smooth. Fold in the toasted nigella seeds, place in an airtight container and keep in the refrigerator for up to 3 days.

Demisec tomatoes
Bring a pan of water to the boil. Use a small, serrated knife to score a cross-shaped incision into the bottom of each datterini tomato. Prepare a large container with iced water. Put the tomatoes in the boiling water for 10 seconds, remove with a slotted spoon and immediately shock them in the iced water, then peel the tomatoes with a small knife and discard the skin. Place the peeled tomatoes in a bowl and toss with the salt, sugar and lemon oil until fully coated. Set up a dehydrator or an oven to 65°C. Put the tomatoes on a tray, making sure they do not touch each other, and dehydrate for 2 hours. Remove from the dehydrator, allow to cool at room temperature and keep in an airtight container in the refrigerator for up to 3 days.

Assemble and serve
Cut the heritage tomatoes in uneven shapes of the same size. Put the cut tomatoes, demisec tomatoes, ginger, chilli, green curry oil and lemon dressing in a bowl. Mix and season with Maldon salt. Place the spiced ricotta in the middle of a bowl and shape into a circle with the back of a spoon. Top with the seasoned tomatoes and garnish with onion slices, herbs and flowers. In a jug, mix the pav bhaji oil with the tomato dressing. Pour the dressing on the side of the bowl to surround the salad.

Shrub

I've already waxed lyrical about the single-farm obsessiveness of Calixta at Flourish Farm in Cambridgeshire. Sam and Harry are like-minded in their desire to deliver the very best ingredients to chefs up and down the A23 from London to Brighton. But that's where the similarities end, because Harry and Sam aren't farmers. While Calixta has her hands in the soil every day, the boys are zipping between a co-operative of farms in Sussex to brochure the best ingredients the southeast can offer.

Also, unlike Calixta, who trained with the best organic and regenerative farmers in the world, the team at Shrub worked in professional kitchens, organic permaculture farms and food-chain logistics. During this time, they identified the desire of chefs to get more connected with their farmers and ingredients, while small, emerging farmers wanted to ensure their hard-grown produce was going to chefs who would show their work the respect it deserves. They decided to do this all during the pandemic. And that's partly because they felt that public perception of farm-to-table truly changed from something that chefs pay lip service to, into a true focus for the best chefs and restaurants in the UK.

One freezing January morning, we set out to West Sussex to meet Harry and visit some of the farms that had joined the Shrub co-operative. I've spent enough time on British farms in the dead of winter to understand what the reality is. It's a challenge we often have with guests who ask why we serve a progression of brassicas and root vegetables like beetroot, celeriac, cauliflower, kohlrabi and turnips on our vegetarian tasting menu. It's because there is literally *nothing* else growing. But there is beauty in these vegetables, which is why we love to use them. Conscious the farms wouldn't be in full bloom, we were expecting to at least see some plant life in the form of leeks, cabbage, some carrots. Maybe the odd polytunnel with micro leaves which tend to keep plugging away during the more barren months.

On this particular morning, the ground still somewhat sodden and frosty from a light snow-fall a week earlier, we saw just how desperate the so-called 'hunger gap' could be. In our naivety we took Anton, our food photographer, along with us to capture some images of the farms, but instead what greeted us was a veritable tundra. It looked more appropriate for the crew of BBC's Planet Earth than some chefs from a swanky Mayfair restaurant and their Leica-wielding, equally swanky photographer.

The positive message is that it isn't always this way. Even in the dead of winter we're still able to source great winter greens and root vegetables through Shrub. Ingredients that are gnarly and odd-sized, sometimes particularly muddy because they are still alive from the soil. These ingredients still taste like fruit and vegetables are supposed to taste. When the season turns, for around nine months of the year, the proximity of these incredible farms across the southeast means that the restaurant is provided with genuinely world-class ingredients as vibrant as the moment they were plucked from the ground. And there are few people I trust more than Harry and Sam to make sure we get the very finest.

Dahi Aubergine

Aubergines are one of the few ingredients that have a surprisingly long season and have adapted to a vast range of growing conditions. However, indigenous to the Indian subcontinent, it's rare to find an aubergine that really tastes of much outside of its native lands. For me, there are only two ways to cook this vegetable properly. Namely, grilled with lots of oil or deep fried. Nobody ever wants an undercooked aubergine; the concept of al dente doesn't really fit this particular member of the nightshade family.

Classic dahi aubergine is usually fried, then topped with copious amounts of yoghurt. Instead, we take the quintessential Chettinad spicing from Tamil Nadu, confit and then grill the aubergines before serving them on top of a tempered yoghurt known as *pachadi*. The salad on top comes from my own love of eating large amounts of leaves and herbs, especially when served alongside grilled meats as this was in the early days of BiBi.

Serves 4

For the imli miso aubergine
250g Japanese long aubergines
2.5g kosher salt
30g MSG Oil (page 221)
100g Imli Miso (page 216)

For the pachadi
120g Hung Yoghurt (page 209)
30g natural yoghurt
120g crème fraîche

Tempering
10g grapeseed oil
5g urad dal
2g black mustard seeds
2g cumin seeds
1g fennel seeds
5 curry leaves
10 dried long Indian red chillies
0.5g black salt
1g kosher salt

For the herb salad
10g picked coriander leaves
10g picked mint leaves
10g picked Thai basil leaves
10g torn red shiso leaves
8g Indian onion, thinly sliced
2g toasted sesame seeds
10g Indian Lemon Dressing (page 216)
Lime Leaf Chaat Masala (page 214), to taste

To serve
250g pachadi
200g grilled imli miso aubergine
6g puffed quinoa (page 226)
60g herb salad
10g Green Curry Oil (page 220)
6g Fried Onions (page 225)

Imli miso aubergine
Peel the aubergines, trim the ends and trim the aubergines to be the same size. In a bowl, mix the aubergines with the salt and let them sit at room temperature for 10 minutes. Drain to remove the excess water coming out of the aubergines, put the aubergines in a vacuum pouch, ladle in the MSG oil and seal. Set up a steamer, or a combination oven, on full steam to 90°C. Place the pouch of aubergines in a steamer tray and cook for 30 minutes until they are cooked but still hold their shape. Cool the sealed aubergines in iced water to avoid them from overcooking. Once cool, remove them from the pouch and cut them into 10–15cm segments. Lay 3 segments in parallel and, using two thin flat metal skewers, skewer them across. Set up a charcoal grill with some binchotan charcoal. Brush the aubergines with the imli miso, then grill for 2–4 minutes until they are fully caramelised and lightly charred.

Pachadi
Combine the hung yoghurt, natural yoghurt and crème fraîche in a bowl.

To make the tempering, heat the grapeseed oil in a frying pan over a medium-high heat. Add the urad dal and fry until the edges start to turn golden, then add the mustard seeds. When the seeds splutter, add the cumin and fennel seeds, curry leaves and dried chillies. Stir for 30 seconds until fragrant. Take off the heat, add the salts and remove the chillies. Pour the tempering over the yoghurt and crème fraîche mixture and fold with a maryse (flexible spatula) until fully incorporated.

Herb salad
Mix all the ingredients in a bowl and season with the lemon dressing and lime leaf chaat masala right before serving.

Serve
Place 4 tablespoons of pachadi on the bottom of a plate and make a well in the middle with the back of a spoon big enough for the aubergine pieces. Remove the grilled aubergine from the skewers and place it in the middle of the pachadi, then cover them with 2 tablespoons of puffed quinoa. Top the aubergines with the seasoned herb salad and green curry oil, and garnish with onion slices and fried onions.

Buffalo Milk Paneer

Living next door to my grandparents was Kumar aunty. As a child, visiting Kumar aunty was like visiting Ursula from The Little Mermaid; she was severely obese – closer to my grandparents' age, but still retained the moniker 'aunty' as is traditional in India – and rarely moved off the *manja* bed in her front room. She had a lot of affection for me, my brother and my cousin, but was surly in her demeanour. As she was the only member of the local swimming pool and sports club – no idea why – we were sent to spend an afternoon with her as payment-in-kind for access to the only pool within walking distance. When it's 30°C+ everyday, this is a small price any eight-year-old would gladly pay.

While the pool was the oasis-like draw, the second benefit would be the chilli cheese toasties served in the clubhouse after our swim. These would be made with grated paneer, fresh Indian onions and spicy green chillies, and be well coated in ghee before being fried in an old cast-iron toasted sand-wich machine. Scalding hot, liberally dusted with the secret 'sandwich masala' and served alongside Maggi tomato ketchup, there was nothing better to eat as the sun drew in another day and we dried off from the relief of the swimming pool.

Note: this cheese, due to the lack of fermentation and salt, spoils very quickly. If you plan to keep the cheese for longer than a few days, I would recommend brining the cheese as we do in the restaurant.

Serves 4

For the buffalo milk paneer
1kg fresh buffalo milk
100g live cultured buttermilk

For the grass-fed ghee
250g grass-fed cultured butter

For the brined paneer
2.5kg water
175g kosher salt
500g buffalo milk paneer

To serve
30g grass-fed ghee
160g brined paneer
20g Indian onion, brunoised
20g green bird's eye chilli, brunoised
Sharmaji Masala (page 215), for dusting

Buffalo milk paneer
Heat the buffalo milk in a large heavy-based saucepan or pot over a very gentle heat, stirring it constantly with a stiff spatula to avoid it scorching. When the milk reaches between 70°C and 75°C, whisk in the buttermilk gently, making sure to not incorporate any air. Heat the milk for 30–40 minutes until the solids curdle into cheese curds, and remove from the heat once there is a clear separation of curds and whey. Leave to cool to about 40°C, then strain the curds over a muslin-lined mould and press the cheese overnight with weights in the refrigerator. Once fully set and chilled, turn out the cheese and portion as needed.

Grass-fed ghee
Cook the butter in a large heavy-based saucepan or pot over a low heat for 15 minutes, without stirring, until the milk solids start to stick to the bottom of the pan. At this point, remove the pan from the heat and allow to rest for 15 minutes. Pass the melted butter through a fine chinois lined with muslin cloth. Store the ghee in glass jars at room temperature for up to 1 month.

Brined paneer
In a pan, mix the water with the salt and bring it to the boil. Cut the paneer into 2cm-thick slices using a cheese wire and place the portioned paneer in a deep heatproof container. Once the brine comes to the boil and the salt has dissolved, pour the solution over the paneer and leave it to brine for 30 minutes. After 30 minutes, remove the paneer from the brine, cool it down, dry it on a cooling rack in the refrigerator for 1 hour, then store it in an airtight container in the refrigerator until needed. Depending on the quality of the paneer, once brined it should keep for up to 7 days in the refrigerator.

Finish and serve
Heat a cast-iron pan to smoking point. Add 3 tablespoons of ghee and place the paneer in the middle. Put the onion and chilli in a metal bowl and set aside. Cook the paneer for 3–5 minutes until the bottom is crisp and caramelised. Remove from the pan. Pour the ghee from the pan over the onion and chilli mix. Place the mix in the middle of a plate and rest the paneer on top, caramelised side up. Pour the remaining ghee over the paneer and dust liberally with Sharmaji masala.

Okra Salan

Second only to aubergine, okra has to be my favourite exotic ingredient. I say exotic because, while most Indians will argue that okra (or *bhindi* as it is more often known) is from the sub-continent, its origins are more likely from the east coast of Africa. Technically, it was all one supercontinent around 150 million years ago so who are we to draw such arbitrary lines?

All I know is that bhindi is something that would almost always be in the fridge at home because of its versatility and how quickly it cooks. When we train new people on the grill section how to cook this dish, we often say it's better to almost forget that you need it, so you cook it right at the last minute, to keep the shape and colour of the vegetable, but making sure any of the slimy parts inside are properly cooked out.

Serves 4

For the peanut and sesame salan
20g white sesame seeds
50g peeled peanuts
3g white poppy seeds
10g desiccated coconut
375g room-temperature water, plus 50g
     extra if needed
100g grapeseed oil
3g cumin seeds
10g garlic, roughly chopped
10g fresh peeled ginger, roughly chopped
1g fenugreek seeds
2g curry leaves
5g Kashmiri chilli powder
5g ground turmeric
2g Garam Masala (page 213)
10g kosher salt
50g Fried Onions (page 225)
20g Tamarind Paste (page 208)
20g jaggery

For the okra chilli mix
25g Indian onion
15g long green chilli, ends trimmed
15g okra fingers, ends trimmed
15g MSG Oil (page 221)

For the peanut podi oil
40g peeled peanuts
1g kosher salt
85g Peanut Oil (page 221)
25g Peanut Oil pulp (page 221)

To serve
10-14 okra fingers
60g okra chilli mix
120g peanut and sesame salan
40g peanut podi oil

Peanut and sesame salan
Preheat the oven to 160°C. Put the sesame seeds on a roasting tray and roast in the oven for 5 minutes. Open the oven, add the peanuts and white poppy seeds to the tray and roast for 10 more minutes or until golden, mixing them every 3-4 minutes to ensure they roast all over. Remove and set aside. Put the desiccated coconut on a separate tray and roast in the oven for 9 minutes, stirring it every 3 minutes to ensure all of it gets golden. Once golden, add it to the peanut and sesame mix. Add the peanut, sesame and coconut mixture to a food processor along with 100g of the water and blend until a butter texture is achieved. Reserve.

Heat the grapeseed oil in a large saucepan over a medium-high heat. Add the cumin and fry until it starts cracking, then add the chopped garlic and ginger and the fenugreek seeds and fry for 1 minute until fragrant. Add the curry leaves and cook until they splutter. Turn off the heat. Add the Kashmiri chilli powder, turmeric, garam masala, salt, fried onions, tamarind and jaggery. Mix in the pan with the residual heat. Put the remaining 275g of water in a blender with the peanut and sesame mixture and the onion and spices mixture. Blend at full speed until smooth, adding 50g more water if needed. Pass through a fine chinois. Cool and store in an airtight container in the refrigerator for up to 5 days.

Okra chilli mix
Thinly slice all the vegetables using a mandoline and mix them in a bowl with the MSG oil. Set up a charcoal grill. Once the charcoal is ready, place the sliced mixture in a metal sieve and cook directly over the charcoal until the onions are translucent. Store in an airtight container at room temperature for up to 3 hours.

Peanut podi oil
Preheat the oven to 160°C. Mix the peanuts with the salt and 10g of the peanut oil. Place the peanuts on a baking tray and roast in the oven for 10 minutes, stirring them every 3 minutes to ensure they colour all over. Remove from the oven and, once cool, place them with the rest of the ingredients in a bowl and mix thoroughly. Keep in an airtight container at room temperature for up to 5 days.

Finish and serve
Set up a charcoal grill. Trim both ends of the okra and, when the charcoal is ready, grill them until blistered and lightly charred all over. Warm up the peanut and sesame salan in a pan. Place the okra chilli mix in the middle of a plate. Put the peanut podi on top of the okra chilli mix. Pour the warm peanut and sesame sauce around the okra chilli mix. Rest the grilled okra on top of the okra chilli mix and serve.

Tushar Dada from Maharashtra

The following memory is laced with warm nostalgia, but also a sadness about the future of Indian agriculture. I was spending a little time in Mumbai and Pune, researching the region's traditional sub-cultures. I had spent so much of childhood in Bombay, as it was then known, so felt fairly confident that I could skip the basics of *dabeli, pav bhaji, ghatti masala*, etc. but needed to get to grips with the more traditional ingredients and preparations from the area. In stepped Ruchi Jain. A college mate of mine at Oxford, but strangely someone who I didn't know until one of India's leading chefs Prateek Sadhu (then of Masque restaurant) introduced us. Then Thomas Zacharias (then of the Bombay Canteen) did the same, then Ranveer Brar, who can only be described as the Jamie Oliver of Indian cuisine… If she had their attention, she definitely deserved mine. In fact, Prateek went as far as to say, 'If you ever need any ingredient from India, Ruchi is the ultimate fixer'.

Bhai jaan (older brother), as I've come to know her, is a kindred spirit. Her family, like mine, is from the Pakistani side of Punjab. She's highly educated, highly opinionated, boisterous, and works just about as hard as anybody I know. You can see why we get on. She runs a company called Taru Naturals, procuring heritage Indian ingredients from independent farms and small farming communities that she found during her time with the World Bank Ministry of New and Renewable Energy in rural India, all based on the research of Ruchi's mother. Sidenote: she just happens to be one of the world's leading authorities on traditional ayurvedic cooking.

Ruchi's driver picked me up one dusky February morning and, despite it being 7am, she was already on the phone to a potential customer in the back, with two giant bottles of water. She covered the mouthpiece: 'So, Chetan, we're going to see Tushar Dada, because his daal is the best but also because he's one of the only farmers left active with all this drought. This isn't going to be like one of your Instagram farm trips, okay?'

For the next four and a half hours Ruchi, with her encyclopedic knowledge of ayurvedic and indigenous ingredients, gave me a one-on-one tutorial about the perilous state of modern Indian agriculture, including droughts, barren monocropped lands, spiraling seed debts and, most chillingly, farmers taking their own lives to avoid defaulting on farm debts. I just wanted to learn how to make *thecha* and maybe see some idyllic fields of millet, but I had inadvertently signed up to a masterclass in rural farm regulations 101.

The drive to Tushar Dada's farm was an eye-opener, and by 'eye-opener' I mean it opened our eyes to the depths of rural poverty, countless free-range chickens and dust. So much dust. We passed through the most rustic parts of Maharashtra, where the roads were so dusty that I started to question whether the entire state was actually a film set for the beginning of Christopher Nolan's *Interstellar*.

Finally, after what felt like an eternity of jostling bumps and trying to keep up with Ruchi's laser-focused conversation, we arrived at Tushar Dada's farm. Tushar Dada, a man who bore the weathered look of someone who had seen sunrises and seasons more vibrant than my urban life ever had, greeted us enthusiastically. He led us through his fields, which were little more than sand dunes at this point, spotted with the sporadic sighting of *tuvar* lentils and the equally unpretentious finger millet. I couldn't quite wrap my head around how Tushar Dada managed to keep these plants thriving, even more so how he managed to feed his growing family with such a measly harvest. '*Sundar hain na?*', he asked, beaming with pride. '*Yeh sirf khana nahin hain, viraasat hain!*' – 'It's beautiful, isn't it? This isn't just food, it's heritage'. Ruchi chimed in, 'And the *tuvar dal* is packed with protein, and millet is a super grain! Super low glycemic index, more nutrient rich than wheat and perfect to grow in drought instead of rice!' There is a real movement among the hipster generation of Indians to pull away from GMO crops, especially rice and wheat, and return to more balanced and complete grains like millets. I'm a little embarrassed to say I never really understood why. Millet requires much more work to become delicious than even the less-polished rice varieties from further south. But, standing in that field, covering our mouths with bandanas to avoid ingesting too much petrified soil, it made perfect sense. There needs to be a shift away from water-intensive crops in these areas, and a much greater focus on hardier minimal-intervention grains.

We returned to Tushar Dada's farmhouse where, with no electricity – anyone who has spent extended time in rural India will know about the dreaded failed generator – we squatted around the kitchen and manually milled our grains for that day's lunch and Dada's daughter-in-law taught me how to use millet flour to make a gruel-like savoury porridge.

I look back on that day with rose-tinted glasses. It was transformative: I learned so much, heard of so many hardships, and had been welcomed with such warmth that the meal was always going to be appreciated. Maybe it was just the fact that there was enough ghee (made from the family's own cows, of course) to lubricate the otherwise quite mealy millet, or that I had spent the previous hour continuously swallowing microdoses of dust, but this truly was one of the most memorable dishes I've ever had. Followed by a glass of fresh buttermilk and a small tasting of ambrosial *puran poli*, I left that humble farmhouse a different chef.

Truffle and Millet Khichdi

Khichdi has ancient roots: Hinduism's 4000+-year-old founding text, the *rig veda*, references *khiccha* as a stewed mix of grains and lentils. In Indian households, khichdi is what you eat when you have nothing else at home, especially when you're not feeling well. It's the definition of balanced *sattvic* cooking. Growing up, we ate split moong daal and broken (cheaper) basmati rice with a tempering of ghee with asafoetida, ginger, green chilli and cumin, and got around its puritan flavour profile by insisting on Punjabi roasted black pepper papad and carrot achar. With the memories of Tushar Dada and the amazing, stripped-back meals with his family, I wanted to create a dish that spoke of humble beginnings, finished with an appropriate level of Mayfair luxury.

Serves 4

For the mushroom base
5g amritsari wadi
50g grapeseed oil
250g button mushrooms, thinly sliced
3g cumin seeds
10g garlic
12.5g fresh peeled ginger, diced
4g green chilli
125g Indian onion, thinly sliced
0.5g asafoetida
1g deggi mirch
1g kosher salt
10g cep mushroom powder

For the smoked ghee
minimum 80g ghee, as needed

For the confit king oyster mushroom
2.5g garlic, finely grated
100g king oyster mushroom, cut into
    1.5cm dice
21.25g kosher salt
50g ghee
0.2g smoke powder

For the khichdi
25g grapeseed oil
4g cumin seeds
20g Indian onion, finely diced
10g fresh peeled ginger, finely diced
100g mushroom base
100g millet
2.5g kosher salt
550g water

To serve
320g khichdi with confit king oyster
    mushrooms
20g smoked ghee, heated to serve
10g Indian onion, brunoised
10g fresh peeled ginger, brunoised
10g chives, finely chopped
black winter truffle, for shaving

Mushroom base
Crush the amritsari wadi to a medium crumb using a pestle and mortar.

Heat 25g of the grapeseed oil in a sauté pan over a high heat. Once the oil is hot, add the sliced mushrooms and cook for 5-10 minutes until caramelised and all the water has evaporated. Remove from the pan and reserve. Add the remaining 25g of grapeseed oil and reduce the heat to medium-high. Add the cumin seeds and crumbed amritsari wadi and fry for 1-2 minutes until the wadi browns and the cumin seeds have cracked. Add the garlic, ginger and green chilli and fry until fragrant for around a minute. Add the sliced onions, lower the heat to medium and cook for 10 minutes, until fully translucent and softened. Add the asafoetida and cook for 30 seconds, then add the deggi mirch, salt and cooked mushrooms. Cook for another 5 minutes until everything is fully combined. Blend the mixture in a high-speed blender or Vitamix until a homogenous paste is formed. Store in an airtight container in the refrigerator for up to 5 days.

Smoked ghee
Light a piece of charcoal in a grill until fully lit and glowing red. Place the ghee in a large metal or glass bowl. Place a smaller bowl inside the big one. Cut a piece of foil big enough to cover and seal the bowl. Place the glowing charcoal in the small bowl, pour 1 tablespoon of melted ghee on the charcoal and cover with foil to keep all the smoke in. Allow to smoke for 10 minutes. Remove the foil and discard the charcoal. Keep the ghee in an airtight container at room temperature for up to 1 month.

Confit king oyster mushroom
Set up a steamer, or a combination oven, on full steam to 100°C. Mix the garlic in a bowl with the diced mushrooms, salt, ghee and smoke powder. Place the mix in a vacuum pouch and seal on full. Place on a steaming tray in the oven and cook for 45 minutes. Open the pouch and discard the juices and excess ghee. Store in an airtight container in the refrigerator for up to 5 days.

Khichdi
Heat the grapeseed oil in a saucepan over a medium-high heat. Add the cumin seeds and fry until they crack, then add half the diced onion and ginger (reserve the rest for serving) and sauté for 5 minutes, until the onions are translucent, and the ginger is fragrant. Add the mushroom base and cook for 5 minutes while stirring, then add the millet, salt and the water and simmer for 30–40 minutes until the millet is soft and the oil starts to split to the surface.

Finish and serve
Add the confit king oyster mushrooms to the khichdi. Ladle the khichdi into a bowl and top with hot smoked ghee, the reserved diced ginger and onion and the chives. Finish the dish by thinly shaving some truffle on the top.

Asparagus and Morel Maggi

This dish is BiBi in a microcosm, taking a comfort food from my childhood and elevating it with technique and amazing produce. It's just a bit of a nightmare to execute in a busy service because we want to match the bounce and chew you get in the best ramen shops, while operating from a kitchen otherwise entirely designed to serve grilled food. There is a reason why you shouldn't order ramen in a yakitori restaurant.

This dish transports me back to after-school snacks my grandmothers made us. In India, we ate it with fresh vegetables; in England we had a frozen Bird's Eye vegetable medley instead. For me, the flavour of Maggi was always tied to something sweet and vegetal. Morels and asparagus are in season simultaneously, during the extended hunger gap of British winter and early spring when little else is around. Later in the year, I'd suggest sweetcorn, squash or pumpkin; anything that can lend a verdant, grassy note, with a little sweetness to help counteract the heat in the spice mixes.

Serves 4

For the confit smoked egg yolk
200g Lapsang Oil (page 221)
4 rich-yolk free-range eggs

For the alkaline noodles
2.5g sodium carbonate
250g strong white bread flour
2.5g kosher salt
100g room-temperature filtered water
potato starch, for dusting

For the maggi chicken masala
450g Reduced Chicken Stock (page 209)
100g MSG Oil (page 221)
10g MSG
10g kosher salt
25g Maggi Masala (page 214)
50g Maggi Tastemaker (page 214)

To serve
24-32 dried morel mushrooms
kosher salt
16 green asparagus tips
240g alkaline noodles
400g maggi chicken masala
4 confit smoked egg yolks
spring onion curls, to garnish

Confit smoked egg yolk
Pour the lapsang oil into a 12cm saucepan and bring it to 63°C. Crack the eggs and separate the egg yolks from the whites. (Reserve the whites for other preparations such as meringues.) Carefully place the egg yolks in the oil and cook for 45 minutes, then carefully remove them from the oil with a slotted spoon. Keep the confit egg yolks in 100g-portion containers with 2 teaspoons of the lapsang oil in each container. Keep refrigerated until needed.

Alkaline noodles
Put the sodium carbonate, flour, and salt in a bowl, then slowly add the water while kneading the dough. The dough will look very dry – this is normal. Knead the dough on the worktop for 10 minutes. Wrap the dough with cling film and allow to rest in the refrigerator for 1 hour. Remove the dough from the refrigerator and knead for another 10 minutes until it starts to become smooth. Roll the dough through the widest setting of a pasta roller twice. Fold the dough in thirds, like a letter, and repeat the previous step. Keep rolling the dough, reducing the thickness until the desired size is reached (1-2mm thick, 4-5mm wide). Using a thin noodle attachment, turn the dough into noodles. Lightly dust the noodles with potato starch to avoid them from sticking. Store in an airtight container in the refrigerator for up to 3 days.

Maggi chicken masala
Bring the reduced chicken stock to a simmer in a saucepan. Add all the remaining ingredients to the stock and mix using a hand blender. Once all the ingredients are fully incorporated, pass the mixture through a fine chinois lined with muslin cloth. Put the stock in a clean pan and warm it up.

Finish and serve
Put the dried morel mushrooms in a bowl of warm water and leave to soak overnight. Once soft, drain and cut them in half lengthways.

Bring a pan of water to the boil and season it with 1% of the water weight in salt. Halve the asparagus tips lengthways and blanch for 1 minute with the morels. Remove and keep aside. Warm the maggi chicken masala in a separate pan. Add the noodles to the boiling water and cook them for 2 minutes, or until al dente. Once the noodles are ready, drain and place in a bowl, making a well in the middle to place the egg yolk. Add the blanched mushrooms and asparagus to the bowl and gently ladle in the maggi chicken masala. Garnish with curls of spring onion.

The Garden

Gujrati Pea Custard

Dried peas are used widely across the Indian subcontinent. From white *safed mattar* in Maharashtrian *ragda* and *hara choliya* in Gujarati *undhiyu* to *chole bhature* in Punjab, every region has its own delicacy based on peas. Kachori is truly a marvel of how dry a food can be – it's designed to survive the desert-like conditions of Gujarat and Rajasthan – but it's still moreish when properly spiced. Our modernised version features a luxurious pea custard and freshness from herbs and mint granita, without sacrificing all the layered flavours of the original.

Serves 4

For the pea tempering
90g grapeseed oil
45g extra-virgin olive oil
5g black mustard seeds
30g fresh peeled ginger, finely diced
10g green bird's eye chilli, finely diced
3g Garam Masala (page 213)
1g ground cinnamon
7g kosher salt
3g white caster sugar
10g sherry vinegar

For the pea custard
4g gold leaf gelatine
500g frozen petits pois
7g kosher salt, plus extra if needed
135g pea tempering
50g oat milk

For the besan chutney
25g besan flour
400g filtered water
15g grapeseed oil
2g black mustard seeds
0.5g asafoetida
2g curry leaves
2 green bird's eye chillies, slit
1g ground turmeric
1g Kashmiri chilli powder
kosher salt
10g white caster sugar, plus extra if needed
10g lemon juice, plus extra if needed

For the mint granita
240g water
50g mint leaves
12g white caster sugar
1g dried mint
20g lemon juice

To serve
80g besan chutney
4 x 80g pea custard
40g garden peas
12 snap peas
kosher salt
10g pea tempering
cornflowers, borage and coriander
    flowers, to garnish
mint tips, to garnish
60g mint granita

Pea tempering
Heat the grapeseed oil and olive oil in a frying pan over a medium-high heat. Add the mustard seeds and fry until they crack, then add the diced ginger and chilli and fry for 1–2 minutes until fragrant. Remove from the heat and add the garam masala, cinnamon, salt and sugar. Allow the mixture to come to room temperature, then add the sherry vinegar. Reserve the tempering for the pea custard and to dress the garden peas for the dish (reserve it in the refrigerator if making it in advance).

Pea custard
Bloom the gelatine in iced water for 5 minutes. Blend the petits pois, salt, pea tempering and 37.5g of the oat milk in a high-speed blender or Vitamix to a smooth purée, then pass it through a fine chinois and adjust the seasoning if necessary. Warm the remaining oat milk in a pan until it reaches 60°C. Add the bloomed gelatine (squeezed of excess water) to the warm milk and mix it thoroughly until the gelatine has dissolved. Slowly add the milk and gelatine mixture to the pea purée and mix with a whisk or a hand blender until fully incorporated. Add 80g of the pea custard to each of the serving bowls and place in the refrigerator for at least 2 hours until fully set.

Besan chutney
Mix the besan flour with half of the filtered water and whisk well, forming a smooth, homogeneous slurry, without any lumps. Add the rest of the water to the bowl, whisk well and set aside.

Heat the grapeseed oil in a saucepan over a medium-high heat, then add the mustard seeds and when they start to crack add the asafoetida, curry leaves and slit green chillies and cook for a couple of minutes until the chillies blister. Add the turmeric and Kashmiri chilli powder, mix for a few seconds, then add the besan and water mixture. Reduce the heat to medium-low and stir for about 2 minutes until the gram flour no longer smells raw and the mixture begins to thicken. Season with the salt, sugar and lemon juice, tasting to adjust as required.

Mint granita
Bring the water to a simmer in a pan. Add all the ingredients except the lemon juice and simmer for 3 minutes. Remove from the heat, add the lemon juice and pass through a fine chinois. Set the liquid in a container and freeze hard.

Assemble and serve
Place 1 tablespoon of besan chutney on one side of each custard. Blanch the garden and snap peas in salted boiling water for 1 minute, then drain and dress them with the pea tempering. Put the seasoned peas over the besan chutney. Garnish the peas with cornflowers, borage, coriander flowers and mint tips. Right before serving, scrape the granita with a fork and place it across the peas.

Southall: Still my home away from home

I grew up in a family-centred household. My grandfather, Ved Prakash, who sadly passed away when my own father was just a toddler, left behind a legacy of two children, a widow and seven siblings. This was in Kenya in the late 1950s, and a few years later my grandmother, with her two boys in tow, moved to Slough (it's pretty close to Heathrow airport) to work in the Mars factory. One of my grandfather's sisters had already settled in Slough, and my dad lived with that family for a little while, then the other sister came, followed by another, followed by another two brothers. Each of these subfamilies then grew - which meant that, just a few short years later, my dad now had 13 first cousins.

Fast forward to the 90s and each of those first cousins got married and had an average of two children, meaning those original eight Sharmas grew to an army of 73 family members who would routinely get together every birthday, Diwali, Christmas and New Year. And sometimes, for no reason whatsoever, on any given Saturday or Sunday afternoon at somebody's house. Throw in a handful of family friends - because at least seven of those 13 first cousins went to the same school / college and had built their own network of friends - and you were talking about feeding 100+ people from a domestic kitchen. If we were lucky, we would hire the scouts hall in Upton Court Park for seven pounds an hour, and take the prepared food over there with us. Even 20 years after starting my career in professional kitchens, I haven't got a clue how our parents did it.

What I do know is that back in the early 90s, if you wanted something Indian, you didn't pop to a local supermarket, you headed to Southall, Birmingham or Bradford. Even on the off-chance that you would find the type of rice that you need, or the vegetables you needed for that evening's feast locally, you would never find it in the quantity or at the price which your parents were after.

The importance of Southall to my parents' generation cannot be understated. During the Windrush generation, Southall became a hotspot for immigrants from the Caribbean and India, especially via Kenya (Southhall too is close to Heathrow). As such, it became an area known for its multicultural community, the site of the first major Sikh and Hindu temples in the UK, as well as the biggest community of Indian-owned restaurants, pubs and businesses in the southeast. Sadly, Southall was also the site of the infamous race riots that ran from 1979-1982, due to some pointedly political rallies from the National Front. Nonetheless, as the country emerged from that particularly dark period, the town began to flourish again with even more Indian-owned businesses - even the sign at the train station was changed into Punjabi.

It was a routine exercise to empty the car, and head to the Dominion car park in Southall, walk over the bridge to Broadway and shop in any one of the massive cash and carry shops designed to feed West London's growing Indian restaurant and retail shops. Or, one house full of Sharmas.

I truly believe my love of weightlifting came from Southall, given my early exposure to ludicrously bulky ingredients needed to cater for our family. At the age of 10, I was being loaded mule-like with a 15kg bag of rice while my older brother, despite being skinnier than me but with the unfortunate pleasure of being significantly (18 months) older than me, would end up with a 25kg sack of flour on his back. My dad would somehow get out of his role in this by either disappearing to play cricket or golf, or pretend he wasn't able to find any parking so would 'have to' sit in the car and ensure he didn't get a ticket.

Conveniently, my dad would always rear his head just in time as we headed back over the bridge to old Southall to join us for much deserved stops at a couple of Punjabi and Kenyan Gujurati shops for a few bites to eat. My mum always wanted the chaats - *sev puri* in particular - while Dad went for *chevda* and *namkeen,* and my brother only ever had eyes for the piping-hot jalebis. For me, the biggest treat was getting a *kachori* from the Gujarati *halwai* which has long since closed. For the uninitiated it seems like a pretty weird dish - a slightly flaky pastry, layered with oil, stuffed with severely overcooked marrowfat peas and served with a slightly chalky chutney made of roasted chickpea flour - it's definitely the kind of food my school friends would never understand but probably has any Gujarati salivating while reading this.

Nashpati Bhel

A few notes on this recipe: please don't worry about the type of grains, the nuts, or making a proper granita if you don't want to. And definitely don't try and cut a block of ice to make it look like it does in the book (unless you really want to).

This is how we make the *bhel* in the restaurant. The key is making sure you get enough toasted warmth through the grains. It's why we love using puffed wheat, oats, spelt or barley as the base. Which grains you use shouldn't really matter, as long as there is a variety of textures and flavours.

This isn't on the dinner menu that often anymore, but we always have all the ingredients in place for whenever Henrietta and Richard come back for a pit stop and a bowl of 'that crazy fucking crunchy ice and pear thing'.

Serves 4

For the bhel mix
neutral vegetable oil, for deep frying
100g puffed oats
20g puffed quinoa (page 226)
20g Thin Sev (page 226)
25g Boondi (page 225)
15g Fried Moong Dal (page 225)
7g Jeera Chaat Masala (page 214)

For the compressed pears and granita
500g pear juice
30g caster sugar
5g citric acid
10g peeled fresh ginger, roughly chopped
5g BiBi Chaat Masala (page 213)
1.3g dried mint
1.5g kosher salt
2.5g black salt
1 nashi pear (Asian pear)

For the roasted walnuts
40g walnut pieces or halves
2g kosher salt

To serve
8g green bird's eye chilli, brunoised
16g Indian onion, brunoised
60g diced compressed pear
20g San Marzano tomato, cut into 2cm dice
40g roasted walnuts
160g bhel mix
Jeera Chaat Masala (page 214), if needed
40g Green Chutney (page 218)
40g Tamarind Chutney (page 219)
40g pear granita
mint tips, to garnish

Bhel mix

Heat enough neutral vegetable oil for deep frying to 190°C in a deep fat fryer (two-thirds to three-quarters full). Fry the puffed oats and quinoa in the oil for 30 seconds to 1 minute, until crispy (there's no need to fry the quinoa a second time if you've already fried it following the Essentials recipe on page 226 – only fry it if using shop-bought). Place the fried puffs on a tray lined with kitchen paper to cool, so the paper absorbs the excess oil. In a bowl, mix the puffed grains along with the rest of the ingredients. Store in an airtight container at room temperature for up to 1 month.

Compressed pears and granita

Put all the ingredients except the pear in a high-speed blender or Vitamix and blend until well mixed, then pass through a fine chinois. Keep back 200g of the liquid mix to compress the pears for the dish, and put the rest in a container and freeze. Once fully frozen, scrape it with a fork to a fine and fluffy granita texture. Peel the pear and quarter it lengthways. Remove the core and cut the end, squaring it off. Place the trimmed pear quarters in a container with enough of the reserved liquid to cover them. Put the container with the pear and the liquid inside a vacuum machine and compress them. Remove from the liquid and cut into 1.5 x 2-cm dice. Store in an airtight container in the refrigerator for up to 3 days.

Roasted walnuts

Preheat the oven to 160°C. Mix the walnut pieces with the salt and place them on a baking tray. Roast in the oven for 10 minutes, stirring them every 3 minutes to roast them evenly. Once roasted, place the nuts inside a tea towel and gently rub them until they are partially peeled. Allow the nuts to cool at room temperature. Store in an airtight container in the refrigerator for up to 1 month.

Finish and serve

Put the chilli, onion, compressed pear, tomatoes, roasted walnuts and bhel mix in a bowl. Mix thoroughly and adjust seasoning with more jeera chaat masala, if needed. Place the mixture on a plate and with the help of a squeezy bottle makes some lines of green and tamarind chutney across the mixture. Put 2 tablespoons of pear granita in the middle of the bhel and garnish with mint tips.

The Sea
Samundar

The source of diminishing returns

Ah, the ocean. The allure of open water has shaped British culture, economy and identity for centuries. With over 12,000 kilometres of coastline, the UK is uniquely positioned to embrace the bounties of its surrounding waters. And for a fair chunk of our history, we did. The British naval system was what enabled Empire to spread all over the world. Imagine a tiny country like ours being able to colonise a quarter of the world's land mass? It all started from the sea.

In the 20th century, lots of traditional cooking methods and appetites were lost for convenience, with only a few truly British delicacies surviving into the new millennia. We really do have an abundance of amazing seafood; consider, for instance, Mylor prawns, Morecambe Bay potted shrimp, Arbroath Smokies, native lobsters, Maldon oysters, jellied eels and Cornish mackerel – and that's before we address the white elephant of fish and chips. Done properly, is there anything more satisfying on a rainy and cold Friday night than a steaming-hot newspaper-wrapped parcel of fish and chips doused in malt vinegar?

Even with all of this in mind, we're still exporting the best British seafood across to the continent. I still remember the first time I saw a delivery of Devon crabs and West-coast turbot make it over to Mugaritz in San Sebastián, the supposed seafood mecca. While people here get by with aqua-farmed sea bass and salmon, the French and Spanish are gladly eating all our best wild seafood like brill, red mullet and gurnard. You have a better chance of finding Scottish langoustines in Spain than you do in even the largest supermarkets in the UK; but rest assured that you'll find half a dozen battered fish brands in the freezer at your local corner shop.

A lot of our poor eating habits with seafood stem from a time where rationing was necessary, and boats wouldn't be able to leave harbours in fear of the Blitz. After that, we never fully recovered our appetite for fish, despite a few notable exceptions in towns still known for seafood like Whitstable, Padstow and Brixham. The fishing industry certainly faces some challenges: it's incredibly hard work, and has historically been uniquely dangerous. To counteract the danger, we built trawlers and giant fishing vessels which blew the little guys almost completely out of the market. As these huge boats head out further and to deeper waters, day-boat fisherman are barely able to get out of the harbour, meaning they can only catch smaller species which come closer to the shore.

Climate change is impacting fish, too, and we've not made things easier for ourselves by overfishing some species and leaving the capture of others unregulated. As stocks dwindle due to unsustainable practices – including trawler-net fishing rather than hook and pole – and changing environmental conditions, coastal communities grapple with uncertain futures. The introduction of sustainable fishing practices and marine protected areas indicates a shift toward a more responsible approach to managing these precious resources, ensuring that British waters will continue to be full of diverse and interesting seafood for future generations. However, we now need to convince people to eat more of the right kinds of fish, and to source their seafood from ethical fishing channels.

In contrast, India, despite being eight times the size of the UK, has a coastline half as long. India's extensive coastlines line the Arabian Sea, the Bay of Bengal, and the Indian Ocean and offer diverse ecosystems brimming with life. Fishing plays a crucial role in supporting the livelihoods of millions of Indians, though it's worth considering that this isn't even 10% of the country - particularly in coastal states such as Kerala and Tamil Nadu. These areas boast a rich tradition of seafood consumption, but the vast majority of Indians rarely eat seafood.

While overfishing is less of an issue in India, aggressive urbanisation of coastal areas has led to high levels of pollution, and habitat destruction, which threatens fish stocks and the health of marine ecosystems. The Indian government has recognised these challenges, emphasising the need for integrated coastal zone management and sustainable aquaculture to protect its marine environment while empowering local communities. However, as is often the case, words are cheap, actions speak louder. And now really is the time for those actions.

As a chef, I'm always going to be passionate about serving the very best ingredients we can. And seafood is a huge part of what we do at BiBi. People come to us for luxuries they don't necessarily have access to at home. Today's menu is roughly eight courses, and eight smaller bites as snacks and second serves. Of these 16 plates, it's fair to assume that at least eight of them are seafood-based. For most of my career, I've worked exclusively with day-boat and Marine Stewardship Council (MSC)-approved seafood. And a few years ago, I couldn't have imagined how far environmentally-focused aquaculture means there is hope that we can still serve great seafood in the long-term, while giving the ocean a chance to recover.

Ultimately, choosing between indulgence and sustainability is no longer an option. As chefs, we have a responsibility to source seafood thoughtfully, educating our customers about their choices and the environmental impacts of their dietary habits. By doing so, we can be a vital part of the solution, helping ensure that our oceans thrive and that the culinary treasures they provide are not lost to future generations. The return on this investment is not just better dishes; it is a thriving planet and a vibrant aquatic tapestry that supports life in all its forms.

Carlingford oysters

Oysters have always had a kind of sophisticated elegance; is there a better start to a fancy meal than oysters and Champagne? Throw in some caviar and you have the perfect opening to an evening, something Thomas Keller realised early on when developing his signature Oysters and Pearls dish. There is something about a raw or lightly poached oyster that is truly singular. We all know that these bivalves have developed a reputation for their aphrodisiac qualities, partly down to the sensory appeal of the slippery texture, but they also contain high levels of zinc which can boost testosterone levels. What else does an oyster contain a lot of? Water. Which is why the source of an oyster is as important as anything else.

The Romans were the first to understand this, and in addition to introducing aqueducts and water management systems to Britain, they also brought us oysters. A normal oyster will filter around 60,000 litres of water in its two- to three-year lifespan, placing a heavy importance on the quality of water flowing through the oyster bed. Over in Carlingford Lough – a glacial fjord forming part of the border between Northern Ireland to the north and the Republic of Ireland to the south – there is a huge tidal exchange meaning that there is freshwater flowing down from the mountains either side of the lough. That chilled, fresh water means that the oysters themselves are shaped like the perfect teardrop, and the flavour has a briny sweetness which can only come about in extreme cold. The EU has recognised this and granted Class A (the highest) grading to the waters around the lough. It's no surprise that oysters have been cultivated in these waters for over two thousand years.

Now it's time to talk about what makes the team at the Carlingford Oyster Company so special. As they describe it themselves, one misty morning in the late 1960s, Peter Louët-Feisser sailed into the lough on a wooden yacht he'd built with his own hands, accompanied by his wife Anna and a couple of chickens. He was enchanted by the lough's beauty and the allure of the Irish way of life, and found a home for his growing family. Peter was always attracted by the sea, having spent time living and sailing in Indonesia and the Netherlands, but didn't really have an interest in fine ingredients or high-end restaurants. It was by chance that he heard about the traditional Roman methods for native oyster cultivation on BBC Radio 4 and thought he would try his hand at it. If nothing else, it got him out on the water every day, but close enough to shore to spend time with his children. And it's a good thing he did, because not only did Peter find a way to refine and perfect the process of oyster husbandry, but kept his children Charm and Kian so involved in the business from a young age that they now run the business day-to-day. This truly is a family business, as now his grandchildren are out on the lough, earning pocket money while helping out around the farm. And Peter? He's still out there a few times a week, despite now being in his late 80s.

Peter's tinkering and continued efforts towards conservation of the purity of the lough's waters have helped him to develop what many consider to be the best oyster in the world, the Louët-Feisser oyster (just don't mention that to the French, because to develop this particular oyster he 'borrowed' some larvae from French waters and slowly crafted the perfect oysters through generations of hybridisation). The Louët-Feisser oyster is celebrated for its rich, creamy flavour and distinctive briny finish. In addition to this, they have a remarkably deep cup and almost entirely flat top, meaning the size of the oyster after three years is deep enough to just fit in the palm of my hand. And, for us, that deep cup gives us the perfect space to fill with the spicy, sour ingredients that work so well with oysters, without losing any of the depth of flavour of these amazing creatures.

Louët-Feisser Oyster and Passion Fruit Jal Jeera

Quite often we stumble on something at BiBi that transports us back to a long-forgotten memory. If the two questions I get asked most often are 'why did you become a chef?', and 'where do your ideas come from?', this is the kind of dish that answers them better than any words ever could. We've already covered my childhood visits to Southall, and my dad's proud Kenyan heritage, but haven't really mentioned Nargis paan shop, just over the bridge as you enter old Southall from the train station. Nargis is a legendary Nairobi restaurant, mainly famed for its grilled items. Its sister restaurant in Southall, which shares little other than the branding, draws out an almost Pavlovian response from me because we only ever ordered two things from there – passion fruit juice and *meetha paan*, normally to take away for our drive back home. Indians love savoury and spicy flavours with fruits, often spiked with a little black salt.

Nargis still, to this day, serves the best fresh passion fruit juice anywhere in the world (I might be biased). Dad claims it tastes just like the juice they would squeeze from passion fruits fresh from the tree in the garden in Kenya. But he also claims he once stared down an adult lion in his back garden, so let's take it with a pinch of salt. In the dead of British winter, when nothing but root vegetables grow, a little exoticism served along with some of Europe's best oysters is a triumphant entry to a meal, as well as a link to a fond memory of my dad and his childhood in Kenya.

Serves 4

For the poached oysters
4 Louët-Feisser oysters

For the oyster emulsion with mango ginger
15g mango ginger
50g poached oyster trim
20g egg yolk
3g dashi concentrate
4g dashi vinegar
0.4g kosher salt, plus extra if needed
1g Pre-Hy (page 212)
1g white rice vinegar
120g grapeseed oil
lemon juice, if needed

For the passion fruit jal jeera granita
100g passion fruit purée
50g water
25g caster sugar
1g roasted ground cumin
0.8g Jeera Chaat Masala (page 214)
1.2g BiBi Chaat Masala (page 213)
0.6g deggi mirch
0.8g black salt
0.8g kosher salt
3.5g Pre-Hy (page 212)

To serve
10g green bird's eye chilli, brunoised
10g Indian onion, brunoised
4 poached oysters
80g oyster emulsion
12g Green Curry Oil (page 220)
60g passion fruit jal jeera granita
4 micro nasturtium leaves

Poached oysters
Set up a steamer, or a combination oven, on full steam to 63°C. Place the oysters on a steamer tray and steam for 45 minutes. Shuck the steamed oysters and trim off the muscle and the skirt. Reserve the skirt trim and the liquor inside the oyster. Keep the oysters in an airtight container in the refrigerator until ready to plate. Set aside the oyster shells for plating.

Oyster emulsion with mango ginger
Peel the mango ginger and juice it with a centrifugal juicer (taste it before using – it can be strong, in which case adjust quantity accordingly). Put all the ingredients except the grapeseed oil in a Thermomix or food processor and blend until a paste is formed. Slowly add the oil to the mixture while blending until emulsified. Adjust seasoning if needed with extra salt and lemon juice. Pass through a fine chinois and keep in a fine-tip squeezy bottle in the refrigerator for up to 3 days.

Passion fruit jal jeera granita
Combine all the ingredients in a blender, then pass through a fine chinois. Place the mixture in a container and freeze. Once fully frozen, scrape it with a fork to a fine and fluffy granita texture.

Assemble and serve
Mix the chilli and onion and place 5g of the mixture on the bottom of each reserved oyster shell. Cover the onion-chilli mix with 20g of oyster emulsion. Place an oyster on top of the emulsion and put a few drops of green curry oil next to it. Just before serving, top the oyster with the granita and garnish with a micro nasturtium leaf.

Raw Bream and Truffle Nimbu Pani

Nimbu pani has become a dish synonymous with BiBi; it is always on the menu when we get citrus and seafood of the right quality, especially when the sweetest seafood, blood oranges and black winter truffles are at their peak in early February. It's a ceviche-like dish, sometimes with hamachi, most famously with scallops, and here with line-caught gilthead bream, an emulsion made of egg whites (so it's lighter than a traditional mayonnaise), a jelly of coconut and dashi vinegar, an Indian lemon and roasted cumin fluid gel, a truffle jelly, a dressing made of coconut water, green chilli, seaweed and fermented fish, our nine-ingredient 'green curry oil' (page 220), our eight-ingredient dish-specific chaat masala, smoked and dried scallop roe and quinoa puffed in oil so hot it's technically illegal. You could argue that the words 'nimbu pani' undersell it, but I think it does exactly what it needs to do.

Serves 4

For the nimbu pani ceviche
20g dashi concentrate
60g Indian lemon juice
125g coconut water
30g grapeseed oil
6g fresh jalapeño juice
2g kosher salt
15g Pre-Hy (page 212)
8g Green Curry Oil (page 220)

For the nimbu pani gel
50g water
25g white caster sugar
25g regular lemon juice, strained
25g blood orange juice, strained
2g agar agar
5g fresh mint
15g Indian lemon juice, strained
1.5g kosher salt
1.5g black salt
1.5g roasted ground cumin

For the dashi truffle jelly
2g gold leaf gelatine
20g water
1.5g kosher salt
10g mirin
40g dashi vinegar
10g truffle water
15g black truffle, finely grated

For the cured bream
800g–1kg gilthead bream
40g Lemon Fish Cure (page 216)
1 litre Vinegar Bath (page 216)

To serve
100g cured bream, diced
5g green bird's eye chilli, brunoised
90g nimbu pani ceviche
Maldon salt
30g dashi truffle jelly
8g puffed quinoa (Puffed Grains; page 226)
2g Lime Leaf Chaat Masala (page 214)
24g Jalapeño Emulsion (page 218)
16g nimbu pani gel
micro purple basil, to garnish
atsina cress, to garnish
20g Green Curry Oil (page 220)

Nimbu pani ceviche
Combine all the ingredients with a hand blender. Pass through a fine chinois and store in a fine-tip squeezy bottle in the refrigerator for up to 5 days.

Nimbu pani gel
Put the water, sugar, regular lemon and orange juices in a saucepan. Using a hand blender, add the agar agar, and bring the mixture to the boil for 1 minute. Add the mint, take the pan off the heat and leave to infuse for 1 minute. Remove the mint, then add the Indian lemon juice and remaining ingredients and mix thoroughly with a whisk. Pass through a fine chinois and place the mixture on a tray. Cool until set. Once solid, blend in a high-speed blender or Vitamix to a smooth, shiny texture. Pass through a sieve, place in a container and remove the air in a vacuum machine. Store in a fine-tip squeezy bottle in the refrigerator for up to 3 days.

Dashi truffle jelly
Bloom the gelatine in iced water for 5 minutes. Heat the 20g water with the salt in a pan until the salt dissolves, then take off the heat and add the bloomed gelatine (squeezed of excess water), mirin and dashi vinegar and whisk well to make sure the gelatine melts. Pour the mixture on the grated truffle. Let it set in the refrigerator, then whisk it with a fork.

Cured bream
Fillet, skin and pin-bone the gilthead bream. Sprinkle the lemon fish cure over the clean bream fillets and let them rest for 5 minutes, then wash the cure off the fillets in the vinegar bath. Cut the bream into 2cm dice.

Finish and serve
Put the diced bream in a mixing bowl with the brunoised chilli and 10g of the nimbu pani ceviche, then mix together and season with Maldon salt. Place the dashi truffle jelly in the middle of a bowl. Cover the jelly with the seasoned bream, making sure the top part is slightly flat, and gently cover the mixture with puffed quinoa and sprinkle the lime leaf chaat masala over it. Make some dots with the jalapeño emulsion and the nimbu gel on top of the quinoa-covered bream. Garnish with micro purple basil and atsina cress. Mix the green curry oil and the remaining nimbu pani ceviche in a bowl or jug and gently pour it around the bream.

ChalkStream Trout Jhal Muri

Jhal muri, like many Indian dishes, leaves so much to interpretation. In Bengali, jhal means 'mixed', and muri 'puffed rice'. Traditionally, jhal muri usually contains mustard oil, chaat masala and often peanuts. Some have green mango, some cucumber or occasionally chana daal. I've seen versions with peas (odd) but never one with seafood, which to me has always been bizarre. Firstly, good mustard oil tastes almost like wasabi, and secondly, maybe more than any other Indian state, Bengalis love seafood. The state sits on top of the Bay of Bengal, which made it a strategic port for the British when establishing the East India Company. The Bay is also one of the best waterways in Asia for species that thrive in brackish waters. Even inland, freshwater fish like basa and ilish are prized despite their sometimes muddy flavour. A similar slanderous label is occasionally attached to trout in Britain. Yes, some brown trout from particularly still waters can be a little... pondy? But, when raised slowly and finished in strong currents, these fish can be amazingly delicate in flavour, but with enough omega-3 fatty richness to stand up to the nose-clearing pungency of mustard oil.

Serves 4

For the jhal muri dressing
25g grapeseed oil
25g coconut oil
25g lime juice
12.5g Tamarind Paste (page 208)
12.5g jaggery
5g Lime Leaf Chaat Masala (page 214)
2.5g kosher salt
10g mustard oil
lemon juice, if needed

For the kasundi mustard emulsion
16g egg yolk
12g kasundi mustard
4g kosher salt, plus extra if needed
15g Worcestershire sauce
7.5g moscatel vinegar
150g grapeseed oil
60g mustard oil

For the jhal muri mix
neutral vegetable oil, for deep frying
16g puffed rice
18g sev
4g Fried Moong Dal (page 225)
8g aloo bhujia
4g Lime Leaf Chaat Masala (page 214)

To serve
45g ikejime ChalkStream trout, diced
12g deseeded diced cucumber
12g breakfast radishes, diced
12g avocado, diced
20g trout roe
8g Indian onion, brunoised
6g bird's eye green chilli, brunoised
80g jhal muri mix
8g roasted peanuts
30g jhal muri dressing
Maldon salt, if needed
lemon juice, if needed
4 Papdi (page 229)
Lime Leaf Chaat Masala (page 214),
    for sprinkling
40g kasundi mustard emulsion
chopped chives, to garnish

Jhal muri dressing
Blend all ingredients using a hand blender until well combined.

Kasundi mustard emulsion
Put all the ingredients except the oils in a Thermomix or a food processor and blend until combined. Slowly add the oils to the mixture, while blending, until emulsified. Adjust seasoning if needed with salt and lemon juice. Store in a fine-tip squeezy bottle in the refrigerator for up to 3 days.

Jhal muri mix
Heat enough neutral vegetable oil for deep-frying to 190°C and fry the puffed rice for 2 minutes until crispy. Remove the rice from the oil and place it on a kitchen paper-lined tray to absorb excess oil. Once cool, mix with the rest of the ingredients.

Assemble and serve
Combine the trout, cucumber, radishes, avocado, roe, onion, chilli, jhal muri mix and peanuts in a mixing bowl, then add the jhal muri dressing. Adjust seasoning with Maldon salt and lemon juice if needed. Place a papdi at the bottom of the serving plate and the dressed trout jhal muri mix on top, forming a small mound, and sprinkle with lime leaf chaat masala. Dot the mustard emulsion on the mixture and garnish with chopped chives.

N25 caviar

Is there anything that better summarises luxury on water or land than caviar? As my head chef Ashkan always likes to remind us, caviar comes from the Farsi 'khavyar', meaning 'fish eggs', but then according to him everything comes from Persia anyway. Anyone who has spent any time in the BiBi will know that whenever I introduce a new dish on the menu, Ash will be close at hand to say, 'you know in the [North/ South] of Iran we have a [rice / meat / fish] dish just like this'. He's often right, but in this instance it's not clear where the tradition of salt curing and preserving sturgeon roe came from. Aristotle is credited as the first person to write about caviar back in the 9th century BC, while the Russians were for many years the largest producers of caviar anywhere in the world. Caviar was a popular peasant food in the Middle Ages around the Caspian. What changed? Tsar Ivan the Terrible took a liking to caviar, keeping much of the finest roe back for the palace, while the sturgeon meat was handed down to the lower classes. One visit from a French aristocrat and, overnight, caviar became the ultimate display of wealth and sophistication across Europe, a luxury affordable only to the uber wealthy. Following the dissipation of the Iron Curtain in the 1980s, Russian imports started to flood back into the West. Now, amazing caviar comes from all over the world, but in many cases, it just isn't very sustainable. In fact, even the Russians completely stopped production of caviar from wild sturgeon after 2008 to allow depleted fish stocks to recover. And that's because in traditional caviar production, a sturgeon needs to grow into its teens in order to reach reproductive maturity – and for an almas (also Farsi, for 'diamond') caviar the sturgeon has to be between 60 and 100 years old. Once at maturity, the fish is killed and eggs processed before being sent around the world at exorbitant costs. A master tin of 1kg caviar can run anywhere from £1000 for a low-grade hybrid, to £50,000 for the golden almas. Consider that, even at peak season, a white truffle sits at £3000 for a kilo - it's safe to say, in general, caviar is still globally the most expensive ingredient.

I first met Hermes Gehen, the soft-spoken half-German, half-Chinese founder of N25 caviar, when he was barely into his 20s and still studying at university in Munich. He was introduced to me by Jeremy Chan from Ikoyi, on the basis that Hermes was looking for some more clients in London, having recently launched his caviar house in Germany. Given that two of his clients were Restaurant Frantzen in Stockholm and Ikoyi in London, I thought it was a meeting worth taking. He stepped into the JKS head office on George Street on a glum summer afternoon and unrolled a beggar's purse filled with caviar and ice packs, and some mother of pearl spoons for tasting.

To be honest, I didn't 'get' caviar. I had just spent the last few years working at sustainability-led British restaurants. Yes, we featured some English caviar, but I never really liked it. Like much of our freshwater fish in England, it was just a little muddy in flavour. So, when the fresh-faced Hermes nervously joined me in the meeting room, a little dishevelled having just flown in from Germany, I can't say I was expecting my opinion on caviar to be changed. Credit to his passion, I've not served a single egg of caviar that isn't N25 since that day.

Hermes's story is an interesting one. He was at university but had a growing appetite for fine dining. He discovered that the best restaurants were increasingly looking to China for high quality caviar. When he returned to China every summer, he would immerse himself in the world of caviar, visiting farms, learning about the ageing process and, of course, tasting a lot of caviar. Along the way, Hermes found a farm in the Yunnan province, 25° north in latitude and immediately knew that he would source his eggs from there. While they now source eggs from a range of aquaculture facilities across China, N25 took its name from this first farm.

What sets N25 apart from other caviar houses is Hermes' meticulous German approach to the maturation of the caviar. All the eggs are shipped to Germany where they are salted, before being packed into master tins at sub-zero temperatures. The ageing process from there is specific to each species of sturgeon and can take months of precision and patience. If you're lucky enough to be one of his clients, Hermes and the team will age the caviar to your own specification. They're now so selective with their caviar that they created a second line which still has the same approach to production, but just doesn't hit the highest standard that N25 brand maintains (similar to a grand vin and second vin).

In that first tasting with Hermes, he presented flavours in caviar that I just didn't know could exist. And moreover, the difference between the varieties is clearer with N25 than any other caviar I've tried. It opened my eyes to the versatility of caviars in savoury but also sweet dishes; though any number of riffs on the classic cultured cream and blini is hard to beat.

At BiBi, while we do work through a range of osscietra, kaluga and a few hybrids, depending on the application, since that first tasting Schrenckii has always been a favourite of mine because of the sweet, acorn-like fat which helps temper the fresh spicy heat that is a signature of our food.

Cornish Bluefin Tuna Belly Pineapple Saaru

For almost 50 years, bluefin tuna was all but extinct in British waters, mainly due to overfishing. Now, stocks are recovering – largely due to altered migration patterns related to climate change – and we feel a little more comfortable about putting them on our menu. We use as many parts as possible: in this dish, it's the o-toro – the buoyant underbelly, full of intramuscular fat – that acts as the perfect creamy counterpoint to the acidic pineapple saaru, which uses fermented pineapple trim, adding layers of complexity to a visually simple dish.

Serves 4

For the smoked candy beetroot
200g candy beetroot
20g rapeseed oil
10g kosher salt

For the pineapple saaru jelly
3.2g gold leaf gelatine
50g Tepache (page 209)
0.8g kosher salt
10g mirin
3g Pickling Liquor Base (page 224)
5g dashi vinegar
45g pineapple juice
10g white caster sugar

For the rassam oil
115g Rassam Masala (page 214)
375g Tomato Oil (page 224)

For the rassam emulsion
30g egg white
25g dashi vinegar, plus extra if needed
50g pineapple juice
5g kosher salt, plus extra if needed
7.5g Pre-Hy (page 212)
240g rassam oil

For the seaweed chewda
neutral vegetable oil, for deep frying
50g wild rice
50g poha
25g Fried Curry Leaves (page 225)
50g toasted white sesame seeds
12g MSG seasoning
10g Nori Mix (page 118)
1g kosher salt

To serve
120g bluefin tuna belly, cut into 2cm dice
40g smoked candy beetroot dice
12g green bird's eye chilli, brunoised
10g grapeseed oil
kosher salt
40g Pepper Fry Sauce (page 127)
80g pineapple saaru jelly
40g rassam emulsion
4 red shiso leaves, cut into a chiffonade
40g seaweed chewda

Smoked candy beetroot
Preheat the oven to 180°C. Cut squares of foil big enough to enclose your beetroot. Place the oil and salt on the foil and wrap it around the beetroot. Place on a tray and bake in the oven until tender: how long they take will depend on their size. Once the beetroots are cool, peel them, trim them and cut into 2cm dice. Using a cold smoking gun and applewood chips, smoke the diced beetroot for 30 minutes.

Pineapple saaru jelly
Bloom the gelatine in iced water for 5 minutes. Heat the tepache and salt in a pan to 60°C, stir to dissolve the salt, then whisk in the bloomed gelatine (squeezed of excess water) until fully dissolved. Take off the heat, add the rest of the ingredients and whisk until combined. Transfer the mixture to a container and allow it to set in the refrigerator. Once set, scrape with a fork. Store in an airtight container in the refrigerator for up to 5 days.

Rassam oil
Put the rassam masala and tomato oil in a saucepan and heat the mixture to 100°C. Cover and cook for 30 minutes at 100°C. Take off the heat and pass the mixture through a fine chinois lined with muslin cloth. Store the oil in an airtight container in the refrigerator for up to 1 month.

Rassam emulsion
Put all the ingredients except the rassam oil in a Thermomix or food processor and blend until combined, then slowly add the oil to the mixture, while blending, until emulsified. Adjust seasoning if needed with more salt and dashi vinegar. Store in a fine-tip squeezy bottle in the refrigerator for up to 3 days.

Seaweed chewda
Heat enough oil for deep-frying to 190°C. Fry the wild rice in small batches for 1–2 minutes per batch until puffed, then drain on a paper-lined tray to remove the excess oil. Fry the poha in batches for 1–2 minutes until crispy, then drain on a paper-lined tray to remove the excess oil. Crush the curry leaves to a flaky texture, then mix all the ingredients together and store in an airtight container at room temperature for up to a week.

Assemble and serve
Put the diced tuna, beetroot and chilli in a mixing bowl. Dress with the grapeseed oil and kosher salt to taste. On each plate, place a large dot of pepper fry sauce, then cover with 1 tablespoon of pineapple saaru jelly. Place the tuna and beetroot mixture in a mound over the jelly. Add 4 dots of rassam emulsion on the surface of the tuna and beetroot mix. Put the chiffonade red shiso on top of the tuna mixture and cover everything with the seaweed chewda.

Malai Cornish Native Lobster

'Why are they so small?' … My American guests are always a little confused when they see the size of our lobsters. I'll admit that the big 2kg-plus lobsters from Maine or Canada can be delicious when roasted in the shell with a butter-based sauce. But you're only really tasting the butter, not the key ingredient itself. We much prefer to use small lobsters – 800g-1.2kg – before they get to breeding age and before they start taking on too much water to molt their previous shell. Nature often amazes me: how the lobster knows to shrink and swell in order to develop a new exoskeleton is nothing short of remarkable. Unfortunately, this swelling tends to result in diluted flavour, which is not what we're after. Selecting lobsters at the right stage, ideally as 'cripples' with a damaged claw (and therefore passed up by less sustainably minded restaurants), means that we get maybe two portions on a tasting menu out of each lobster. In season, you're likely to see 50 lobsters being dispatched in our kitchen every morning. We do this humanely, but it's a gory scene nonetheless. Like so much of what we do at BiBi, it's a labour-intensive job.

Having done all the hard work in sourcing, we then really don't want to get in the way of the lobster's own flavour. Malai marinades are commonplace in North India, though the use of *jaivitri elaichi masala* is distinctly Awadhi. It has a sophisticated and regal air about it, so it made perfect sense to pair it here with the most celebratory of seafoods.

Serves 2

Ajwain pumpkin purée
200g peeled violina pumpkin, cut into
   3-4cm-thick wedges
25g unsalted butter
2g roasted ajwain seeds
25g unsalted brown butter
2g kosher salt

For the bisque sauce base
50g rapeseed oil
0.6g green cardamom pods, smashed
0.4g mace blades
0.8g fennel seeds
0.8g coriander seeds
0.4g black peppercorns
5g garlic cloves
5g fresh ginger, smashed
6g Indian onion, sliced
0.5g lemongrass stick, smashed
6g brandy
40g plum tomato, diced
5g tomato purée
4g Kashmiri chilli powder
100g langoustine heads and shells,
   lightly grilled over the grill
0.1g saffron
1g kewra water
400g Fish Stock (page 209)

To finish the bisque sauce
40g rapeseed oil
16g lemongrass, smashed
16g fresh ginger, smashed
400g bisque base
160g whipping cream
kewra, to taste
kosher salt, to taste
5g Pre-Hy (page 212)

Ajwain pumpkin purée
Put the pumpkin wedges in a vacuum pouch with the first 25g butter and roasted ajwain and seal. Set up a steamer, or a combination oven, on full steam to 100°C. Place the pouch inside and cook for 30-40 minutes until soft. Once cooked, open the pouch and discard the butter and liquids. Blend the cooked squash in a high-speed blender or Vitamix and slowly add the brown butter and salt until it forms a smooth purée. Add the salt. Store in a fine-tip squeezy bottle in the refrigerator for up to 3 days.

Bisque sauce base
Heat the rapeseed oil for the bisque base in a large pot over a medium-high heat, then add all the whole spices and fry for 2-3 minutes until fragrant. Add the garlic, ginger, onion and lemongrass and cook until soft, then deglaze the pan with the brandy. Add the tomatoes, tomato purée and Kashmiri chilli powder and cook for 10-30 minutes over a medium-low heat until the oil splits to the surface. Add the langoustine heads and shells, saffron, kewra and fish stock and cook over a low heat for 30 minutes, then strain and discard the solids. Return the bisque base to the pot and cook until it reduces by a third.

Bisque sauce
Heat the rapeseed oil for finishing the bisque sauce in a different pot over a medium heat, add the lemongrass and ginger and cook for 2-3 minutes until fragrant. Once the bisque base is reduced, add it to the pot of ginger and lemongrass, along with the cream. Reduce the mixture by half, then finish with kewra and salt to taste. Blend in the pre-hy and load into an isi gun with two nitrous oxide charges. Keep warm until ready to serve.

Beef-fat ratte potatoes
Add the whole potatoes and beef fat to a pan and confit at 90°C for 45-60 minutes until the potatoes are cooked through. Remove the potatoes from the fat and let them cool to room temperature, then peel and cut into 1cm dice.

The Sea

Beef-fat ratte potatoes
200g ratte potatoes
beef fat, melted, to cover

For the pickled fennel
100g baby fennel, washed and thinly sliced
    (keep the fennel tops)
100g warm Pickling Liquor Base (page 224)

For the smoked eel emulsion
175g grapeseed oil
20g smoked eel bones (leftover from dicing
    the smoked eel)
20g egg white
10g dashi vinegar
grated zest and juice of ½ lime
2g kosher salt
5g Pre-Hy (page 212)

To serve
kosher salt
1 lobster tail (about 240g)
30g Malai Marinade (page 215)
8g pickled fennel
20g diced smoked eel
12g smoked eel emulsion
60g diced beef-fat ratte potatoes
8g Fennel Oil (page 220)
8g Lemongrass Oil (page 221)
40g ajwain pumpkin purée
bisque sauce

Pickled fennel

Put the thinly sliced fennel and tops in a container and pour over the warm pickling liquor. Leave to pickle in the refrigerator for a minimum of 4 hours, ideally 2-3 days. Once the fennel is pickled, it can last up to a week.

Smoked eel emulsion

Put 75g of the grapeseed oil in a container with the eel bones. Using a dehydrator or an oven, place the container inside at 70°C and infuse for 12 hours. Pass the infused oil through a fine chinois and discard the bones. Combine the remaining 100g grapeseed oil and the eel-infused oil and set aside. Put the egg white, dashi vinegar, the lime juice and zest, salt and pre-hy in a blender and blend to combine, then slowly add the combined oils to the blender until fully emulsified. Store in a fine-tip squeezy bottle in the refrigerator for up to 3 days.

Finish and serve

Bring a pot of salted water to the boil. Wedge the handle of a spoon between the shell and the meat of the lobster tail (this will keep it straight when blanching it) and blanch for 30 seconds. Remove the lobster from the water and place in iced water to stop it from cooking any further. When cool, take the tail off the shell and skewer it lengthways with a metal skewer.

Set up a charcoal grill. Once the charcoal is ready, brush the lobster with some of the malai marinade and cook it over the grill (keep back some marinade for brushing it while it cooks). Meanwhile, put the pickled fennel, diced smoked eel and diced ratte potatoes in a mixing bowl and dress with a few drops of fennel oil and lemongrass oil and kosher salt to taste. Place the potato mixture in the middle of each plate and dot it with eel emulsion and pumpkin purée.

Once the lobster is cooked, cover the plated mixture with aerated bisque sauce from the isi gun and rest the lobster on top.

Pictured on p.109

The Sea

Khatti Meethi Hake

I completely fell in love with hake during my time in the Basque country. Of course, we've always had access to it in Britain, but the Basques live and breathe seafood, and hake is often at the top of the wish list. In particular, if you ever make it to a traditional *sidrería*, you're likely to have two staples – salt cod with eggs, and hake served with fried peppers.

It's an incredibly ugly fish, not quite on the level of monkfish but also definitely not in the running for a seafood beauty pageant. It can also be riddled with worms (spoiler – some experts estimate that 99 per cent of white fish are), especially in the egg sacks, which is why it often stands in as a 'poor man's' cod. The interesting thing for me is that hake is considerably more versatile in the kitchen than most white flaky fish. It also has a really delicate flavour, mainly due to the low levels of fat and high water content. Brining or salting hake isn't essential, but it does help firm up the fish, especially if you want to grill it. However, with a strong enough marinade, like the imli-miso, *khatti meethi* (sour and sweet) marinade we use, you can skip this stage and grill it directly. We love serving it with a drop dosa – something in between a crispy dosa and a steamed idli. I think the slightly lactic tang and creamy mouthfeel helps carry the flavour of the marinade into every bite, while remaining cleansing at the same time.

Serves 4

250g hake fillet
120g Imli Miso (page 216)
240g Dosa Batter (page 212)
60g Peanut Podi (page 226)
120g Coconut Chutney (page 218)
Fried Curry Leaves (page 225)

Set up a charcoal grill.

Skin, pinbone the hake and portion it into 40–50g pieces, ideally about 12cm long.

Brush the portions of hake with imli miso, retaining about 20g of imli miso to put inside the dosa. Once the charcoal is ready, grill the hake until it is fully cooked through and lightly charred around the edges.

Heat a non-stick pan over a medium-high heat until smoking hot. Ladle 60g of dosa batter in the middle of the pan and, with the help of the back of the ladle, spread it in a circular motion until you get a dosa about 12cm in diameter. Reduce the heat to medium-high and cook for 2 minutes until the batter is fully set and the bottom is golden. Place the dosa on a plate and spread it with 5g of imli miso. Put the cooked hake in the middle of the dosa. Cover with peanut podi, fold it in half and serve with coconut chutney garnished with a fried curry leaf. Repeat with the remaining dosa batter, plating as directed.

Green Chilli Turbot

Time for a confession – this is not really my dish. It is a BiBi one, nonetheless. Before we opened, I had come across *chukh masala* in India, a kind of fermented red chilli paste that we explore in more detail on page 130. I had decided that cooking this paste in a heavily reduced chicken stock, split with really high-quality ghee, would be a spicy introduction to a new type of Indian-ish cooking, which was definitely the style of BiBi 1.0.

Keiran, our former head chef, was making the papads (page 28), which contain pickled green chillies, and asked if I had ever tried to make the chukh sauce green instead of red. So we made it, and tried it with some grilled chicken but decided it just didn't work in the same way. At the end of the day, we also had some Dover sole in the test kitchen so we cooked it slowly over the dying embers of the grill, and given there was some of the green chilli sauce left, basted and glazed the fish with that. And, just like that, a new dish was born.

Serves 4

For the spinach purée
200g spinach
2.5g kosher salt, plus more for blanching
    and if needed
5g rapeseed oil
50g shallots, thinly sliced
50g whipping cream
5g Pre-Hy (page 212)

For the celeriac purée
200g peeled celeriac
60g grapeseed oil
2.5g kosher salt, plus extra if needed
2g ajwain seeds, toasted
rice vinegar, to taste, if needed

**For the razor clam butter emulsion
and clams**
8 large razor clams
200g filtered water
salted butter, to emulsify

For the green chilli sauce
50g green chukh masala
5g kosher salt
200g Reduced White Chicken Stock
    (page 209)

For the fish preparation
25g Lemon Fish Cure (page 216)
250g turbot fillet
500g Vinegar Bath (page 216)

To serve
kosher salt
4 x 60g turbot portions
200g green chilli sauce
8 prepped and sliced razor clams with
    butter emulsion
12g Green Curry Oil (page 220)
4 sea beet leaves
80g picked monk's beard
40g spinach purée
40g celeriac purée

Spinach purée
Blanch the spinach in salted boiling water, then cool immediately in iced water. Once cold, remove and squeeze out the water. Heat the rapeseed oil in a sauce-pan over a medium heat, add the shallots and cook until translucent and soft. Add the cream and reduce by half, then blend in a high-speed blender or Vitamix until smooth. Leave to cool. Once cool, blend it with the spinach, the 2.5g salt and pre-hy until smooth. Pass through a chinois. Adjust seasoning if needed.

Celeriac purée
Cut the peeled celeriac into 1cm-thick slices. Add the celeriac, oil, salt and toast-ed ajwain to a vacuum pouch and seal. Set up a steamer, or a combination oven, on full steam to 100°C. Steam the mixture for 40 minutes, or until soft. Once cooked, strain the oil and set aside. Blend the celeriac in a high-speed blender or Vitamix, adding some of the cooking oil and juices. Adjust seasoning with salt and vinegar if needed and store in a squeezy bottle in the refrigerator for up to 3 days.

Razor clam butter emulsion and clams
Leave the clams in a container under running water to remove sand. Heat a pan over a high heat, add the clams and water and cover. Steam for 1 minute, or until all the clams are fully open. Remove the clams from the pan and reduce the liquid by half, then add the same amount of butter as there is liquid, and whisk to emulsify. Trim and slice the clams thinly diagonally. Set aside the emulsion and clam meat.

Green chilli sauce
Blend everything in a high-speed blender or Vitamix and pass through a fine chinois.

Fish preparation
Sprinkle the lemon cure over the filleted turbot and let it cure for 5 minutes, then wash off the cure in a vinegar bath. Cut the fish into 60g portions.

Assemble and serve
Set up a charcoal grill and a pot with salted boiling water for blanching. Grill the turbot over the charcoal (when the coal is ready) until fully cookec. Once cooked, peel off the skin (it should come off easily). Warm the green chilli sauce in a pan, then add the razor clams and the butter emulsion and remove from the heat and mix in the green curry oil. Blanch the sea beet leaves and monk's beard in the salted boiling filtered water. Place the fish in a bowl, and next to it place one large dot each of spinach purée and celeriac purée. Garnish with the blanched herbs and gently spoon the sauce with the razor clams around the fish.

Frazer Pugh and his scallops

Frazer Pugh of the Hand Picked Scallop Company is a terrifically attractive man. Handsome, rugged, hirsute, with a perma-tan from a life spent on boats and diving in the freezing salinity of the English Channel. Basically, all the things I wish I could be but never had the physical ability to attain.

Did you know that a scallop will always taste better if it comes from cold water because the scallop develops higher levels of the essential amino acid glycine which acts as a natural anti-freeze but has the (unfortunate) benefit of tasting sweet to a human? Frazer does. In fact, I'd wager there is very little about scallops that he doesn't know.

Aside from my now obvious man-crush on him, Frazer also dives for some of the best scallops in the world. Only ever hand-dived, selected from well-maintained 20–25-metre-deep sites, he and his divers have honed their skills to consistently deliver scallops of pristine purity. We serve his scallops raw at BiBi so there really is little room to hide when the scallops aren't at their very peak. Frazer knows this, which is why some months we just won't receive anything from him. He knows what we're looking for, despite having never eaten any meat or seafood in the restaurant – he only eats what he kills himself. Plus, he's always too busy out on the water or processing the scallops for delivery to any number of high-end restaurants around the country.

He started selling his scallops exclusively through an online marketplace but as soon as chefs tasted them, we all clamoured for accounts with him. So much so that there is rarely a day where he isn't 'treasure hunting', as he calls it, in the waters of Torbay.

Ajwaini Orkney Scallop

The smell of ajwain is one that will forever be linked to my *dadima*. Ajwain is one of those miracle cure-alls that pop up in traditional and herbal medicine. A quick google search will tell you that there is evidence that it boosts your metabolism, reduces joint inflammation, lowers blood pressure, relieves symptoms of asthma and even regulates menstrual cramps and irregular periods. For Punjabis, it's the ultimate post-meal tonic, chewed on as seeds, infused in water or added to chai. It also shows up quite often in fried goods such as *mathiya, pakore, bhajia,* etc. and, of course, most famously for us, with seafood – without ajwain, there is no fish *tikka*, no Amritsari macchi. This odd little seed, closely related to oregano and fennel, exclusively grows in the most barren and dry parts of Asia and North Africa. How it made its way into coastal cooking in India is beyond me; it really is the antithesis to the old adage, 'what grows together, goes together'.

Whenever I taste the sauce pre-service, I can only think of my grandmother's ajwain-filled Tic Tac box, hidden in the depths of her handbag.

Serves 4

For the nori ajwain seasoning
10g ajwain leaves
15g curry leaves
26g nori sheets
5g ajwain seeds
3g MSG
0.1g citric acid
4g kosher salt
3g caster sugar

For the ajwain sauce
24g Indian onion, thinly sliced
3g kosher salt
30g salted butter
300g button mushrooms, thinly sliced
12g garlic, chopped
1g ajwain seeds
100g Noilly Prat
250g Fish Stock (page 209)
130g full-fat milk
130g whipping cream
3g yellow chilli powder
Pre-Hy (page 212)

For the tepache gel
125g pineapple purée
63g Tepache (page 209)
25g mirin
5g chilli or tarragon vinegar
1g kosher salt
1% agar agar

To serve
4 Orkney scallops
rapeseed oil, to coat
200g Dashi Resting Butter (page 212)
nori ajwain seasoning
24g tepache gel
40g ajwain pumpkin purée
Thai basil leaf tips
20g N25 Schrenckii caviar
ajwain sauce isi

Nori ajwain seasoning
Set up a dehydrator or an oven to 70°C and dehydrate the ajwain and curry leaves and nori sheets overnight. Toast the ajwain seeds in a pan over a medium heat until fragrant. Let the ajwain, nori and curry leaves come to room temperature. Add the MSG, citric acid, curry leaves, ajwain and nori to a spice grinder or a Vitamix and blend to a smooth powder. Mix the powder with the salt and sugar and store in an airtight container at room temperature for up to 1 month.

Ajwain sauce
Put the onion, salt and butter in a saucepan over a medium-high heat and sweat for about 10 minutes until the onion is soft, with no colour. Add the mushrooms garlic and ajwain and cook for 10–15 minutes until all the water released from the mushrooms has evaporated. Add the Noilly Prat and reduce by two thirds, then add the fish stock and reduce by a third. Add the milk and cream, bring to the boil and simmer for 10 minutes. Strain the mixture and discard the solids. Season with yellow chilli powder and blend in 2g of pre-hy per 100g of sauce. Load the sauce in an isi gun with two nitrous oxide charges. Keep warm for up to 2 hours.

Tepache gel
Put all the ingredients except the agar agar in a high-speed blender or Vitamix and blend until homogenous. In a pot, whisk the mixture with the agar agar wel (to avoid lumps). Bring to the boil and boil for 2 minutes, then cool in a container in the refrigerator for 20–30 minutes until fully set. Once solid, blend in a high-speed blender or Vitamix to a smooth, shiny texture. Pass through a sieve, place in a container and remove the air in a vacuum machine. Store in a fine-tip squeezy bottle in the refrigerator for up to 3 days.

Assemble and serve
Heat a cast-iron pan to smoking point. Coat the scallops with rapeseed oil and sear on one side on the cast-iron pan. Melt the resting butter and once the scallops are 90 per cent cooked, put them in the butter and allow them to rest in a warm place for 3–5 minutes. Remove the scallops from the resting butter and dust generously with the ajwain nori seasoning. Cut them into four slices. Place the scallop in a bowl and dot with tepache gel and pumpkin purée. Garnish with Thai basil tips and quenelle the caviar on top of the scallop. Cover the scallop with the ajwaini sauce from the isi gun.

The Pasture
Shikaari

Why so much beef?

First, a confession to my bibis – sorry, but we can't pretend anymore – I eat meat. By most standards, not that much, but I'm not the good Brahmin boy you thought you were raising. I grew up a vegetarian. Before hitting my teens, I had the occasional piece of chicken tikka at a family party, or the even more occasional chicken and mushroom pie from the school canteen, but between the ages of 14 and 18 I was what is known in India as a 'pure veg'; a vegetarian who ate dairy and honey, but was otherwise essentially a vegan. Both my grand-mothers lived their whole lives this way, but I went one step further by abstaining from products that contained eggs, meaning no cakes for those fallow years. I'm not sure what brought about this decision. Maybe it was a weird form of teenage rebellion; for years, I was convinced I would become a Hindu priest, then, the day I turned 18, like a light switch, I lost all faith in religion. I called Hirsh, an old school friend who my dad often referred to as his 'adopted Yiddish son', and said, 'I want a Nandos today'. A true friend, Hirsh dropped everything and sped over in his banged-up old Proton before I had a change of heart.

I've not looked back since then. The best part of 20 years, literally the latter half of my life, has been spent as a meat eater. Let's face it: meat is delicious. Plant-based food is en vogue, but it's undeniable that we have evolved to be omnivores. It's just about finding a balance.

Having grown up without meat, I've always had a tinge of guilt about eating it. Probably be-cause we were raised being told meat is 'dirty', and 'cruel', I approach it with the mentality that any meat that I serve or consume has to pass a few non-negotiable criteria:

1. The animal has to live a good, healthy and happy life
If an animal has lived a fulfilled life, we remove some of the guilt around rearing meat purely for consumption. Whenever I visit any of the meat or poultry farms we work with, I always look for the signs that the farmers are almost a little sad to see their animals go off to the abattoir, but then still enjoy the fruits of their labour. Farmers who care about their animals are the only ones we're interested in working with.

Also, happy animals taste better. When I was in the Lake District, I remember one farmer who lined his transport vehicles with lamb's wool, so that when he loaded up his herd for their final journey, they felt comforted by being surrounded by other sheep, as if it was any other day. Tests on their meat showed a lower level of lactic acid build-up, which is usually caused by stress. If you've ever suffered from a muscle cramp, you know what the feeling of lactic acid build-up is – there is no way that translates to good flavour. There is also the argument that older, healthier animals produce much tastier meat (with the exception of veal). A long life with mixed feed means more intramuscular fat, and bigger muscles which makes the meat juicier and tastier. The old adage is true – fat is flavour.

2. The impact of an animal's life should be maximal for flavour, minimal for the environment
There is so much misinformation, half-truths and bad science around meat production.

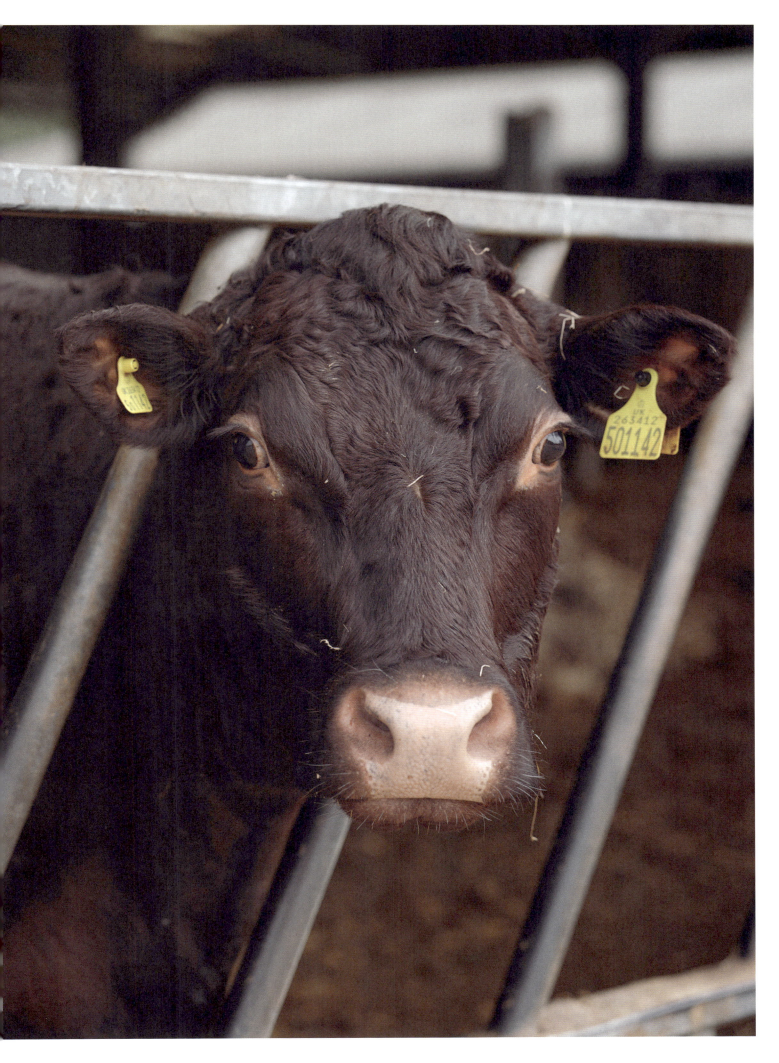

It's also hard to accurately measure its output. Methane gas is the key issue when it comes to harmful output, from beef production in particular. When a cow produces methane – as do you and I – it turns into carbon dioxide, which can be processed one of two ways: it is either released into the environment where it can hang around for about a decade before decaying, or, if that cow is raised on a regenerative farm, it is absorbed by plants in the local environment, photosynthesised into more plant matter, then eaten by the next generation, in what is known as the biogenic carbon cycle. With intensively-raised cattle, flat fields are cleared then built on, meaning the methane has no chance to be sequestered locally. And on those farms, the feed is also likely to be shipped from every corner of the planet, with much famously coming in as soybeans from the Amazon basin. No trees, no carbon cycle.

Of course, this comes at a cost, which is why the meat we use at the restaurant is some of the most expensive in the country. We could make more money by serving cheaper meat, but what's the long-term cost of that to the planet?

3. Meat, like any ingredient, has seasons, and those should be respected
The taste of a plum farmed in Kenya that's shipped to us in winter, versus one picked straight from the tree in the height of English summer, are worlds apart. The same goes for meat. In the UK lambs are around from late February to April, pork soon after that into the summer, then game season starts in autumn (along with a second coming for lamb and goat), before we hit peak beef season. Chickens are mostly available all year round. Availability is connected to breeding cycles, the animal's age, and when their food also hits peak season. I prefer lamb in the second wave in autumn as they've spent the whole summer eating wild grasses and herbs, while also developing a thicker layer of tasty subcutaneous fat.

You might wonder why we serve beef in the summer at BiBi, when winter is when it is typically considered to be 'in season' and at its best. Well, quite often we age meats far past the industry norms. Supermarkets proudly boast their meat is heavily 'dry-aged' after as little as 21 days, but I think the furthest we've taken the meat post-slaughter is 100 days: ageing helps to tenderise and break down the protein, and means that we can serve the meat three months after the season is over.

4. Use as much of the animal as possible
I'm not wild about most offal. I eat it because I feel I should (probably because I didn't grow up eating meat and never developed a palate for gamey flavours), but there are some cuts that I adore and sweetbreads are one of my favourite. India has a long history of eating offal – Kaleji [liver], maghaz [goat brain] and paya [trotters] line pretty much any non-vegetarian food market across the country – but it is often masked by other flavours, mainly the heavy masala they're cooked in. At BiBi, we often take trim from a prime cut and lace it with a little offal. For example, with chicken keema, the base is often chicken breast trim, with extra chicken skin for fattiness and 20% of the mixture consisting of chicken hearts. It's a nice way to use less desirable bits, without having to eat a bowlful of hearts, which is probably not going to be for everyone.

5. Never forget how lucky we are
To have the luxury to choose whether to eat meat, or if we want to source it from an intensive chicken factory or from a family-run operation where chickens eat herbs from the farm next door, is a First World problem. Just because bad meat is readily available, doesn't mean we should fall back on it. I do not intend to vilify plant-based diets, but it's important to recognise that consuming meat has been part of the human story for millennia. It is delicious, sustaining and experiential. We need to do our bit to ensure we strike a balance.

Raw Beef Pepper Fry

Have you ever tried the real pepper fry in Kerala? This is probably about as far removed from it as possible. But sometimes you need a title for a dish that settles people a bit. And the reality is there is an inherent distrust from people to eat cooked beef in Indian restaurants anyway; throw in the fact that it is a tartare, and this would be a non-starter in any other Indian restaurant. So, we do our best to add some familiarity to what is otherwise a completely unfamiliar dish.

Why go through the difficulty of having to trick guests into eating this? Because pepper is to spices what Lionel Messi is to football. It's the GOAT spice. It was such a tasty and valuable addition to boring western cookery that Europeans in the Middle Ages called it 'black gold'. Imagine a spice so delicious that you would get on a ship for nine months risking scurvy, sodomy and shipwrecks just to get your hands on it. If pepper didn't grow so well in Kerala, there is a chance that India would have never been colonised. Of course, I want to celebrate an ingredient which quite literally redirected the course of history.

The problem with a real pepper fry - as delicious as it is with its fragrant, complex, woody black pepper - is that the meat is always cooked to a point where it is unrecognisable. I remember distinctly having one rendition in Madurai and for the life of me I have no idea what the meat was. We wanted to flip that on its head and serve a version which can still scream with peppery heat, but lets the meat come through, too. Most people use fillet for a tartare, but thanks to L'Enclume and Moor Hall, I've always favoured a cut with a little more age and fat, so we tend to go with a well-aged sirloin, ideally from a bigger cow, like a Ruby Red / Devon or Dexter. Not only are they quite literally made to grow well on British pasture, but they develop slowly, so all the meat is well marbled with intramuscular fat, meaning we can age them further to bring out all the funk needed to stand up to the seasoning in this dish.

Serves 4

For the beetroot compression liquid
500g beetroot juice
1g sherry vinegar
1g smoke powder

For the compressed beetroot
1 large beetroot
2 tablespoons rapeseed oil
1 tablespoon coarse rock salt

For the onion oil and burnt onions
125g brown onions, sliced
40g grapeseed oil

For the onion ash
12.5g onion oil
125g maltodextrine
7.5g burnt onions
7.5g kosher salt
2g citric acid
20g BiBi Chaat Masala (page 213)

For the burnt milagi podi
24g urad dal
24g chana dal
12g white sesame seeds
12g coriander seeds
24g desiccated coconut
10g Reshampatti chilli powder
12g deggi mirch
10g asafoetida

Beetroot compression liquid
Reduce the beetroot juice in a saucepan over a medium heat to 250ml. Remove from the heat and, once cool, stir in the sherry vinegar and smoke powder.

Compressed beetroot
Preheat the oven to 180°C. Cut squares of foil big enough to wrap around the beetroot.

Put the rapeseed oil and the rock salt on the foil and wrap it around the beetroot. Place on a tray and bake until cooked - how long this will take will vary depending on its size. Remove from the oven and, once cool, peel and trim, then cut into 1cm dice. Place the dice in a container or bag with the compression liquid and compress in a vacuum machine. Strain and store in an airtight container in the refrigerator for up to 3 days.

Onion oil and burnt onions
Put the sliced onions and grapeseed oil in a saucepan and cook over a low heat for 3 hours until completely soft. Remove from the heat and leave to cool, then strain the onions, retaining the oil.

Preheat the oven to 250°C. Spread the onions out on a baking tray and bake in the oven until burnt and blackened, then dehydrate at 65°C overnight.

For the salli potatoes
250g agria potatoes, peeled and cut into
 thin julienne strips with a mandoline
kosher salt
rapeseed oil, for deep frying
burnt milagi podi, to taste
freshly ground black pepper

For the lapsang dressing
85g Lapsang Oil (page 221)
85g grapeseed oil
42g Indian lemon juice
2g kosher salt
20g onion ash
1g freshly ground black pepper

For the pepper fry sauce
30g coconut oil
4g split white urad dal, rinsed and soaked
 in water for minimum 1 hour
4g black mustard seeds
6g curry leaves
2g black peppercorns
10g fresh peeled ginger, chopped
10g garlic, chopped
2g green bird's eye chilli, chopped
200g Indian onion, sliced
76g coconut cream
4g kosher salt

For the tartare mix
150g beef sirloin, cut into 1cm cubes
50g compressed beetroot, cut into
 1cm cubes
20g Indian onion, cut into small dice
20g Tendli Pickle (page 224), finely diced
8g green bird's eye chilli, finely diced
8g chives, thinly sliced
60g Lapsang dressing
4g Maldon salt

To serve
80g pepper fry sauce
8 fermented tellicherry green peppercorns
320g tartare mix
60g Curry Leaf Jalapeño Emulsion
 (page 218)
salli potatoes
black peppercorns, for grinding
onion ash, to garnish
burnt milagi podi, to garnish

Onion ash
Measure out 12.5g of the onion oil and reserve the rest for another use. Blend the onion oil with the maltodextrin and burnt onions in a Thermomix or food processor until they form a fine powder. Season with the salt, citric acid and chaat masala.

Burnt milagi podi
Mix all the ingredients together and grind to a coarse powder, then roast in a frying pan over a high heat for 2–3 minutes, stirring, until very deep brown. Store in an airtight container at room temperature for up to 1 month.

Salli potatoes
Put the julienned potatoes in a container under cold running water until it runs clear. Make a 2% cold brine with cold water and salt, place the julienned potatoes in and leave in the refrigerator overnight. Heat enough rapeseed oil for deep frying to 160°C in a deep fat fryer (two-thirds to three-quarters full). Remove the potatoes from the brine, place in a cloth and squeeze until most of the water comes out. Deep fry in small batches for 3 minutes per batch until crispy and golden. Place on a tray lined with kitchen paper to drain the excess oil. Season with burnt milagi podi, black pepper and salt.

Lapsang dressing
Combine all the ingredients using a hand blender. Store in a fine-tip squeezy bottle in the refrigerator for up to a week.

Pepper fry sauce
Heat the coconut oil in a sauté pan or saucepan over a medium-high heat, add the drained urad dal and fry for 1–2 minutes until light golden, then add the mustard seeds and curry leaves and cook until they splutter. Add the black peppercorns, ginger, garlic and chilli and cook for 2 minutes until fragrant. Add the sliced onion and cook for 5 minutes until tender – it should still have a bite. Add the coconut cream and salt and cook for 5 minutes, then blend in a high-speed blender or Vitamix until smooth.

Tartare mix
Mix all the ingredients together.

Assemble and serve
Place a large dot of pepper fry sauce on a plate and place a couple of fermented peppercorns in the middle. Place 80g of tartare mix forming a mound on top of the pepper fry sauce. Dot the top with curry leaf emulsion. Cover the tartare with 5g salli potatoes and grate some fresh black pepper and sprinkle a little onion ash and burnt milagi podi on top.

Pictured on p.129

Veal Sweetbread in Chamba Chukh Masala

When I was travelling around India on a research trip, my wife's school friend was getting married in Jaipur, so I took a short break from research, so we could attend the wedding together before heading over to some farms on the Haryana / Rajasthan border. It was my first time out from a particularly challenging trip and I was more than happy to take a few days off from intensive eating and pause for a few days at her *massi's* house.

Fortunately, my wife's massi didn't think I deserved a break. And so, for the few days we stayed with her, she was keen for me to try as many local delicacies as possible. There were some good things, like *ghewar*, a kind of fried honeycomb pastry from Rajasthan, designed to stay moist for long treks in the desert. But, on the whole, they were things I had already heard or read about during my own research. One morning we sat down to a late Punjabi breakfast of *parathas* and fresh *dahi* with a few achars and condiments on the table. As if struck by inspiration, massi got up from the table and fetched a mysterious oil in a red jar for me, suggesting if I liked spicy food, I should try this stuff she found on a recent trip to Himachal Pradesh. A pretty deadly paste called *chukh*.

Most of my food references are quite high-end, but I swear to you this paste tasted identical to Nando's extra-extra hot sauce. It transpires that the high elevation of the Chamba region, where the paste is made, means that the chillies are exposed to extreme temperature variations – very hot days, very mild nights – just like the region of Mozambique where peri peri originates from. When we opened BiBi, we served chukh sauce with a 'slaw' of baby gem lettuce and slowly grilled chicken thighs. This affectionately became known as 'the other Sharmaji's chicken' – named after our regular Dr. Vik Sharma (no relation).

Unfortunately, there is no way to buy chukh outside India; just hope you're lucky enough to know someone who'll smuggle it in for you.

Serves 4

For the chamba chukh sauce
25g red chamba chukh
2.5g kosher salt
100g Reduced Chicken Stock (page 209)
50g Pre-Hy (page 212)
10g thinly chopped chives

For the dressed baby gem salad
1 head baby gem lettuce
35g buttermilk
15g crème fraîche
0.5g kosher salt

For the sweetbread
200g veal sweetbreads, soaked in iced water
    for 2½ hours
kosher salt
rice wine vinegar, for brine
40g Red Chamba Chukh Marinade
    (page 215)
20g rapeseed oil
20g salted butter

To serve
dressed baby gem salad
200g veal sweetbreads
100g chamba chukh sauce
finely chopped chives

Chamba chukh sauce
Blitz the chamba chukh until smooth in a Thermomix or food processor, then blend it with all the other ingredients until smooth.

Dressed baby gem salad
Remove the foot of the lettuce, discard and thinly slice the rest. Mix the buttermilk, crème fraîche and salt until fully homogenous. Dress the sliced lettuce with the buttermilk dressing.

Sweetbread
Wash all the scum off the sweetbreads under running water. Make a 1.2% brine solution with cold water and salt and add 5% of rice vinegar. Cover the sweetbread in a saucepan with the solution and, starting from cold, lightly poach them, simmering until they reach an internal temperature of 85°C. Cool them quickly in an ice bath, then peel them carefully. Heat a cast-iron pan to smoking point. Coat the sweetbread in the chukh marinade. Add the rapeseed oil to the pan and sear the sweetbreads for 4–5 minutes until crispy, lower the heat to medium, add the butter and 20g of the chukh sauce and baste for 2–3 minutes until fully cooked.

Assemble and serve
Place the dressed baby gem salad in the middle of a plate. Carve the sweetbread and place on top of the lettuce. Gently place the sauce around the sweetbread and garnish with chopped chives.

Goodbye, little friend: understanding where our food comes from

As I've already mentioned, I grew up mostly vegetarian. With this in mind, my first exposure to meat – real meat, not the stuff wrapped in plastic at the supermarket which has lost all resemblance to the animal it came from – was in India. My grandfather was being sent out on some errands and asked if I wanted to go with him. This meant the opportunity to jump on the back of his motorcycle and zip through the bustling streets of suburban Mumbai, so I was always game. Andheri, the district they lived in, was a neighbourhood close to the glamour and luxury of Juhu beach; India's answer to Malibu (my grandparents' house was barely 20 minutes away from where Soho House now sits, which probably tells you everything). In contrast, within a 10-minute drive was one of the poor areas of the city – not quite a slum, but street children, open sewage systems and stray dogs were a common sight. And of course, stereotypically, you'd see the odd cow sat in the middle of the road, going about her business.

On this particular day we crossed all the way down to Mahim, back then one of the poorer districts of Mumbai, and one which was a distinctly Muslim area. There are a few tell-tale signs when you cross from Hindu- to Muslim-dominated areas of Indian cities. One is the sound of the Imam belting out the call to prayer from the Masjid, and the other is the number of cats. It's a historical artefact of Muslim invasion; Hindu areas have stray dogs, Muslims have stray cats. And the archetypal relationship between those two animals also neatly sums up how the relationship between those two religions worked for so many years. Mahim back then (which is *very* different to now) felt like the abandoned Wild West: pot-hole-ridden roads, peeling paint and almost a guarantee that every shop sign would be missing – a never-ending dust bowl.

We stopped along the way to pick up whatever it is Grandmother had requested, and as my grandfather stopped at a kiosk to pick up cigarettes, I wandered across the road and down a wide, shaded alley lined by flats with a never-ending row of clothes flung over balconies to dry. I'm not sure why, but I found myself drawn to the sound of a goat, so headed in that direction. As I got closer, I could make out that the goat was distressed, and heard a bit of a skirmish. Rounding the corner, I saw two men holding the goat down, while a bear-like man in a knitted kufi and stained grey *kurta* came out of the shadows inside, wielding a rusty cleaver. With a sharp strike, the butcher tore through the goat's jugular then, suddenly, silence. The goat twitched a little as the blood poured out into the street, quickly rinsed away with water from a bucket by the butcher's assistants. I'm not sure there is a stillness like the one where an animal's life has just been taken. I swear I could hear the newspapers rustling in the distant wind.

I've often wondered if that memory cemented my position as a vegetarian in my formative years. It all felt quite disconnected from reality. In the middle of an underdeveloped but overpopulated city, there was this goat living its final moments, surrounded by dust and concrete that had no semblance to its natural environment. In sharp contrast, the first time I was somewhat 'involved' in livestock farming when working for Simon Rogan in the Lake District, we had a herd of heritage sheep – the famously feisty Herdwick sheep – in a picture-perfect setting of lush grass, rolling hills and thick, wild plants and flowers for them to feed on. This made more sense to me. Sheep naturally bred to thrive in its own conditions, eating food they have always eaten, breathing the same clean air they have always needed.

As brutal as that first exposure to animal death and the ensuing whole-animal butchery in Mumbai was, it certainly gave me an appreciation of where our meat comes from, and maybe where it should come from too.

Aged Swaledale Lamb Barra Kebab

This dish illustrates the debt I owe to Karam Sethi for teaching me so much about Indian food. We were in the Middle East, recruiting a head chef for a JKS project, in 2018. We met with Tamba (a chef who impressed us so much that he became head chef at Brigadiers in London) at Gazebo in DIFC, a Dubai institution, and I spotted *burra* kebab on the menu. I remarked to Karam that it was a weird name for a kebab – 'barra' in Punjabi literally means 'big'. He gently corrected me, telling me that burra in Mughlai cooking refers to mutton meat and often specifically to the chops or waist region. I will never forget the embarrassment: I had given myself away as an imposter. I was only just getting to grips with the vast lexicon of Indian cooking and that lunch was a clear reminder that I had, and always will have, work left to do.

In Britain we like meat cooked pink (with lamb I actually prefer medium-well). Our animals spend plenty of time on lush pasture giving their meat more fat and flavour than their subcontinental counterparts.

Serves 4

For the ver masala oil
25g Ver Masala (page 215)
225g grapeseed oil

For the lamb chops
1 x 400–600g rack of aged Swaledale lamb chops, French-trimmed
60g First Marinade (page 215)
60g Barra Marinade (page 215)

For the Tokyo turnip
1 Tokyo turnip, leaves/tops trimmed and set aside
30g MSG Oil (page 221)

To serve
Maldon salt, to taste
5g ver masala oil
4 wedges of Tokyo turnip, plus 4 reserved leaves (quickly blanched and squeezed of excess liquid)
2 portioned and marinated double lamb chops
60g Walnut Chutney (page 219)
60g Green Pepper Sauce (page 219)
ghee, for basting

Ver masala oil
Put the paste and oil in a high-speed blender or Vitamix and blend thoroughly, then place in a metal container. Set a dehydrator or an oven to 70°C and cook for 15 hours. Pass the mixture through a fine chinois and store the oil in a fine-tip squeezy bottle in the refrigerator for up to 1 month.

Lamb chops
Remove the fat cap from the rack of lamb and trim it down to the eye of the meat. French-trim the bones and remove every other bone to get more meat per bone once portioned. Wrap the remaining bones with foil to avoid them burning. Divide the rack into three portions of two bones each. Coat the lamb chops in the first marinade and allow them to rest for 30 minutes in the refrigerator. Transfer them to a different container, discarding the remaining juices from the first marinade, and rub the barra marinade around the meat of the chop (retaining 30–40g for brushing them later as they cook). Allow to marinate in the refrigerator for about 2 hours before grilling.

Tokyo turnip
Set aside some of the turnip tops for the green pepper sauce and the best leaves for using as garnish. Peel the turnip and cut it into 6–8 wedges, depending on size. Set up a steamer, or a combination oven, on full steam to 100°C. Place the turnip in a vacuum pouch with the MSG oil, seal and steam for 15 minutes. Remove from the bag.

Finish and serve
Set up a charcoal grill. Once the charcoal is ready, place a sieve on top of the grill over the charcoal and finish cooking the turnip wedges in the sieve, letting them develop some colour. Once fully cooked, season with the ver oil and Maldon salt.

Cook the lamb chops over the charcoal, brushing them with the remaining marinade as needed. Cook to medium-rare, ensuring the outside is lightly charred around the edges. Take off the heat, baste generously with ghee and allow the lamb to rest for 5–7 minutes before carving it.

Place 2 large dots each of walnut chutney and green pepper sauce on a plate. Place the carved lamb chop next to the dots. Place the warmed turnip wedge coated with ver oil and cover it with a blanched and lightly grilled turnip leaf.

Hogget Haleem

There are versions of *haleem, halim, harisa, kichra* all the way from Eastern Turkey through to Hyderabad in the south of India. In principle, it's a pretty ancient food. Grains and meat cooked into a thick, nutritious porridge to be enjoyed throughout the colder months, or as it is inherently a Muslim dish, eaten during Ramadan when people practice the most extreme and diligent form of intermittent fasting throughout the daylight hours. It is also a recipe that requires very little skill or equipment: essentially fire, a thick-bottomed pan and a wooden mallet to emulsify the fat and grains into a paste.

I'm probably not selling it very well. I promise if you go through the effort of making this dish, which is probably one of the more achievable dishes in this book, you will be pleasantly surprised at how tasty something so simple can be. The recipe essentially involves two key steps; one is making sure the mix is thoroughly broken down and the other is whipping it as we do with a whisk or stand mixer. The other challenge is making sure there's enough freshness to cut the monotonous texture of a well-made haleem: you don't want to be caught short on the ghee, raw and fried Indian onions, lemons and fresh herbs.

Serves 4

25g chana dal, rinsed and soaked overnight
25g split white urad dal, rinsed and
    soaked overnight
100g grass-fed ghee
125g Indian onions, thinly sliced
75g onion paste
25g Ginger and Garlic Paste (page 208)
7.5g coriander stem, finely chopped
7.5g green bird's eye chilli, finely chopped
2.5g deggi mirch
2.5g yellow chilli powder
2.5g ground turmeric
1.3g ground royal cumin
5g Garam Masala (page 213)
3g ground cumin
2g ground coriander
250g boneless hogget neck, diced
50g natural yoghurt
2.5g mint leaves, thinly sliced
6g kosher salt
50g fine bulgur wheat

To serve
320g haleem
12g fresh peeled ginger, julienned
8g Indian onion, thinly sliced
4g Fried Onions (page 225)
12g mint leaves
12g coriander leaves
8g Indian Lemon Dressing (page 216)
seasonal flowers, to garnish

Drain the soaked chana dal and urad dal and cook together in a pressure cooker with water – 3–4 times the volume of dals – at high pressure for 22 minutes, then drain the excess water.

Heat the ghee in a pot over a medium-high heat. Add the onions and fry for 8–10 minutes until they are deep brown, then add the onion paste, ginger and garlic paste, coriander stem and chilli and cook for 5–10 minutes until the ghee splits and settles on the surface. Add all the dried spices and cook for 5 minutes until the mix is a dark brown colour with a bit of yellow. Add the hogget and sear until brown, then add the yoghurt and mint and cook for 10–15 minutes until it splits again. Add the salt, cooked dal, bulgur wheat and enough water to cover the wheat by 2.5cm. Once the wheat is cooked, after about 15 minutes, put the mixture in a stand mixer fitted with the whisk attachment and whisk for 5 minutes at speed 2 until the mixture has achieved a thick texture and all the wheat and meat has broken down. Return to a pan and warm through.

Serve
Plate the haleem and garnish it with the julienned ginger, onion slices, fried onions, mint and coriander leaves dressed with lemon dressing and flowers.

Hussainbad Mutton Seekh Kebab

I'm always grateful that I was raised British and Indian – not one or the other, but also not half of each. I fully embraced my English side in the sports I played, my circle of friends, the music I listened to in my teens and even the way I dressed. However, on weekends, I was still surrounded by family, knew members of the local Indian community, could speak the languages of my heritage and thankfully knew about my own culture and the history of India. I am also grateful that I knew Indian food wasn't just a spicy curry on a Friday night. That said, when you're 17 and it's a Friday night after football practice, there are few more wholesome activities than going for a mixed grill and a pint (or three) of Cobra with your team. An Indian mixed grill is invariably terrible. It's almost impossible to cook lamb, chicken and seafood to the perfect *cuisson*, then put it on a raging-hot sizzler platter and send it out across a pub without getting at least one of them wrong. The only saving grace – other than those onions taking on all the meat juices – was the *seekh* kebab.

It's a pretty nondescript name; seekh just means skewer. It's typically minced mutton, sometimes chicken, and can be as simple as the Peshwari versions that contain a few herbs and cumin, or as complex as the Jawahari version that we stuff into chicken wings whenever I'm feeling particularly mean to the chefs working on the grill section (see page 152). The Hussainabad seekh is inspired by the famous Karachi street food and the small foodie neighbourhood of Hussainabad. The key ingredient that keeps this kebab juicy is the ground almonds, which not only lends it sweet fattiness, but also swells with the meat juices as it cooks. And to bring about some of that Friday night magic, I've stolen a trick from Kian at Berenjak and baste the kebab and add a small herb salad with a tomato water dressing for extra umami and moisture.

Serves 4

For the tomato pav bhaji dressing
50g reduced Tomato Water (page 209)
2.5g Pav Bhaji Masala (page 214)
25g cold-pressed sunflower oil
0.4g dried mint
1g coriander stem

For the dressed herb salad
12g coriander leaves
12g mint leaves
8g Thai basil leaves
4g pickled burgundy wood sorrel
8g Indian onion, thinly sliced
8g tomato pav bhaji dressing

For the mutton seekh kebab
2.5g coriander seeds
2.5g deggi mirch
1.3g royal cumin seeds
1.3g black peppercorns
0.8g black cardamom seeds
7.5g fresh peeled ginger, finely diced
5g garlic, finely diced
5g kosher salt
2.5g black salt
5g green bird's eye chilli, finely diced
10g coriander stem, thinly sliced
5g mint leaves, cut into a chiffonade
250g mutton shoulder (30% fat)
10g ground almonds

To serve
8 x 150g mutton seekh kebab
50g dressed herb salad

Tomato pav bhaji dressing
Blend all the ingredients in a high-speed blender or Vitamix until smooth. Pass the dressing through a fine chinois.

Dressed herb salad
Mix all the herbs with the onions and dress the salad with the pav bhaji dressing just before serving it.

Mutton seekh kebab
Preheat the oven to 160°C and lightly roast the coriander seeds on a tray for 3 minutes. Grind to a fine powder with the rest of the spices. Mix the spices, diced ginger and garlic, salts, green chilli and herbs with the mutton shoulder and mince through the thick disc of a meat mincer once. Portion into two 150g balls. Wet your hand and shape into a kebab along a wide metal skewer. Repeat to make three more kebabs.

Set up a charcoal grill. When the charcoal is ready, grill the kebabs, rotating regularly, until fully cooked.

Serve
Serve each kebab along with the dressed herb salad.

Galouti kebab

In a world of wellness, the quest for longevity and restricted eating windows, it's always encouraging to hear stories from a bygone era, where unabashed indulgence was seen as a positive trait, rather than being recklessly irresponsible. I try to live my life by the motto 'carpe diem' – seize the day – and to grab every opportunity that comes my way and generally consider the risks later. But I also don't want to keel over in my forties, so I go to the gym, try to eat a balanced diet and don't drink too much. Nawab Asaf-ud-Daula (1748-1797) had a much more steadfast dedication to the carpe diem life. One of a long line of the Awadhi hedonists, the Nawab lived in the resplendent luxury of Lucknow, in the final throes of Indian indulgence before the British descended on the country. Asaf-ud-Daula was famous throughout the Awadh and Mughal dynasty for his opulence, especially when it came to his diet. He had built a reputation for a notorious obsession with shahi or 'royal' cuisine and rich meat-based curries in kebabs. He is responsible not only for much of the beautiful architecture of Lucknow, including the Imambara, the high court, but also for installing a military department in the kitchen of his palace, much like Escoffier did in France several hundred years later. Their brief was to create a plethora of rotating stews, breads and kebabs to entertain the Nawab and his cohorts. Legend has it that due to his overindulgences – predominantly with a particular poppy-derivative from Mughal-controlled Afghanistan – the Nawab lost all his teeth. Not a man to let that slow him down, his chefs developed a recipe for a kebab so soft that he could gum it into submission. They even played a little joke on him by using poppy seeds in the recipe.

These days, other than at BiBi, of course, if you ask any right-minded Indian where the best galouti kebabs are, they will surely recommend that you can only find them in Lucknow. Sorry for those reading from Delhi. Delhi's are not bad, but get in the car, drive those eight hours to Lucknow and try the real deal. The very best place for them is Tunday Kebab in Khayali Ganj, on a narrow offshoot of the Old Nazirabad Road. Tunday comes from the Urdu word tunda, meaning crippled – like our toothless prince, the founding father of this kebab restaurant was one-armed, and generations of his apprentices still pay homage to this, as they only use one hand when shaping the patties. So prized are these kebabs, that Lucknowis living in London will now ask any visiting relatives to swing by Tunday to pick up a box of galouti kebabs, freeze them, then pack them in their hold luggage. By the time they reach London they are still just frozen.

You cannot imagine, when we first put the galouti on our menu, how quickly people flocked to the restaurant in the hope to have a little taste of home. In the early days, it brought me immense pride when guests would say, 'these are as good as or better than the ones from Tunday' (if you know your Indian food, you know Tunday).

The way we recommend guests eat the galouti is based on the way I was shown by the waiter at Tunday; you open up an ulta-tawa paratha (or roomali roti for us), layer in some Indian onions with a mint kebab chutney, then spread the kebab like a paté on a piece of toast. You then roll up the roti, ingeniously keeping all of the aroma from the onions, meat and chutney off your hands, and eat it like a thin burrito. People go crazy for them, almost as if they're addicted in the same way the original recipient was hooked to his own addictive substance of choice.

We've had guests from India order thirty of these kebabs, along with a bottle of Champagne and a tin of caviar to have with papads. It is still Mayfair, after all. We've also had to try to explain the ritual of opening up the roomali roti and spreading the galouti on there to guests from all over the world. Once, a Japanese guest sat alone on the counter and just wasn't getting the story (and this was in the days where our team didn't include a native Japanese speaker) so I took the liberty of assembling the perfect roll for him, to which he said, 'Oishi. Like Indian sushi roll'.

Ex-Dairy Goat Galouti Kebab

This dish is ever-present on the BiBi menu and has little chance of being taken off. Why? Because it's delicious (that's always the first answer), it gives our guests a true hit of Indian flavour and it allows us to tell a story of Indian cuisine, using lesser-loved cuts or animals. For a year or so, we made the dish with lamb, focussing on using belly and saddle trim taken off other parts of the menu. Then, our sous chef Alessandro suggested it might be fun to say 'goat galouti' forty times a night (it's not), so we tried out some ex-dairy goat from a farmer we knew in Devon. As the dish developed, we got into the realm of basically buying whole goats, just for this one dish, the hides of which go into our leather products at the restaurant.

Sustainable. Delicious. Nostalgic. Everything the perfect BiBi dish should represent.

Serves 4

For the galouti kebabs
2g white poppy seeds, soaked in water
    for 30 minutes to 1 hour
6g Cashew Paste (page 208)
2.4g Garam Masala (page 213)
2g Ginger and Garlic Paste (page 208)
1.5g Kashmiri yellow chilli powder
6g ghee
6g Roasted Besan Flour (page 212)
3g kosher salt
1.5g kewra water
6g tenderiser paste (1g green papaya
    powder mixed with 5g water)
100g goat shoulder, diced
50g goat belly, diced

To serve
4 x 30g galouti kebab
40g Indian onion, cut into 5mm-thick rings
3g green bird's eye chilli, brunoised
10g Indian Lemon Dressing (page 216)
2 Roomali Roti (page 229)
60g Green Chutney (page 218)

Galouti kebabs
Drain the poppy seeds. Put all the ingredients except the goat in a blender and blend to form a paste. Mix the diced meat with the paste in a mixing bowl, then pass the meat mixture through a mincer fitted with the finest disc four times. Place it in an airtight container and let it rest in the refrigerator for 1 hour, then shape into six 30g balls.

Finish and serve
Heat a non-stick frying pan over a medium heat and cook the kebabs for 4 minutes on each side, or until the core temperature reaches 75°C. Put the Indian onion rings and brunoised chilli in a mixing bowl and season with the Indian lemon dressing. Serve the kebabs with roomali roti, green chutney and the seasoned onion rings.

Achari Middlewhite Pork Belly

We're really lucky that we found our home in Mayfair, on what was an up-and-coming street, sandwiched between Grosvenor Square and Selfridges. I can't imagine a more perfect location for what BiBi has become; a high-end but fun restaurant ... admittedly with a price point that matches the postcode. People from all over the world come to and stay in Mayfair, meaning that the restaurant has been discovered by every nationality under the sun. Unfortunately, what that also means is that we can rarely ever feature pork on our menu which, religion or dietary choices aside, is a big shame for me personally because I love it. It's probably my single favourite meat and it is just so versatile. Cured and preserved as salami, jamon and bacon, chops cooked over charcoal, slow-smoked pulled pork or a braised belly ... each one is so distinct but has the single thread of piggy deliciousness. And we haven't even mentioned bangers and mash!

Achar is just a generic word for pickle in India, though when discussed with meat it most often refers to a spice mix with mustard, nigella, fennel and fenugreek seeds. Each one brings its own flavour and also helps to preserve the main ingredients, whether it's fruit, vegetables, meat or fish. In our case, we make a garlic achar and forget about it for about a year before moving onto the next stage (which is much shorter by comparison). The wakame salad is not traditionally Indian, and you could make it with cucumber if you prefer, but it's essential for cutting all the fatty, pungent heat from the pork sauce.

Serves 4

For the sesame chutney
20g peanuts
30g white sesame seeds
80g freshly grated coconut
5g coconut vinegar
10g Tamarind Paste (page 208)
3 whole red Kashmiri chillies
15g garlic
240g water

For the confit pork belly
250g pork belly (skin on)
25g coarse kosher salt
125g Achari Marinade (page 215)

For the seaweed salad
120g fresh wakame, washed well and cut
  into 2–3mm-thick ribbons
½ cucumber, cut into 2–3mm-thick ribbons
  (avoid core and seeds)
20g sesame chutney

To serve
250g portioned confit pork belly
120g dressed seaweed salad
pork belly sauce (juices and marinade)

Sesame chutney
Preheat the oven to 160°C. Roast the peanuts and sesame seeds on a tray for 10 minutes, stirring every 3 minutes until light golden. Place all the ingredients in a high-speed blender or Vitamix and blend until smooth. Store in an airtight container in the refrigerator for up to 3 days.

Confit pork belly
Coat the pork belly on both sides with the salt and leave it to rest in the refrigerator for 2 hours. Brush off the salt and rub the belly with 75g of the achari marinade. Place in a vacuum pouch and seal. Set up a steamer, or a combination oven, on full steam to 72°C and cook it for 12 hours. Once cooked, strain the juices and set them aside. Chill the confit belly in the refrigerator overnight, pressed with a weight on top. Remove the skin and set it aside. Portion the pork in about 2 slabs of 8 x 4cm (how many slabs you get will depend on the shape of the belly).

Set up a charcoal grill. Heat the pork belly cooking juices and 25g of the achari marinade in a saucepan and reduce until the sauce coats the back of a spoon. Reserve the sauce for serving. Once the charcoal is ready, brush the pork with the remaining marinade. Grill the belly until it's warmed all the way through and lightly charred around the edges.

Seaweed salad
Mix the wakame, cucumber and sesame chutney in a bowl.

Serve
Carve the pork belly and put it off-centre on a plate, place the seaweed salad next to the pork and gently pour the sauce on the side around the pork.

Sharmaji's chicken

Sharmaji's Lahori Chicken. This dish is as iconic, I would now argue, as any modern dish at any new-ish restaurant in London, such as Da Terra's Caviar and Cachaca Baba, Ikoyi's Plantain, or Kol's Langoustine Taco. In the early days, we had guests from all over the world who couldn't speak English showing us a photo of the chicken from Instagram as the closest thing to ordering it. So popular is the dish that Topjaw even made a special video about it, which pretty quickly catapulted to over four million views; even more than when I cooked it on BBC One's Saturday Kitchen.

My grandfather introduced me to this famous kebab. He was part of that generation who suffered the pain of partition. He was fourteen (we think; of course, there is no birth certificate) when Mountbatten drew his arbitrary line and the biggest mass migration of people in modern history took place over a few months. My family left their ancestral home in Lahore – historically the capital of Punjab – and headed east to the now-Indian side of Punjab. My grandfather stuck with his mum, while his father took my great aunt across the border. Separating the family gave them the best chance of survival. They had heard horrific stories of honour killings, rape and theft, and decided that separating the men as protectors was the right decision for the women of the family. My grandfather and great grandmother ended up in a refugee camp just outside Amritsar before being reunited quite miraculously with the remaining family in Delhi two years later. This is truly miraculous, as they estimate nearly 15 million people moved across the new borders in 1947 alone, while anywhere as many as another two million perished trying.

So, you can understand why my notoriously quiet grandfather was especially reticent to delve into the pain of that period. What he did open up about was the food of his childhood home of Lahore. Unlike the more veg-driven cities of Amritsar and the Hindu parts of Delhi, Lahore is one of the kebab capitals of the world. (Though anyone from Karachi will tell you it's garbage, it's like trying to get a Parisian to admit there is world-class food in London.) But for Sharma ji, as my grandfather was always known, there was nothing like the *sigree*-driven, charcoal-imbued *kebabs* of Lahore. In particular, there was one *kebabchi* down the Ferozpur road who would grill *teetari* [small poussin-like birds] and lather them in a sauce made of cashews, *methi* and fatty, sour yoghurt.

Over the years, journalists have over-romanticised this story, claiming that my grandfather cooked this dish for me during my childhood visits to India. This is probably as good a place as any to set the record straight. My grandfather, a carnivore pre-marriage, was placed firmly under the thumb of his wife and made to abstain from any non-veg. We would never be allowed to cook or eat meat anywhere near either of my grandmothers. Certainly not within their respective homes. And Sharmaji never cooked the dish, he just told me about it once, briefly, the night before my brother's wedding.

The true genesis for this dish came from the combination of his story, a legendary dish from the Muslim-quarter in Old Delhi, and the eye-watering amount of yoghurt whey being thrown away every day at Indian restaurants. To make the rich, yoghurt-y marinades so common in Indian food, we hang yoghurt overnight in muslin, leaving behind a rich *labneh*-like curd and a pool of sour yoghurt whey. From my time working in modern European restaurants, I know that this whey is really flavourful, especially when it's reduced down to a caramel with its nutty sourness and just a tiny bit of sweetness. I also know that because it's so acidic that it's also harmful to tip this whey down the sink, or – even worse – direct into waterways: it has been suggested that the amount of whey released into the Adriatic has caused a significant shift in aquatic migration patterns. Something to think about next time you have a bowl of Greek yoghurt for breakfast.

Knowing that BiBi would be producing a fair amount of yoghurt whey – we are a grill-led Indian restaurant, after all – I set about combining all these different influences to make something that would use up both the thickest and most difficult to cook shoulder parts of the chicken breasts from the whole birds we bought, and the few litres of yoghurt whey we generated from our other marinades. Maybe we would run it for lunch a couple of days every fortnight.

Little did I know.

This is the only dish that has survived BiBi's many facelifts and rebrands since we opened nearly four years ago. I know you're not supposed to have a favourite dish, just like you're not supposed to have a favourite child. But this is mine. Like a favourite child, this dish can do no wrong. Summer, winter, it doesn't matter – I'll probably never tire of the gasps of excitement from guests when we present this at the table. We continue to try to evolve and improve the dish – at the time of writing, we are serving it with a mushroom and truffle paste, and wild greens cooked down with smoked nutmeg, but after nearly 75,000 chicken breasts served in just a few years, I think it's safe to assume if you're eating at BiBi, you're probably eating Sharmaji's Lahori Chicken.

As the whole restaurant is named after my grandmothers, it's only fitting that my grand-father gets our most famous dish named after him.

Sharmaji's Lahori Chicken

If you want to make this dish taste the same as the restaurant, you need to … One: use really good yoghurt for the whey, ideally homemade. If you're making it yourself, use an Indian bacteria strain as this makes the curd stiff, leaving behind lots of acidic whey. The role of hung yoghurt in the marinade is to tenderise the meat – acid does this better than neutral solutions. Two: buy the best chicken you can afford. We only use white meat for this dish (utilising the rest of the bird in other ways) because we want to show off how tender we can make the breast – it's possible, you just have to cook it *à point*. And breast has a cleaner flavour and texture than the dark meat. Spatchcock a bird and go from there, but remember you need to skin it, as the fat in the skin stops the marinade from binding to or tenderising the meat. Finally, like any meat, cooked chicken needs resting. We have the custom-made *sigree* in the restaurant, with levels and pulleys to carefully control the heat, but at home just rest the chicken for at least half as long as you cook it, ideally in a warm spot.

I don't think any chef ever sets out to create a recipe that becomes a signature – think Jeremy Lee and his eel sandwich, Michel Roux Jr's cheese souffle, Heston Blumenthal's Sounds of the Sea – but this chicken has become BiBi's. Sometimes, in the desperation to innovate as a chef, we're itching to change things up, but a bit of grilled chicken and a sauce that hugs it like a weighted blanket doesn't need to be messed with. After all the conceptual, sometimes challenging flavours and combinations earlier in the meal, doesn't everyone just want a little comfort to finish the night?

Serves 4

For the Sharmaji butter
100g salted butter, softened
5g Sharmaji Masala (page 215)

For the cashew whey sauce
360g Yoghurt Whey (page 209)
180g double cream
2g green cardamom pods, crushed
24g fresh peeled ginger, crushed
60g Cashew Paste (page 208)
1.5g Kashmiri yellow chilli powder
100g Sharmaji butter, warmed
15g fresh peeled ginger, brunoised
15g coriander stem, finely chopped

For the creamed kale
400g double cream
6g freshly ground nutmeg
14g freshly ground white pepper
100g picked green kale leaves (250-300g
    untrimmed), thinly sliced
kosher salt

To serve
40g First Marinade (page 215)
2 free-range cornfed boneless, skinless
    chicken breasts
80g Awadhi Marinade (page 215)
ghee, for basting
50g creamed kale
Sharmaji Masala (page 215)
50g Sharmaji butter, melted
200g cashew whey sauce

Sharmaji butter
Put the softened butter and masala in a food processor and blend until homogenous. Store in an airtight container in the refrigerator for up to 1 week.

Cashew whey sauce
Put the yoghurt whey in a large saucepan with the cream and crushed cardamom pods, bring to the boil, then reduce the heat to medium and reduce by two thirds. Add the crushed ginger to the mixture, remove from the heat and allow the ginger to infuse for 20 minutes. Pass the mixture through a fine chinois, add the cashew paste and yellow chilli powder and blend with a hand blender until homogenous. Just before serving, add the warm Sharmaji butter and chopped coriander and brunoised ginger.

Creamed kale
Put the cream, nutmeg and white pepper in a saucepan and simmer over a medium-low heat until reduced by half. Blanch the kale in a pan of salted boiling water for 3 minutes, before draining and squeezing out the excess water. Bring a separate pan to a medium heat and add 200g of blanched kale. Cook until all the moisture has evaporated, then add the reduced cream and cook for another 5 minutes. Season with salt.

Finish and serve
Set up a charcoal grill. Put the first marinade and the chicken in a mixing bowl. Mix and allow to sit for 30 minutes in the refrigerator. Transfer the chicken to a different bowl, leaving behind the liquid in the bowl, adding 60g of the awadhi marinade and mixing thoroughly. Grill the chicken over the charcoal (once it is ready), brushing it with the remaining awadhi marinade as needed. Once the chicken is cooked, remove it from the grill, baste it generously with ghee and allow it to rest for 5 minutes before carving it. Add the creamed kale to the bottom of a bowl and place the carved chicken on top. Dust liberally with Sharmaji masala. Mix the melted butter with the cashew whey sauce and pour it over the chicken.

Jawahari Stuffed Chicken Wing

We've already had the story of the Nawab who lost his teeth; the inspiration behind this kebab is even more unusual. Jawaharlal Nehru (1889-1964) was a Kashmiri pandit who studied at Harrow, followed by Trinity college, Cambridge, and finally became a barrister at Inner Temple. If colonialists ever argue that they couldn't see the end of the Raj coming, maybe they shouldn't have educated Nehru and his fellow Indian nationalist Mahatma Gandhi in the best ways to take down the British government. Because Nehru became the leader of the Indian nationalist party, eventually being elected as the first prime minister of free India for 16 years.

Nehru's other secret passion – aside from Edwina Mountbatten (also a great way to get rid of the Raj) – was eating meat, smoking cigarettes and drinking wine away from the judgemental and prying eyes of the electorate. History tells us that he would even have minced koftas or kebabs stuffed inside *nadru* (lotus roots) so that he could enjoy meat without anybody apart from the cooks in his home knowing. There is no recipe for this, but we took inspiration from the story, and the even more historic *noorani* (daughter-in-law) kebab. The story for that dish involves taking goat mince and stuffing it inside a *pasanda* cut (from the leg), which is marinated and grilled over charcoal. Traditionally, a new bride would make it for her mother-in-law to show off her cooking skills in her new home.

Similarly, boning out chicken wings only to stuff a chicken farce back inside is a pretty efficient way of testing the skills of any budding chef.

Serves 4

4 extra-large chicken wings
20g Ginger and Garlic Paste (page 208)
20g Indian onion, grated
10g coriander stem, finely chopped
6g green bird's eye chilli, brunoised
180g boneless chicken thighs
16g chicken skin
16g chicken fat
8g Jawahari Masala (page 214)
2g roasted cumin seeds, cracked

To serve
4 x stuffed chicken wings
ghee, for brushing
Sharmaji Masala (page 215)

Bone out the chicken wings, being very careful not to break the skin and leaving the wing tip intact.

Place the garlic and ginger paste, grated onion, coriander stem and chilli in a muslin cloth and squeeze the mixture to drain as much water as possible from it. Add the drained mixture to a mixing bowl along with the remaining ingredients except the chicken wings and ghee. Mix it thoroughly. Using a meat mincer with a coarse attachment, mince the mix once, then stuff the chicken wings, making sure not to tear the skin.

Set up a steamer, or a combination oven, on full steam to 100°C. Steam the stuffed chicken wings for 12 minutes.

Finish and serve
Set up a charcoal grill. Once the charcoal is ready, brush the wings with ghee and grill for 5 minutes, until fully cooked and crispy golden all over. Dust with Sharmaji masala.

Creedy Carver Duck Khaas Nihari

Nihari, from the Arabic word for morning (*nahaar*) is a dish typically eaten for breakfast after the morning prayer across the north of India and Pakistan. It is thought to originate in the 14th century sultanate of Delhi. And this was the first place I ever tried the most famous variation, the *nalli nahari*, which is a bone-in mutton shank curry with an almost sticky, gelatinous sauce and melting, fall-off-the-bone-tender meat. Eaten with a *gilafi kulcha* (a little like a puff pastry that is baked in a cast-iron *tandoor*), it's as comforting and indulgent as Indian food gets. Probably only a close second to a proper *dum biryani*. Like the biryani, however, the heaviness of the traditional versions means they will never comfortably fit in a tasting menu.

We've always been keen to stay away from the trap of modern ethnic restaurants, westernising our food to separate protein and sauce, just to reintroduce them at the table. Is a langoustine that is grilled and dressed with *moilee* really any better than a langoustine cooked in moilee? In fact, is it not markedly less delicious? However, in the case of the duck, we find that not only can we cook the crown perfectly by 'deconstructing' the original nihari, we can retain the velvety richness of the sauce and have enough acidity in the glaze for the duck to make sure both add up to be greater than the sum of their individual parts.

Serves 4-6

For the duck roast masala
5g fennel seeds, cracked
5g cumin seeds, cracked
5g coriander seeds, cracked
5g royal cumin seeds, cracked
5g black peppercorns, cracked
2g ground green cardamom seeds
1g ground black cardamom seeds
2g ground cloves
3g ground mace
1.5g ground nutmeg
3g ground cinnamon
5g deggi mirch

For the duck roast and marinade
1kg duck crown
40g First Marinade (page 215)
40g ghee
100g reduced duck stock
20g duck roast masala
40g fresh peeled ginger, roughly chopped
50g Tamarind Paste (page 208)
10g kosher salt
20g jaggery
20g deggi mirch

For the duck sauce
150g duck marinade (leftover from the
    duck crown)
150g Hung Yoghurt (page 209)
kosher salt, if needed
Tamarind Paste (page 208), if needed

To serve
1 duck roast
240g duck sauce

Duck roast masala
Preheat the oven to 160°C. Put the fennel, cumin, coriander, royal cumin and black peppercorns on a tray and roast in the oven for 3 minutes. Allow the spices to cool, then crack them to a rough texture using a pestle and mortar. Mix all the masala spices together and set aside.

Duck roast and marinade
Set up a steamer, or a combination oven, on full steam to 65°C. Probe the crown in the thickest part of the breast and cook in the steamer until the probe reads 58°C. Remove the duck from the steamer and chill immediately, ideally in a blast chiller. Once completely cold, score each of the breasts diagonally (3mm between each line) with a razor blade. Rub the first marinade all over the crown and leave at room temperature for 20 minutes.

To make the duck marinade, melt the ghee and the stock together in a saucepan, then put them in a high-speed blender or Vitamix with the ginger, tamarind paste, jaggery, salt, deggi mirch and 10g of the duck roast masala and blend to a smooth, thick marinade. Put the duck on a rack set in a roasting tray. Rub 100g of the marinade all around the duck and keep 50g to brush while cooking. Reserve the remaining 150g to make the duck sauce.

Preheat the oven to 225°C then roast the marinated crown for 18 minutes, brushing the rest of the marinade over it every 6 minutes. On the last coat of marinade, cover the crown with the remaining 10g of duck roast masala. Once cooked, remove from the oven and allow to rest for 10 minutes before carving.

Duck sauce
Put the duck marinade and hung yoghurt in a saucepan with any resting juices from the duck crown and stir over a medium-high heat. Once the mix starts to simmer, keep cooking for 5-10 minutes until the ghee and oil start to split to the surface of the sauce. Remove from the heat and pass the mixture through a fine chinois. Adjust the seasoning with salt and tamarind if needed.

Serve
Carve the roast at the table after presenting it with the flowering herbs.

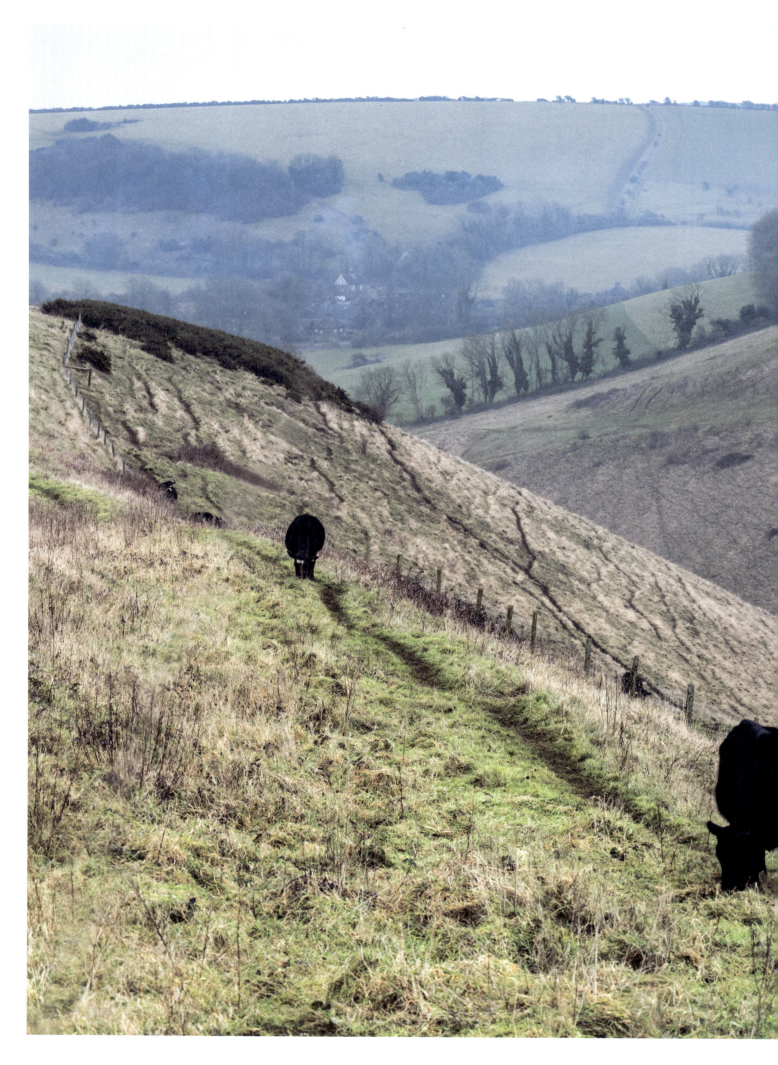

Desserts
Meetha

The end of a meal

Brett Graham of The Ledbury once said to me, 'That 80-year-old neighbourhood regular, she doesn't want a light-roast acidic hipster coffee, or a cup of earl grey she doesn't recognise. She'd be much happier with something comforting that she recognises after 20 experimental dishes through a tasting menu.' Your first thought is probably; 'The Ledbury has neighbourhood regulars?!' But we have to remember, like Mayfair, Notting Hill is a residential area and lots of people live there and stop in for lunch once a month or so. Regulars are what keep your restaurant ticking over year round, even more than celebrities or out-of-town diners who splash out on wines and supplements.

This conversation was based around my push to introduce 'better' teas and coffee at The Ledbury. Brett, much in the way he approached desserts back then, was always in favour of comfort at the end of the meal rather than pushing boundaries. And I now approach the end of the meal in the same way. For what it's worth, most great restaurants now just use really good Nespresso pods for an end-of-meal coffee. Difference Coffee supply our coffee pods and beats all small-batch artisan roasters as well as avoiding the inconsistency of a coffee made by a busy waiter. It's way more expensive but it's a 10/10 every single time.

Put yourself in a diner's shoes; you've had the novel and playful papad, followed usually by a handful of snacks that sometimes feature challenging ingredients. Whole prawns that you eat the head and shell of? Chicken hearts stuffed inside a kulcha? Spreadable ex-dairy goat? Are you likely to want to eat an experimental dessert rather than a nice warm choc-olate mousse with rice ice cream?

We have an exercise at BiBi called 'three good, three bad'. It's something we do as seniors when we discuss what we've eaten at a restaurant of similar calibre / ambition to BiBi. It needn't be something dramatic; an example of a 'good' point could be the temperature of the room, an element of storytelling in the meal, the pace of the meal. A 'bad' point could similarly be something as subtle as the waiter not noticing that my wife is left-handed and so setting her cutlery wrong, or maybe my still water was topped up with sparkling. In at least two thirds of instances, one of the bad points is the end of the meal. Which is so counter-intuitive to me for a few reasons. Firstly, I started my career as a pastry chef and it is the most scientific part of a kitchen so, for me, in some ways, it's the easiest course to be con-sistent with. Secondly, you put in all this effort through the meal to treat ingredients so carefully, sourcing the best of the best, ensuring that it is delivered to a table at the right time at the right temperature. Then, desserts come around and they are either too sweet, not sweet enough, not seasoned, don't have enough texture or just generally unloved. I wonder, 'has the chef actually sat down and eaten this with the same cutlery and without the distraction of a dessert wine or coffee?'.

It's the final touch-point you have as a chef / restaurant with your guests; surely it has to be at least as good as everything else, if not better.

Indian desserts

Disclaimer: Indians love sweets but historically we don't really do 'dessert'. When most people think about Indian sweet dishes, they think of sickly, sticky, syrupy dishes, or copious amounts of milk reduced down to a solid. I love them, but they aren't traditionally enjoyed as desserts; they are usually eaten in the middle of the afternoon with a strong and equally sweet and milky cup of tea. At BiBi, the genesis of all our desserts comes from one of three places:

1. a nostalgic memory of a particular sweet dish or something from my childhood.

2. the desire to use incredible fresh, heritage Indian fruits, like the alphonso mango or victoria pineapple.

Yes, I know the pineapple is South American, but chillies are from Central America and I doubt any eyebrows are raised when we include those in this book. For the record, many of the fruits we think of as Indian – chickoo (sapodilla), amrood (guava) and sitaphal (custard apple) – aren't, but oranges are. Go figure.

3. the focus on championing lesser-known varieties of spices, like vanilla from the Malabar Coast (which has a musky, nutty flavour), cassia leaves from Nagercoil (often confused for bay leaves) or intensely smoky black cardamom from Sikkim.

What these spices all have in common is that they would never be used in sweets in India, but we're in Mayfair so we have a little more freedom. We then also use Gujarati fennel, Keralan cardamom and Kashmiri saffron in abundance to balance the dishes with a little more recognisable Indian flavour.

When it comes to designing a dish, along with my head pastry chef Irene, we'll try to achieve a balance of all three of the above. In all cases we don't skimp on the quality of our produce sourced from the UK. We have some of the best ingredients in the world here, so we need to use them liberally across the menu. Flour from Cambridgeshire, butter from the South Downs, milk from Lancashire and eggs from Oxfordshire really are staples for the pastry team.

The perfect dishes for me are the ones that don't require shoehorning 100 textures and techniques, but instead tell the story of the restaurant while using knockout produce along the way. That ethos goes for the whole menu, but sometimes I feel like it's even more important to remember that right at the end of the diner's experience.

Alphonso Mango Lassi

In the early days, guests wouldn't really know what they were in for when they sat down at BiBi (it's baffling how often this still happens): 'the food is fusion', 'it's not authentic Indian', 'why no naans or biryani?'. One customer – who is now a regular – came in for the first time and, without looking at the menu, asked for a mango lassi. In my opinion, ordering a mango lassi with a tasting menu is no different than going to, say, The Clove Club, and asking for a smoothie with your scallop, clementine and truffle (delicious). I'm all about doing our best for the guests, and part of that is not filling them up with a thick, sweet mango lassi before hitting them with 20 plates of (hopefully) well-balanced dishes. Anyway, eventually we did run a dessert inspired by flavours of the mango lassi, hopefully meaning we won't have to answer that request again.

Serves 4

For the mango sorbet
30g sunflower seeds
12g white caster sugar
5g dextrose powder
83g cold water
10g prosorbet
40g Kissan alphonso mango pulp
grated zest of ½ lime
2g lime juice
0.2g ground green cardamom seeds
0.1g kosher salt

For the compressed cucumber
½ cucumber, peeled and cored (keep the
   cucumber skin, seeds and trims)
25g Malibu
2.5g mint
50g water
50g caster sugar
5g lime juice
0.125g ascorbic acid

For the tapioca pearls
45g small tapioca pearls
735g water

For the tapioca coconut and vanilla
½ vanilla pod
120g coconut milk
40g double cream
20g caster sugar
kosher salt
2.1g pectin jaune
20g full-fat yoghurt
15g Malibu
15g maple syrup
0.3g Sosa smoke powder
150g cooked tapioca pearls

To serve
24 pieces of compressed cucumber
24g Passion Fruit and Mango Gel
   (page 232)
240g tapioca coconut and vanilla
4 quenelles of mango sorbet
20 x 1cm Meringues (page 232)
Thai basil leaf tips, to garnish
allysum flowers, to garnish

Mango sorbet
Preheat the oven to 160°C and roast the sunflower seeds on a baking tray for 4 minutes. Blend the sunflower seeds with the sugar, dextrose and the water to a paste consistency in a high-speed blender or Vitamix. Add the rest of the ingredients and blend until incorporated. Pass through a chinois and freeze in a Pacojet beaker overnight. Spin in the Pacojet and put back in the freezer at least 1 hour before using it.

Compressed cucumber
Use a 12mm Parisienne scoop to create mini cucumber spheres. Alternatively, cut the flesh into 1cm dice. Blend all the ingredients for the compression liquid in a high-speed blender or Vitamix. Pass through a fine sieve and compress the cucumber flesh in the liquid.

Tapioca pearls
Put the tapioca pearls in a saucepan with 135g of the water, place over a medium heat, and cook for 8–10 minutes, stirring, until the mixture thickens. Strain and cool under cold running water. Boil the tapioca pearls in the remaining 600g water for 20–25 minutes until cooked through. Rinse in a sieve under cold running water and store in the refrigerator until ready to serve.

Tapioca coconut and vanilla
Smoke the vanilla pod over a charcoal grill (or using a cold smoking gun and oak smoking chips) for 30 minutes.

Heat the coconut milk, cream, 16g of the caster sugar and salt in a saucepan to 40°C. Mix the pectin with the remaining 4g of sugar, then add to the coconut mix and bring to the boil while whisking. Take off the heat, blitz with a hand blender and bring to the boil once more. Remove from the heat and leave to cool. Once the mix reaches 40°C again, blend in the rest of the ingredients, except the tapioca pearls. Leave to cool in the refrigerator. Hand blend before serving and fold in the cooked tapioca pearls.

Assemble and serve
Place 6 pieces of compressed cucumber and 4 dots each of passion fruit and mango gel in the middle of a bowl. Cover with 4 tablespoons of tapioca coconut and vanilla, place a quenelle of mango sorbet over the gel and garnish with 5 meringues and some Thai basil tips and allysum flowers.

Amrood Ka Meetha

This dessert makes an appearance on the BiBi menu like clockwork every September. The main reason, other than my love of guavas, is because my mum won't stop hounding me about how I've ruined her garden. When I was 17 and still living with my parents, I bought a small indoor fig tree. I took this tree with me first to Camden, then to Oxford as I worked my way through university. The tree never grew beyond knee height, and it very rarely had more than a handful of leaves, but I had a strange bond with it so didn't want to let it go. Before leaving England for San Sebastián, I suggested we plant the tree outside in my parents' garden, thinking that it might survive the winter and become hardier over a few years.

Fast forward 12 years, and that tree is now over 3 metres tall and has become so dominant in that corner of the garden that nothing can grow anywhere near it. Other than some not-so-wild wild garlic I planted soon after the fig tree. And so, inevitably, with my birthday in late August, my mum will give me anywhere up to three bin-bags full of fig leaves for my birthday to take and process in the restaurant. They have a remarkable coconut-y flavour, which works so well in oils, vinegars, alcoholic infusions and dried then powdered, as they are for these meringues.

Serves 4

For the fig leaf ice cream
3 or 4 fig leaves, washed thoroughly
200g Coconut Sorbet Base (page 196)

For the guava fluid gel
100g guava purée
100g water
25g white caster sugar
1.6g agar agar
0.5g citric acid

For the guava granita
216g guava purée
216g water
35g caster sugar
1g Kashmiri chilli powder
3.2g lime juice

For the pecan shortbread crumb
50g caster sugar
5g glucose
30g pecans, roughly chopped
60g crustless white bread, cut into
    1-2cm dice
45g unsalted butter
40g icing sugar
30g cornflour

For the buttermilk pudding
4g gold gelatine leaves
160g whipping cream
80g white caster sugar
0.4g strip of orange zest
0.4g strip of lime zest
seeds scraped from ½ vanilla pod
240g buttermilk
4g lemon juice

Fig leaf ice cream

First, dehydrate the fig leaves (you want 1.3g powdered, dehydrated fig leaf): put the clean leaves in a dehydrator at 70°C for up to 2 days, or until completely dry. Crush the leaves, discarding the stem parts, and use a spice grinder to blend the dried leaves to a fine powder. Mix the fig leaf powder with the sorbet base and decant into a Pacojet beaker. Freeze until solid. Spin in the Pacojet and put back in the freezer at least 1 hour before using it.

Guava fluid gel

Mix the guava purée, water, sugar and agar agar in a saucepan and bring to a simmer for 1 minute, then blend in the citric acid using a hand blender. Pass through a fine chinois, set in a container and cool in the refrigerator until jellified. Blend the jelly in a high-speed blender or Vitamix until smooth, place in a vacuum machine to remove the air, then transfer to a fine-tip squeezy bottle and store in the refrigerator for up to 3 days.

Guava granita

Put all the ingredients in a high-speed blender or Vitamix and blend until thoroughly mixed, then pass through a chinois. Put the liquid in a container and freeze hard. Scrape with a fork to serve.

Pecan shortbread crumb

Make a caramel with the caster sugar and glucose, heating it to 180°C in a saucepan. Add the pecans and leave to set on a silpat. Once cool, finely chop it. Dehydrate the diced bread overnight in a dehydrator or oven at 50°C.

Preheat the oven to 160°C. Melt the butter and mix the chopped pecan caramel and butter with the icing sugar and cornflour. Spread the mix out in a baking tray and bake for 20-25 minutes until golden, mixing it and breaking it apart every 5 minutes to obtain a crumble texture. Store in an airtight container at room temperature for up to 1 week.

To serve
4 x buttermilk pudding
40g pecan shortbread crumb
60g guava granita
4 quenelles of fig leaf ice cream
24g guava gel
20 fig leaf meringue sticks (page 232)
purple allysum flowers

Buttermilk pudding

Bloom the gelatine in iced water for 5 minutes. Put 60g of the cream in a saucepan with the caster sugar, zests and vanilla seeds and bring to a simmer, then take off the heat and whisk in the bloomed gelatine (squeezed of excess water) until dissolved. Whisk in the buttermilk and lemon juice and allow to cool. In a separate mixing bowl, whip the remaining 100g cream to soft peaks. Once the buttermilk mixture is cool, fold in the whipped cream. Portion 60g in serving bowls and allow to set in the refrigerator for at least 2 hours.

Serve

When the buttermilk pudding has fully set, add 1 tablespoon of pecan shortbread crumb and cover it with guava granita. Place a quenelle of fig leaf ice cream in the middle of the bowl and 5 dots of guava gel on top of the ice cream and around it. Garnish with fig leaf meringues and purple allysum flowers.

Pictured on p.168

Pineapple Tipsy Cake

I have no qualms about ripping off this dish. I think there are five perfect desserts in the world. My chachi's rasmalai, Dani García's torrija, La viña's tarta de queso, The Ledbury's brown sugar tart and Dinner by Heston's tipsy cake. For the uninitiated, tipsy cake is a sweet sponge slowly fed a custardy mixture of alcohols as it bakes. 'Feeding' the sponge means that you slowly develop a texture not dissimilar to a *pain perdu*, and this is served with a rum-glazed pineapple, slowly caramelised over several hours. This dish requires patience.

Now, my stance on colonialism is pretty clear. So as I sat in Dinner, which celebrates the history of British food, and ate a dish obviously inspired by empire – pineapples from Africa, spices from India, sugar and rum from the plantations in the Caribbean – it dawned on me that I can completely reclaim this 'British dish' by using exclusively exotic produce from India, so it certainly can fit on the BiBi menu. If they can take the crown jewels, surely I can just borrow a cake?

Serves 4

For the grilled rum-soaked pineapple
100g demerara sugar
1g fennel seeds
0.5g star anise
1g Maldon salt
25g water
25g lime juice
50g Havana 7 rum
¼ pineapple

For the brown sugar crumb
100g unsalted butter, cold
100g light brown sugar
100g plain flour
7g ground cinnamon

For the brioche balls
4g fresh yeast
35g full-fat milk
155g whole egg
270g bread flour, plus extra for dusting
8g kosher salt
30g white caster sugar
170g unsalted butter, cubed and softened

For the tipsy cakes
350g unsalted butter, melted
200g golden caster sugar
24 brioche balls
Havana 7 dark rum, for brushing
Tapioca Coconut and Vanilla (minus the
    cooked tapioca pearls) (page 164)

To serve
4 x tipsy cakes
12 slices of grilled rum-soaked pineapple
40g brown sugar crumb
4 x 30g quenelles of Coconut Sorbet
    (page 232)

Grilled rum-soaked pineapple
Put a heavy-based saucepan over a medium heat, add half of the demerara sugar and spread it out in a thin layer. Let it melt until it starts to change colour, then add another layer using the remaining sugar. This time, cook until the sugar has completely melted and turn to a dark golden caramel (177°C). Do not stir the mixture as this will crystalise the caramel. Add the spices and Maldon salt to the caramel, then add the water to make a syrup. Remove from the heat and add the lime juice and rum, then pass through muslin cloth. Peel and core the pineapple. Keep the peel and core to use in other recipes like the tepache on page 209. Cut the quarter in three pieces and compress it in the syrup in a vacuum machine.

Set up a charcoal grill. Grill the compressed pineapple, basting it with the syrup. Remove from the grill, allow to cool to room temperature, and dice into 1 x 4cm pieces.

Brown sugar crumb
Preheat the oven to 170°C, fan setting 3, 0% humidity. Put the cold butter, light brown sugar, plain flour and cinnamon in a stand mixer fitted with the paddle attachment and blend to a fine crumb. Spread the crumb over a baking tray lined with a silicon mat and bake for 25 minutes, stirring it every 10 minutes. Remove from the oven and allow to cool at room temperature.

Brioche balls
Put the fresh yeast, milk and 125g of the egg in a bowl and stir to dissolve the yeast. Put the bread flour, kosher salt and caster sugar in the bowl of a stand mixer fitted with the dough hook attachment, add the egg mixture and mix at low speed. Once the ingredients have formed a dough, increase the speed to medium and mix for 15 minutes. Reduce the speed of the machine to slow and add the remaining 30g of egg. Once the egg is incorporated, slowly add the cubed butter and continue mixing until fully combined. Switch off the machine, place the dough in a large container that has been lightly dusted with flour, cover with cling film and rest the dough overnight in the refrigerator.

The next day, remove the dough, flatten it to a thickness of 2cm and cut it into 24 small 12g squares. Place the squares on a tray and put back in the refrigerator for 30 minutes. With plenty of flour in your hands, roll each piece of dough into a ball using the work surface and the palm of your hand to shape it. Place the balls in a container and freeze them overnight.

Tipsy cakes

The next day, put the melted butter in a large bowl, making sure it is completely melted but not hot. Put the golden caster sugar in a separate bowl. Dip the frozen dough balls in melted butter, then roll them in the sugar until fully coated. Place 6 balls each in 10cm diameter mini cast-iron pans, cover with cling film and put in a warm place (20-24°C) for 2-3 hours to proof until the brioche doubles in size and some sugar cracks form.

Preheat the oven to 180°C. Place the cast-iron dishes in the oven. Bake for 15 minutes. Remove the dishes from the oven, use a knife to make an incision between the brioche pieces and pour 25g (per dish) of coconut custard into each incision. Place back in the oven and bake for 5 more minutes. Repeat the previous step twice more, with only 15g of coconut custard. Brush the brioche with rum as soon as it comes out of the oven.

Serve

Place the sliced pineapple in a separate bowl with a tablespoon of the brown sugar crumb next to it and a quenelle of the coconut sorbet on top of the crumb. Serve alongside the tipsy cake.

Pictured on p.169

Kashmiri saffron

Europeans scoured the world for spices and exotic produce, eventually colonising India for its peppercorns and tea. I love peppercorns, as I do tea, so I can understand it to some extent – though in no way condone or justify it – but why the hell didn't they take the saffron back with them? Now known as the 'golden spice' it is by far the most expensive ingredient in the world gram for gram. Of course, one gram of saffron is enough for a dish that feeds a family of four; you'd find it hard to get one gram of caviar to stretch the same way. Saffron has a distinct and sometimes polarising aroma, but has been cultivated for thousands of years, ever since the Persians found a cornucopia of applications for it in food, medicine and textiles.

Here's a good one for you... Where was Europe's leading production centre for saffron during the Roman Empire? Croydon! The south London suburb takes its name from the Latin for the saffron flower, *Crocus sativus*. Fortunately, the spice spread across the Middle East and into the subcontinent around the same time; and production in Kashmir has continued uninterrupted ever since. Now, this is where me and Ash, our head chef, will never agree. He holds premium Iranian saffron up as the very best, even smuggling it into the restaurant from time to time. But the Kashmiri stuff holds a very special place in my heart, for its flavour, cultural relevance and the symbology of an ingredient that can help unite a disputed territory.

The production of saffron is notoriously difficult. The flowers need to be carefully hand-harvested – specifically the three thread-like stigmas are removed from each flower, usually at dawn when the flowers are most accessible, then air-dried and processed slowly to preserve the intense colour and aroma. Saffron grows best in cooler climates and, in the Northern hemisphere, are best harvested between October and November.

Kashmir's saffron is often regarded as superior due to the natural growing conditions in the region. The temperature (especially the cold winters), the altitude, soil composition, and the historically free-flowing waters are ideal for cultivating saffron. The saffron-growing areas in Kashmir, such as Pampore, located on the banks of the Jhelum River, are often referred to internationally as the 'Saffron Bowl' due to the high quality of the spice produced there.

Kashmiri saffron comes in two grades: *laccha*, thinner strands with a light colour and milder flavour usually exported to people who don't know better, and *mogra*, thick and deep crimson strands, with an unmistakable heady aroma, which the Kashmiri's keep for themselves. The consistent tension and recent drought conditions in this region mean it's almost impossible to get a consistent supply of *mogra* Kashmiri saffron anywhere outside of the state.

Despite travelling extensively throughout India, I've only made it up to the state of Jammu and Kashmir once, and of course never to the Pakistani side of Azad [free] Kashmir. I was eighteen at the time. My parents decided it would be a good idea to take my brother and I off the beaten path and away from the cities of India, insisting we hike the famous Vaishno Devi shrine in Jammu. Partly a religious pilgrimage, this was also a chance visit a lesser known part of India and challenge ourselves away from the cityscapes of Delhi and Mumbai, and the flat farmland of Punjab. For me the climb was quite easy - at eighteen most minor physical challenges seem relatively easy - but slightly less mobile pilgrims were jumping on the backs of particularly scrawny-looking donkeys as they trundled up the cliff-face. Surely no level of religious epiphany is worth that level of peril?

We climbed the mountain, visited the holy cave on which the larger temple was built and, as the sun drew in, checked into a hostel. As we settled into our shared room, we set our alarms for five hours later so that we could get up and head back down the mountain before the sun reached its peak position. Of course, we're up the side of a mountain in rural Kashmir, so I'm not sure what made me think there'd be readily flowing hot water - or any water really for that matter - and electricity. The following morning, I washed myself with pure mountain melt water by candlelight. It sounds very romantic, but I was sharing a bed with my adolescent brother with my parents in the bed next to ours. You know the kind of cold that give you chills right to the bone? The kind that settles into your lungs, drawing your breath shorter? That was my memory of that morning. As we set back off down the mountain with the sun barely on the horizon, we stopped where a man was selling Kashmiri *noon chai*. A saffron-rich rose-pink tea, in this occasion, served with a piece of *girda* and rose jam. That was the first time I tasted Kashmiri saffron, and now every time we infuse it in the kitchen, I'm sent back to that mountain in the freezing cold, restored by the warmth of the world's most luxurious ingredient in one of its most unsophisticated settings.

Shah Babur's Saffron Egg

If some guests had their way, this would be a staple on the BiBi menu all year round. I love the flavours and textures of the dish. But what I really love is the story. Shah Babur was the first Mughal emperor of India. Originally from Central Asia, he brought with him an opulent love of aromas and heady spices. At a celebratory feast, where a mind-bending one thousand dishes are said to have been served, the centrepiece was whole chickens, fed saffron for 100 days, stuffed with rice and cooked over charcoal. What the Shah didn't know is that his canny house manager was stashing away the saffron-laced eggs for weeks. So, while the nobles feasted on the flesh, the cooks created a sweet noodle dish (*seviyan ki zarda*) finished with a saffron-yolk sabayon.

Serves 4

For the blood orange insert
1g gold leaf gelatine
100g Boiron blood orange purée
10g caster sugar

For the frangipane discs
50g unsalted butter, softened
50g white caster sugar
50g eggs
0.2g kosher salt
50g ground almonds
50g Boiron passion fruit purée
20g gluten-free plain flour

For the ghee-roasted kataifi
80g kataifi pastry
50g ghee
20g icing sugar

For the lemon saffron gel
50g caster sugar
100g water
0.2g saffron
5g agar agar
100g lemon juice

For the yoghurt saffron mousse
2.4g gold leaf gelatine
130g whipping cream
grated zest of ¼ lemon
0.1g saffron
70g white chocolate, broken into pieces
80g natural stirred yoghurt
6g caster sugar

To serve
yoghurt saffron mousse
4 x 20ml blood orange insert
4 frangipane discs
White Chocolate Dip (page 196),
    for dipping
80g ghee-roasted kataifi
24g saffron lemon gel
cornflowers, to garnish
micro lemon balm, to garnish

Blood orange insert
Bloom the gelatine in iced water for 5 minutes. Warm a small amount of the purée with sugar. Add the bloomed gelatine (squeezed of excess water) and melt it. Add the remaining purée and take off the heat. Set into 4 x 20ml semi-sphere moulds and freeze.

Frangipane discs
Put the softened butter and sugar in a stand mixer fitted with the paddle attachment and mix until creamed and airy. Reduce the speed of the stand mixer to medium-low and gradually add the eggs. Once the eggs are incorporated, add the salt, ground almonds, passion fruit purée and gluten-free flour and mix until incorporated. Heat a combination oven to 170°C, fan 3. Spread the mixture out on a baking tray lined with parchment paper to a thickness of 1cm and bake for 10–15 minutes, until golden brown. Remove from the oven and allow to cool, then, using a pastry cutter, cut the frangipane into 4 discs as big as the egg mould you are using. Store the discs in an airtight container in the refrigerator for up to 5 days.

Ghee-roasted kataifi
Preheat the oven to 180°C. Coat the kataifi with the ghee and 10g of the icing sugar and bake for 7 minutes, then remove from the oven. Mix, dust with the remaining icing sugar and bake for another 7 minutes until golden. Allow to cool to room temperature.

Lemon saffron gel
Put the sugar, water and saffron in a saucepan and bring to the boil. Take off the heat and leave to infuse for 20 minutes, then bring back to the boil and blend in the agar agar. Take off the heat and add the lemon juice. Pass through a fine chinois and set the gel in the refrigerator. Once set, blend in a high-speed blender or Vitamix until smooth.

Yoghurt saffron mousse
Bloom the gelatine in iced water for 5 minutes. Put half of the cream in a saucepan with lemon zest and bring to a low simmer, then remove from the heat, add the saffron and let it infuse for 10 minutes before passing the mixture through a fine chinois. Add the bloomed gelatine (squeezed of excess water) and warm the mixture until the gelatine is fully dissolved. Melt the white chocolate in a microwave or using a bain marie and pour the warm saffron cream over it. Mix the yoghurt with the sugar then add it to the infused cream and chocolate mix. Allow the mixture to reach room temperature. Whip the remaining cream to firm peaks and fold it into the mix, a third at a time. Transfer to a piping bag.

Assemble and serve

Pipe the saffron mousse in the egg mould, filling it to half its capacity. Push the blood orange insert in and cover it with a frangipane disc. If there are any gaps left, fill them with more saffron mousse. Smooth the surface of the mould and clean the edges with a pallette knife. Place the filled egg moulds in a blast freezer until frozen solid. Demould the eggs, stick a toothpick on the top part of the egg and dip it in the white chocolate dip. Once the white shell has set, sprinkle some chocolate dip to emulate the stains on natural eggs. Keep the dipped eggs in the refrigerator for at least 4 hours before serving, to allow the filling to reach the right temperature and defrost. Place the egg in the chosen plate and surround it with ghee-roasted kataifi pastry for a 'nest'. Put 5 dots of saffron lemon gel on the kataifi around the egg and garnish with cornflowers and micro lemon balm.

Pictured on p.178

Desserts

Sweetcorn and Blackberry Shrikhand

Occasionally the classification of ingredients can be incredibly misleading. The tomato is a fruit that acts as a vegetable. Chilli peppers are also fruits but are often treated as a spice. And corn? For so long, it was only seen in Europe as a vegetable. Even after centuries of selective breeding, corn is a grain. We separate out maize as the grain crop, and sweetcorn as a vegetable, but they are one and the same. And if this dish was called 'rice and blackberry shrikhand' nobody would think twice.

Sweetcorn has an amazing honey-like quality to it, and in the last throes of autumn, just as the best summer fruit is fading out, sweetcorn is a final remnant of natural sugars, before we hit colder months when the only natural sugars left to harvest come from squash and root vegetables. It's not unusual to use grains for their sweetness – consider, for instance, how barley and wheat are used for their sugars in beer production. We often use corn kernels in savoury applications, but we still want to use the whole product across the menu, so we make corn oil from the discarded cobs, toast the corn husks to a dark, flavourful ash, and make this corn pudding. This approach allows us to make full use of the season – the corn needed here can be much hardier and more fibrous than the corn we would use (for example) for the Sweetcorn Kurkure on page 30. Of course, all that honey-sweet flavour needs to be tempered and balanced, so we naturally turn to the last of the summer berries to provide this. The association between sweetcorn and blackberries has long been etched into my mind, from summers spent at the back of my *Chacha's* house in Berkshire, where blackberry thickets lined the neighbouring cornfield… all sepia tinted and very Tom Sawyer. Walking back from the nearby park, the late summer air was thick with the scent of corn husks and meadowsweet, while we gorged ourselves on fresh blackberries off the hedgerow.

Serves 4

For the yoghurt mousse
30g full-fat milk
15g whipping cream
20g procrema
12g inverted sugar (trimoline)
7g dextrose
105g Hung Yoghurt (page 209)
6g yoghurt powder
6g milk powder
0.3g kosher salt

For the blackberry granita
35g caster sugar
220g water
35g lemongrass
0.7g lemon verbena
0.1g freshly ground black pepper
5g gondhoraj lebu lime juice
215g Bioron blackberry purée

For the corn ash
6 corn husks

For the coffee oil
100g grapeseed oil
5g instant coffee granules
1g kosher salt
2g corn ash

Yoghurt mousse
Mix all the ingredients using a hand blender and chill in the refrigerator. An hour before serving, whisk by hand to soft peaks. Load in an isi gun with two nitrous oxide charges.

Blackberry granita
Put all the ingredients, except the blackberry purée, in a saucepan and bring to the boil. Take the pan off the heat, add the blackberry purée, and allow the mixture to cool. Once cool, thoroughly mix, then pass through a chinois. Set the liquid in a container and freeze hard. Scrape with a fork just before serving.

Corn ash
Dehydrate the corn husks overnight in a dehydrator or an oven at 70°C. Place the corn husks in a large metal container and char them using a blowtorch until blackened. Once cool, blend to a fine powder using a Vitamix or spice grinder. Decant the ash into a shaker, ready to serve.

Coffee oil
Mix all the ingredients with a hand blender until fully incorporated. Store in a fine-tip squeezy bottle at room temperature for up to 1 week.

For the corn milk
380g corn cobs (just the cobs, no kernels,
    but retain 40g kernels)
400g full-fat milk
170g double cream
0.02g saffron
0.8g crushed black pepper
0.4g kosher salt
20g caster sugar
⅛ vanilla pod
8g honey

For the corn panna cotta quenelles
3g gold gelatine sheet
120g corn milk
45g mascarpone
40g whipping cream

To serve
14g crystallised puffed oats
    (see Crystallised Garnishes, page 232)
4 corn panna cotta quenelles
16g coffee oil
80g yoghurt mousse
blackberry powder, for dusting
8 large blackberries
40g blackberry granita
micro lemon balm, to garnish
apple marigold, to garnish

Corn milk

Put the corn cobs, milk and double cream in a saucepan and heat to 90°C. Cook for 1 hour, then remove from the heat, leave to cool and let it infuse overnight in the refrigerator. The next day, pass the mixture through a fine chinois. Heat 140g of the corn-infused milk and the saffron in a Thermomix to 80°C, then add the remaining ingredients, including the corn kernels, and blend. Pass through a fine chinois and keep in an airtight container in the refrigerator until ready to use for the corn panna cotta.

Corn panna cotta quenelles

Bloom the gelatine in iced water for 5 minutes. Warm the corn milk in a saucepan to 50°C and add the soaked gelatine (squeezed of excess water). Take off the heat and hand-blend in the mascarpone. In a separate bowl, whip the whipping cream to soft peaks. Once the mascarpone milk mix has come to room temperature, fold in the whipped cream. Divide the mixture among four 30g quenelle moulds and freeze. Once frozen, demould and plate in the chosen bowl. Leave it for 2 hours in the refrigerator to allow it to come to the right temperature.

Assemble and serve

Place 1 teaspoon of crystallised puffed oats next to each corn quenelle, add 3 drops of coffee oil over the oats and cover them with the yoghurt mousse in the isi. Dust blackberry powder over the yoghurt espuma. Halve the blackberries lengthways and dress them in coffee oil. Place them next to the oats and cover them with blackberry granita. Garnish the corn quenelle with micro lemon balm and apple marigold.

Pictured on p.179

Desserts

BiBi Ka Baba

The key flavours of a *gulab jamun* are cardamom, sometimes saffron, sugar and heavily reduced milk (or *khoya*). To achieve some of those notes, we toast milk powder until it turns a light nut brown and add it to an otherwise conventional baba or savarin batter. After the babas have risen and baked, we introduce the other flavours in the baba syrup. At this stage it tastes like a classic gulab jamun, just without the dense texture and sickly sweetness of the original. A coffee jelly and Chantilly filling surprises guests as they slice through the baba and, eaten together, it takes your mind to several different but equally comforting places all at once. Which is kind of the point of a BiBi dessert.

Serves 4

For the Chantilly
¼ vanilla pod
60g whipping cream
6g light muscovado sugar

For the coffee jelly
2g silver leaf gelatine
65g brewed espresso coffee
30g white caster sugar
5g Havana 7 rum

For the saffron bavarois
2.5g gold leaf gelatine
55g white chocolate, roughly chopped
100g whipping cream
10g inverted sugar (trimoline)
10g glucose
1g saffron
150g whipping cream, whipped to
    soft peaks

For the BiBi Babas
50g eggs
6g white caster sugar
50g strong white flour
4g toasted milk powder
4g fresh yeast, crumbled
1g kosher salt
30g unsalted butter, melted

For the Baba syrup
1kg water
pared rind of ¼ lemon (no pith)
1.5g green cardamom pods, smashed
125g white caster sugar
0.1g saffron or 2.5g saffron extract
100g dark rum

To serve
4 BiBi babas
Baba syrup, to fully soak the baba
40g coffee jelly
60g Chantilly
80g saffron bavarois
seasonal flowers, to serve (we use dianthus
    in image opposite)

Chantilly
Prepare a charcoal grill. Toast the vanilla pod over charcoal embers. Scrape the seeds from inside the vanilla pod and place them in a bowl with the cream and muscovado sugar. Whip to soft peaks before serving.

Coffee jelly
Bloom the gelatine in iced water for 5 minutes. Heat the coffee and sugar to 60°C in a saucepan and mix until the sugar has dissolved. Remove from the heat, add the bloomed gelatine (squeezed of excess water) and rum and mix until dissolved. Cool down and set in a shallow container in the refrigerator, then - once set - break into small pieces with a fork.

Saffron bavarois
Bloom the gelatine in iced water for 5 minutes. Melt the white chocolate with the cream, inverted sugar and glucose in a saucepan over a low heat. Once melted, dissolve the bloomed gelatine (squeezed of excess water) in the mix, along with the saffron. Allow to cool to room temperature, then fold the whipped cream one third at a time through the mix. Store in a piping bag fitted with the star nozzle and refrigerate until ready to serve.

BiBi Babas
Beat the eggs and white caster sugar in a stand mixer fitted with the whisk attachment until combined. Gradually whisk the flour, milk powder, yeast and salt into the batter, then slowly pour in the melted butter until incorporated. Fill each of 4 silicone baba moulds with 25-30g of the batter and proof at about 25°C - or a warm room temperature - until doubled in size. Preheat the oven to 165°C, then bake the babas for 15 minutes until golden brown. Allow to cool for 5 minutes in the moulds then transfer to a wire rack to cool for 5 more minutes.

Baba syrup
Put all the ingredients except the saffron and rum in a saucepan and bring to a simmer. Once the sugar has dissolved, add the saffron, remove from the heat and leave to steep for at least 15 minutes. Pass through a fine chinois and add the rum to the mixture.

Assemble and serve
Add the babas to the warm syrup and soak them for about 30 seconds or until almost doubled in size. Leave the babas to cool on a wire rack. Once cool, trim the wider end, making sure the cut is straight as that part will be the base of the baba, then hollow out the inside of the baba, making sure there aren't any holes on the sides. Add 1 teaspoon of coffee jelly inside each baba and fill the rest with freshly whipped Chantilly. Put the baba on a flat plate using the side as a base. Pipe the saffron bavarois on top of the baba in a swirl pattern. Garnish with flowers.

Desserts

Mason & Co.

Not many people think of India when they think of chocolate. And not many people think of chocolate when they think of India. I was the same. Back in 2018, before embarking on a life-changing trip around the southern states of Tamil Nadu and Kerala, I knew that amazing spices, coconuts, rice varieties and a whole range of indigenous ingredients like elephant yams came from this part of India, but there was much I didn't know. North Indians tend to erroneously group anything south of Mumbai as 'Southie'. Malayalam, Telugu, Tamil, Konkani, Kannada – they all sound the same to our untrained ears. Northern languages generally come from the ancient language Sanskrit; and while Gujarati is distinct from Hindi, which is distinct from Punjabi, there is generally a common thread across all these languages. Danta, danth, or dunth. All three words mean 'tooth' in their respective language. Just like in Spanish a tooth is 'diente', in French it's 'dent' and Farsi it's 'dandan'.

In Malayalam, the official language of Kerala, a tooth is a 'pallu'. In Tamil it's 'pal'. That's because most of their languages evolved from Dravidian languages. It's why Northern Indians, many times conquered by Europeans dating back to Alexander the Great, see ourselves as a genetically and culturally distinct civilisation. Lahore, where my family is from, is closer as the crow flies to Tehran than it is to Trivandrum in the south. And while we all now sit under the umbrella of one country, we couldn't be more different. The majority religion is the same in name, the gods we worship are very different.

To many North Indians, then, all 'Southie' food is dosa, curry leaves, coconut and mustard seeds. When we opened BiBi we had a chef from Kerala named Sandeep working with us. To this day, if we have to fry some curry leaves in the restaurant it's still called 'Sandeep tempering'. Which is why setting off on a journey zigzagging all the way from Andhra Pradesh down to Kanyakumari – so far south that you've passed half of Sri Lanka – and then back up the Western coast through Kerala and Karnataka was essential to me gaining a better understanding of the complexities of the food from this area. An area which, I should mention, is more than five times bigger than the entire landmass of Greece.

I set off particularly keen to hit some real food hot-spots: Hyderabad, with its Nizami cuisine – the southern equivalent to the royal kitchens of Agra and Lucknow, the Nizams (kind of princes) had a love for fiery, rich dishes and claim the throne for the *kacchi biryani*; Madurai, the city of temples, has amazing vegetarian food, and is a city that uses coconuts in more ways than any other in the world; Kochi, a historic port city in Kerala which is still one of the main export sites for spices from the Malabar coast through to the Middle East and beyond. There, they have lots of interesting sub cultures, like the toddy shop – a rough, men only fisherman's pub where guests regularly go blind from all the methanol in the ropey eponymous toddy – and the Syrian Christian community who have a welcomingly mild cuisine for this part of the world. However, what interested me most was Puducherry. Inside Tamil Nadu, Puducherry was once colonised by the French and the district capital renamed to Pondicherry. The street signs are still in French to this day, and the residents qualify for dual citizenship. Full disclosure - my first night there was spent in a room infested with bed bugs. I went full angry Punjabi on them and don't think I'm welcome back in that hotel ever again. I also saw a cow swim, which was a beautiful sight.

On my second day, I'm pretty sure that's where the idea to name the restaurant after grandmothers came from. Because I visited the inimitable Pushpa of Chez Pushpa. She is a national treasure, and many high-end chefs from across the country recommended I visit her. While she mainly spoke Tamil, we managed to communicate through enough broken kitchen French for her to show me the riches of their cuisine. Milagai podi, Manathakalli berries, nannari and vadagam (the real, non-watered down 'vadouvan', which three-star French chefs love using). As her daughter Anita sat with us for dinner - thankfully, Anita lived in London and Paris so could seamlessly switch between English, French and Tamil - she told me that I should visit a potter in nearby Auroville.

Auroville is a weird hippy commune about 10km out of Pondicherry city. It's a centre for free love and artistic expression, a remnant of the French that didn't want to leave after independence. There is still a nudist community there, and it was there that I had perhaps the best croissant I've had outside of France. While Anita and I visited the potter, a grizzly old man producing lovely Japanese-style ramen bowls, she also suggested I try the newish local chocolate producer, Mason & Co. We drove a little further into what can only be described as a tropical jungle, before parking up and walking on foot. Real Indiana Jones shit. When we finally arrived at the factory, we were greeted by a few local women, before a Frenchman named Fabien popped out.

Fabien and his business partner Jane had the same struggle with Indian chocolate that I did; most of it isn't very good, with terrible commodity beans being processed en masse in Cold War-era machinery and pumped full of so much milk and sugar that it bears relatively little resemblance to the artisan chocolate they were so used to enjoying in Europe. They began to experiment in their homes, speaking with local farmers and producers to fine-tune how they selected their beans. They opened Mason and Co., employing only local women - many of whose husbands had left to work on cruise ships and in the Middle East - empowering them with chocolate-making training and their own source of income. In those early days all the beans were grown in Tamil Nadu, but as the company has grown, they've started to work directly with farmers and co-operatives in Kerala and Karnataka.

In that first tasting, Fabien showed me there was so much more to the Indian chocolate than I had previously known. That there was a desire and growing knowledge base to produce chocolate at the highest standard, while maintain all the corporate social responsibility that growers in Central America and West Africa can often leave behind.

Since that chance meeting seven years ago, we have loyally worked with Mason & Co., featuring some of their chocolate on the menu all year round. We were already their biggest customers anywhere in the world, until last year we finally realised the dream of producing our own chocolate bar with them, flavoured with cardamom and coconut sugar. Now, not only do guests get to try the amazing product from this tiny ramshackle factory in the jungle when the dine in the restaurant, but they also receive a bar to take home with them. A piece of tropical Auroville from our often-grey little corner of London.

Pondicherry Hot Chocolate

This is a hybrid of my life both as a chef and as an eater. It's probably why we're always keen to bring this dish back on the menu more than any others (generally in colder months, when citrus fruits flourish and a richer style of dessert seems most fitting), just making little tweaks to reflect our evolving style at BiBi. We wanted to represent Mason & Co. in the best way possible, so I started to scan the annals of my mind for the great desserts of the world.

The starting point had to be the chocolate. I'm not usually a fan of cooked chocolate, but when it is warmed gently, all the complex aromas emerge. The truest way to enjoy chocolate is to just let it melt slowly in your mouth while you breathe out of your nose to force the aroma around your olfactory bulb. Remembering that people are in restaurants to eat and not to be lectured, the best way for us to showcase the chocolate is in the form of an aerated chocolate mousse. Just cream and chocolate – no eggs or sugar to change the flavour.

I mentioned earlier that Dani García's torrija is one of the best desserts anywhere in the world. Essentially a custardy pain perdu, it really is a joyous plate of food. If you're ever in Madrid and have an hour to spare, go to Bibo and try it for yourself. He uses berries to cut his; we wanted a milder type of acidity, but still freshness, so we turned to mandarins. They're a little sweeter than orange but also more aromatic. The fluid gel has a little bit of zest that just lifts it a little. I think back to my first visit to Mason & Co., and how ingenious I thought it was that they used rice grinders to conche chocolate. Along with the fact that Pondicherry is very much a rice-eating part of the country, I wanted to utilise toasted rice as the base of the ice cream, as well as puffed rice to bring some texture to an otherwise soft and luxurious dish. a chocolate espuma that really is just BiBi.

Serves 4

For the mandarin oil
100g grapeseed oil
5g pared mandarin rind (no pith)

For the warm chocolate mousse
90g double cream
150g 65% Mason & Co. chocolate,
    roughly chopped into small pieces
90g egg whites

For the mandarin gel
100g Boiron mandarin purée
50g white caster sugar
1.4g agar agar

For the toasted rice ice cream
125g jasmine rice
500g full-fat milk
85g double cream
335g condensed milk
50g procrema

For the wild rice crumb
30g unsalted butter, chilled
36g demerara sugar
30g gluten-free plain flour
8g cacao powder
neutral vegetable oil, for deep frying
0.2g Maldon salt
1.5g wild rice

Mandarin oil
Set up a dehydrator or an oven to 70°C. Place the grapeseed oil and the zest in a metal container and cook at 70°C overnight. Strain the mixture, discard the solids and store the oil in an airtight container in the refrigerator for up to 1 month. Transfer to a fine-tip squeezy bottle before serving.

Warm chocolate mousse
Heat the cream in a saucepan until it simmers, then add the chocolate, remove from the heat and whisk the chocolate with the cream. Add the egg whites to the chocolate cream and whisk together loosely, to combine. Add to an iso gun and add two canisters of nitrous oxide. Place the iso into a water bath at 65°C for 1 hour, shaking the canister every 15 minutes to fully incorporate the mixture.

Mandarin gel
Put the mandarin purée, caster sugar and agar agar in a saucepan, bring to a simmer and let it cook for 2 minutes until the sugar dissolves, then blend with a stick blender in the pan. Pour into a container and cool in the refrigerator until solid. Blend in a high-speed blender or Vitamix until smooth. Place in a vacuum machine to remove the air. Store in a fine-tip squeezy bottle in the refrigerator for up to 3 days.

Toasted rice ice cream
Preheat the oven to 160°C and toast the rice, spread out on a baking tray, for 30 minutes until golden. Bring the milk to a simmer in a saucepan, add the toasted rice and let it infuse in the refrigerator overnight. The next day, pass the rice milk through a chinois. Blend the rice milk, cream, condensed milk and procrema with a hand blender. Set in Pacojet beakers and spin 2 hours before serving.

For the pao perdu
250g full-fat milk
90g double cream
75g whole eggs
0.5g ground green cardamom seeds
1g ground cinnamon
1g fennel seeds, ground
40g light muscovado sugar
20g pao, cut into four 2.5 x 5cm discs
icing sugar, for dusting
ghee, for frying

To serve
4 discs of pao perdu
12 drops of mandarin oil
40g wild rice crumb
4 quennelles of rice ice cream
40g mandarin gel
50g warm chocolate mousse

Wild rice crumb

Preheat the oven to 170°C, fan setting 3, 0% humidity. Mix the butter, demerara sugar, flour and cacao to a fine crumb in a Thermomix or food processor, then spread out on a baking tray and cook for 25 minutes, mixing it every 10 minutes. Leave to cool.

Heat enough neutral vegetable oil for deep frying to 190°C in a deep fat fryer (two-thirds to three-quarters full). Fry the wild rice in the oil for about 1 minute until puffed, then drain on kitchen paper to absorb excess oil, and leave to cool. Combine the crumb, Maldon salt and puffed wild rice.

Pao perdu

Blend all the ingredients together, except the pao, icing sugar and ghee. Soak the pao in the pao perdu mix for 30 seconds, then remove and dust both sides with a thin layer of icing sugar. Warm a 1cm depth of ghee in a frying pan to 150°C. Fry the soaked pao in the pan for 2 minutes on each side, then place on a rack and dust with icing sugar again on both sides. Fry the pao a second time, 1 minute per side. Keep at room temperature on a wire rack until needed.

Assemble and serve

Place a piece of pao perdu in the middle of a bowl and add 3 drops of mandarin oil to it. Cover the pao perdu with 1 tablespoon of wild rice crumb. Place a quenelle of rice ice cream in the middle of the bowl. Put the mandarin gel over the rice ice cream in a zigzag pattern, and cover everything with warm chocolate mousse using the isi gun.

Pictured on p.188

Desserts

Malai rabri kulfi

It's funny how history skews our perceptions of certain dishes and their origins, often to suit a Eurocentric view of the world. Most people think that ice cream comes from Italy, food geeks will argue that its roots lie in the Moorish practice of eating mountain ice as sherbets. But did you know that two hundred years before that, the Mughals had already made kulfis the de-facto summertime dessert in Delhi? For the uninitiated, a kulfi is a kind of ice cream made from heavily reduced milk – basically, cooked until it crumbles – which is usually flavoured with cardamom and, at its best, saffron.

I've spent a lot of time studying the science behind ice creams (I can't recommend Robin and Caroline Weir's seminal work, *Ice Creams, Sorbets & Gelati: The Definitive Guide*, more highly), and even proudly developed an Excel spreadsheet which contains a matrix for soft-serve ice cream. This has become so widely distributed that I've been told it has appeared everywhere from London's Dorchester Hotel to a Michelin-starred restaurant in Macau. Stripped back to its most basic form, an ice cream is a stable emulsion of fats (including lipoproteins), non-fat solids (mostly proteins such as casein and albumin) and sugars (usually lactose and sucrose). All of these solids are dissolved and held in an emulsion with water. Traditionally, the base of ice cream in western kitchens is an anglaise mixture – a dairy custard thickened and stabilised by eggs – however, other mixtures can perform the same function. It's equally possible to replace the dairy fat with plant-based fats (as we do for our coconut kulfi base overleaf) and for the stability to come from a mix of hydrocolloids like locust bean gum, xanthan gum and a variety of seaweeds.

On the other end of the scale, removing ourselves from all the technical jargon and science of ice cream, we find ourselves looking for inspiration from traditional Indian ice cream. Nestled in the bustling lanes of Delhi's old quarter, there are a multitude of small, unassuming shops selling all of the city's most beloved treats, and on a dusky summer's day, there is no shop more popular than Miyan Ji's kulfi shop, tucked away on a quiet street, barely noticeable amidst the chaos of everyday life. The aroma from the shop, rich with the scent of reducing milk, cardamom and saffron, wafts across Delhi 6 and draws people in from neighbouring streets.

The shop has been there for over seventy years, passed down from one skilled *kulfiwala* to another. Miyan Ji had learned the art of making kulfi from his father, who himself had learned from his great uncle, an Indian nationalist like so many of the Muslim population in this neighbourhood. On my first visit, hoping to meet the legendary Miyan Ji, I was greeted by Miyan's grandson, Sameer, who was barely sixteen but was already carrying on his family's tradition. Making them fresh every day, and dipping them in a vat of thick *rabri* (reduced milk), Sameer's kulfi was still the perfect balance of richness and sweetness, each bite a little piece of heritage. Except for the one he gave me with marijuana in it as a joke.

Sameer, unlike his grandfather, likes to play with tradition, changing up the flavours of his kulfi and straying from the classics such as saffron, pistachio and more recently mango, in favour of contemporary flavours, like *phalsa* (Indian blueberry), *shakargandi* (sweet potato) and *nolen gur* (a type of palm sap, almost maple syrup-like). And of course, *bhang* (marijuana). It's not as strange as it sounds: around the festival of Holi, it's traditional to drink milk muddled with sugar and marijuana. In the vein of the Lord Shiva, the calming effects of the drug would help you still your mind in order to meditate. However, it often comes out as a form of elation. Taking a step back, I guess it makes sense that you would need to be on something to dance in the streets and throw paint at each other all day.

In any case, I needed to test out whether it had been the best kulfi I had ever tried, or if I was just so high that I looked back on it with rose-tinted glasses. So, the next time I was in Delhi, I wound my way back through the streets lining Jama Masjid - India's most famous mosque - passing up the opportunity to eat at Karim's (purveyor of the best *nihari* and *bheja* in Delhi) but never missing Aslam restaurant's butter chicken, and ended up back at the kulfi shop. Miyan Ji was perched on a chair outside the shop. Sameer and his father were both hard at work reducing milk with a couple of assistants. Through all of this, small tasters were shown to the ageing kulfiwala - he was so experienced at making kulfis that just the way the milk falls off a ladle back into the pan is enough for him to make a call on whether the mix is ready or not (so much for my magic Excel sheet). Miyan Ji spared some time to talk me through the history of his family and the business, as well as explaining to me what he's looking for whenever his grandson brings over the reduced milk. In the end, the key seemed to be the slightest change in colour, as the milk turns from a milky white to a pale straw. Only at this point, off the heat, does Miyan Ji take the saffron out of his small pouch - I've already mentioned just how expensive the best Kashmiri saffron is - and grind it into a few tablespoons of room-temperature water, before adding it into the pot with the milk. The team leaves it to cool, before loading it into an ancient-looking set of ice-lolly moulds.

To unmould the frozen kulfis, Miyan Ji would dip the case in warm water, then into cool water to stop any excessive melting. As he's getting ready to hand you the denuded kulfi, he dips it into more rabri and sprinkles it with roasted, crushed almonds. I can confirm, it wasn't just the weed that made this small shop so special.

Kulfis

I've written a fair bit about the traditional, sepia-tinted, romantic ways of making kulfi. An old man, his grandson in tow, reducing milk over a low flame, slowly stirring it to ensure it doesn't catch on the pan, the smells of Delhi 6 and the low-tech lanes surrounding the Jama Masjid. We don't try to recreate any of that at BiBi. In fact, we don't even reduce the milk. We tried it – it's tasty – but it's just not necessary with modern technology and ingredients. And also not really the right flavour for a space like BiBi; it's just too rich and heavy as a flavour profile. Instead, our most classic kulfi flavours are based on already-reduced milk, in the form of condensed or evaporated milk, whole-fat milk powder, roasted until slightly nutty, or even just crumbled *khoya* (a kind of reduced milk cake) and paneer. And, like the best vegan foods, we developed a vegan version unintentionally, just wanting to lighten things up with coconut milk rather than animal dairy.

In order to achieve the texture we need, we use a very expensive blast chiller – essentially an overpowered freezer fitted with a giant fan to speed up freezing below -20°C – and a Pacojet, a Swiss tool which basically functions as a powerful blender and shaves ice crystals into such a fine texture that it comes out like an ice cream on the other side. This kulfi / ice cream – stabilised by hydrocolloids (viscous thickening substances) – is then re-frozen and dipped into a flavoured chocolate shell. It's a fun and playful way to bring your experience with us to an end, not to mention the most Instagrammed thing in the restaurant.

The basic components:

For the dark chocolate dip
100g cocoa butter
100g 70% dark chocolate, broken into
    pieces

Melt the cocoa butter, add the white chocolate and blend with a hand blender until smooth.

For the white chocolate dip
100g cocoa butter
100g white chocolate, broken into
    pieces

Melt the cocoa butter, add the white chocolate and blend with a hand blender until smooth.

For the coconut sorbet base
400g Boiron coconut purée
36g caster sugar
40g prosorbet
4g lime juice

Mix the purée, sugar, prosorbet and lime juice together and blend until incorporated.

For moulding each kulfi
After spinning the base mixture in the Pacojet and folding through any additional ingredients, place the mix in a piping bag, insert the kulfi stick in the mould (we use mini Magnum-style mini ice lolly moulds) and fill them up. Tap the mould on the worktop to ensure there aren't any air pockets in the kulfis and place the mould in the freezer until the mixture is solid.

All variations pictured on p. 200 and 201

Toasted Vanilla Kulfi

Makes 10–12 kulfi

For the peanut caramel
50g white caster sugar
80g whipping cream
10g unsalted butter
10g smooth peanut butter
1g Maldon salt

For the peanut crumb
100g peeled, blanched peanuts
1g kosher salt
20g white caster sugar
crystallised dark chocolate (see Crystallised
    Garnishes, page 232)

For the base
5g vanilla pod
480g coconut sorbet base (opposite)

To finish
dark chocolate dip (opposite)

Peanut caramel
Take the caster sugar to 180°C in a heavy-based saucepan to make a dry caramel, then deglaze with the whipping cream and cook until it reaches 105°C. Reduce the temperature until the mixture reaches 70°C, then add the unsalted butter, peanut butter and Maldon salt. Mix with a hand blender and cool at room temperature. Store in a fine-tip squeezy bottle in the refrigerator for up to 5 days.

Peanut crumb
Preheat the oven to 175°C. Mix the peanuts and kosher salt on a tray and roast for 15 minutes.

Remove from the oven and cool, then blitz to a coarse powder in a food processor. Sift to get rid of larger pieces, then mix the sieved peanuts with the caster sugar. Store in an airtight container at room temperature for up to 1 month.

Toasted vanilla base
Preheat the oven to 200°C. Put the vanilla pod on a tray and roast for 14 minutes, then remove and, once cool, blend with the coconut sorbet base in a high-speed blender or Vitamix, pass through a chinois and fill up a Pacojet beaker. Freeze and, once frozen solid, spin in the Pacojet.

Finish
Melt the dip and keep it at 40°C in a large enough container to dip the kulfis. Set up your dipping station with the dip and garnishes. Once the mixture is fully frozen, demould the kulfis and dip them twice in the chocolate. While the chocolate is still runny, garnish with crystallised chocolate, 5 dots of peanut caramel and a sprinkle of peanut crumb. Store in an airtight container in the freezer until needed.

Conference Pear Kulfi

Makes 10–12 kulfi

For the coconut and pear base
240g Boiron coconut purée
160g Boiron conference pear purée
40g white caster sugar
40g procrema
20g prosorbet

For the pear gel
200g Boiron conference pear purée
30g white caster sugar
3g agar agar
0.4g ascorbic acid

To finish
dark chocolate dip (opposite)
crystallised dark chocolate (see Crystallised
    Garnishes, page 232)

Coconut and pear base
Put all the ingredients in a container and mix thoroughly with a hand blender. Put the base mix in a Pacojet beaker. Once frozen solid, spin in the Pacojet.

Pear gel
Put the pear purée and sugar in a pan and bring to the boil. Add the agar agar and mix until fully incorporated, then take off the heat and mix in the ascorbic acid. Cool down in a container in the refrigerator until set. Once solid, blend in a high-speed blender or Vitamix to a smooth, shiny texture. Pass through a sieve, place in a container and remove the air in a vacuum machine. Store in a fine-tip squeezy bottle in the refrigerator for up to 3 days.

Finish
Melt the dip and keep it at 40°C in a large enough container to dip the kulfis. Set up your dipping station with the dip and garnishes. Once the mixture is fully frozen, demould the kulfis and dip them twice in the chocolate. While the chocolate is still runny, garnish with crystallised dark chocolate and 5 dots of pear gel. Store in an airtight container in the freezer until needed.

Tutti Frutti Kulfi

Makes 10–12 kulfi

For the tutti frutti mix
250g water
1g Earl Grey tea leaves
64g raisins
64g candied orange peel
32g stem ginger, finely chopped

For the tutti frutti kulfi
500g coconut sorbet base (opposite)
75g tutti frutti mix

To finish
dark chocolate dip (opposite)
crystallised dark chocolate (see Crystallised
    Garnishes, page 232)
diced candied orange peel (4–6 dice
    per kulfi)

Tutti frutti mix
Heat the water to 85°C and brew the Earl Grey tea for 4 minutes. Strain the tea leaves and soak the raisins and candied orange peel in the tea in the refrigerator overnight. Pass the tutti frutti mix through a chinois and discard the liquid. Put the tutti frutti mix in a food processor and blend until finely chopped. Fill a Pacojet beaker with the coconut sorbet base and freeze until fully solid. Once frozen solid, spin the coconut sorbet in the Pacojet. Fold the tutti frutti mix through the coconut sorbet and leave to set.

Finish
Melt the dip and keep it at 40°C in a large enough container to dip the kulfis. Set up your dipping station with the dip and garnishes. Once the mixture is fully frozen, demould the kulfis and dip them twice in the chocolate. While the chocolate is still runny, garnish with crystallised chocolate and candied orange. Store in an airtight container in the freezer until needed.

Black Sesame and Sultana Kulfi

Makes 10-12 kulfi

80g sultanas
100g coconut milk
430g coconut sorbet base (page 196)
60g black sesame tahini
22g crystallised black sesame seeds
    (see Crystallised Garnishes, page 232)

To finish
dark chocolate dip (page 196)

Soak the sultanas overnight in coconut milk in a bowl in the refrigerator.

Once fully hydrated, drain (discarding the milk) and roughly chop the sultanas with a knife. Put the coconut sorbet base and black sesame tahini in a Pacojet beaker. Once frozen solid, spin in the Pacojet then fold through 20g of the crystallised black sesame seeds.

Finish
Melt the dip and keep it at 40°C in a large enough container to dip the kulfis. Set up your dipping station with the dip and garnishes. Once the mixture is fully frozen, demould the kulfis and dip them twice in the chocolate. While the chocolate is still runny, garnish with the remaining 2g of crystallised black sesame seeds. Store in an airtight container in the freezer until needed.

Mint Chocolate Chip Kulfi

Makes 10-12 kulfi

430g coconut sorbet base (page 196)
45g mint leaves

To finish
dark chocolate dip (page 196)
20g crystallised cocoa nibs (see Crystallised Garnishes, page 232)
1-2g crystallised dark chocolate (see Crystallised Garnishes, page 232)
1-2g crystallised mint (see Crystallised Garnishes, page 232)

Fill a Pacojet beaker with the coconut sorbet base and mint leaves. Freeze until fully solid. Once frozen solid, spin in the Pacojet and mix. Refreeze. When frozen solid, spin for a second time, then fold through the crystallised cocoa nibs.

Finish
Melt the dip and keep it at 40°C in a large enough container to dip the kulfis. Set up your dipping station with the dip and garnishes. Once the mixture is fully frozen, demould the kulfis and dip them twice in the chocolate. While the chocolate is still runny, garnish the front side of the kulfi with the crystallised chocolate and mint. Store in an airtight container in the freezer until needed.

Black Winter Truffle Kulfi

Makes 10-12 kulfi

430g coconut sorbet base (page 196)
18g black truffle, freshly grated
20g crystallised cocoa nibs (see Crystallised Garnishes, page 232)
crystallised dark chocolate (see Crystallised Garnishes, page 232)

To finish
dark chocolate dip (page 196)
shaved truffle, to garnish

Put the coconut sorbet base and grated truffle in a Pacojet beaker and freeze. Once frozen solid, spin in the Pacojet then fold through the crystallised cocoa nibs.

Finish
Melt the dip and keep it at 40°C in a large enough container to dip the kulfis. Set up your dipping station with the dip and garnishes. Once the mixture is fully frozen, demould the kulfis and dip them twice in the chocolate. While the chocolate is still runny, garnish with crystallised dark chocolate and shaved truffle. Store in an airtight container in the freezer until needed.

Grapefruit and Timur Kulfi

Makes 15-20 kulfi

300g Boiron coconut purée
200g grapefruit juice
50g white caster sugar
50g procrema
25g dextrose
60g candied orange, finely chopped

To finish
white chocolate dip (page 196)
0.3-0.6g cracked pink peppercorns

Put the purée, juice, caster sugar, procrema and dextrose in a container and mix using a hand blender. Transfer to a Pacojet beaker and freeze. Once frozen solid, spin in the Pacojet, then fold through the chopped candied orange.

Finish
Melt the dip and keep it at 40°C in a large enough container to dip the kulfis. Set up your dipping station with the dip and garnishes. Once the mixture is fully frozen, demould the kulfis and dip them twice in the chocolate. While the chocolate is still runny, garnish with the cracked pink peppercorns. Store in an airtight container in the freezer until needed.

Desserts

Indian Lemon and Hazelnut Kulfi

Makes 15-20 kulfi

For the chilli hazelnut crumb
75g blanched hazelnuts
22g white caster sugar
3g lemon zest
0.5g Korean chilli flakes

For the lemon kulfi base
300g Boiron coconut purée
200g Indian lemon juice
50g white caster sugar
50g procrema
25g dextrose
60g candied orange, chopped into
   small pieces

To finish
 white chocolate dip (page 196)

Chilli hazelnut crumb
Preheat the oven to 160°C. Put the hazelnuts on a baking tray and roast for 10 minutes until golden. Remove from the oven and leave to cool, then add them to a Thermomix or food processor along with the sugar, lemon zest and Korean chilli flakes. Pulse until a large crumb is achieved. Sift the mixture and discard the powder. Store in an airtight container for up to 1 month.

Lemon kulfi base
Put all the ingredients, except the candied orange, in a container and mix using a hand blender. Place the lemon kulfi base in a Pacojet beaker and freeze. Once frozen solid, spin in the Pacojet, then fold through the chopped candied orange.

Finish
Melt the dip and keep it at 40°C in a large enough container to dip the kulfis. Set up your dipping station with the dip and garnishes. Once the mixture is fully frozen, demould the kulfis and dip them twice in the chocolate. While the chocolate is still runny, garnish with the chilli hazelnut crumb. Store in an airtight container in the freezer until needed.

Alphonso Mango Kulfi

Makes 15-20 kulfi

For the mango kulfi base
100g water
45g white caster sugar
14g dextrose
12.5g procrema
12.5g prosorbet
235g Kissan alphonso mango pulp
10g lime juice
2g lime zest
0.4g ground green cardamom seeds
1g kosher salt

For the caramelised white chocolate
2g white chocolate

To finish
white chocolate dip (page 196)

Mango kulfi base
Place all the ingredients in a container and mix using a hand blender. Place the base in a Pacojet beaker. Once frozen solid, spin in the Pacojet.

Caramelised white chocolate
Preheat the oven to 120°C. Place the white chocolate on a baking tray and cook for 10 minutes. Remove the chocolate from the oven and spread it around with a maryse (flexible spatula). Repeat this process five more times, until the chocolate has a crumbly texture and a deep golden-brown colour. Allow to cool at room temperature. Store in an airtight container for up to 1 month.

Chop the caramelised white chocolate into small pieces.

Finish
Melt the dip and keep it at 40°C in a large enough container to dip the kulfis. Set up your dipping station with the dip and garnishes. Once the mixture is fully frozen, demould the kulfis and dip them twice in the chocolate. While the chocolate is still runny, garnish the kulfis with the chopped caramelised white chocolate. Store in an airtight container in the freezer until needed.

Buffalo Milk Paneer Kulfi

Makes 15-20 kulfi

200g full-fat milk
0.1g saffron
200g Buffalo Milk Paneer (page 70)
48g white caster sugar
8g glycerine
40g procrema
8g toasted milk powder

To finish
white chocolate dip (page 196)
2-3g crystallised pistachios (see
   Crystallised Garnishes, page 232)

Heat the milk and saffron in a saucepan to 80°C.

Blend the paneer with the saffron milk in a Thermomix or food processor until smooth. When cool, mix in the remaining ingredients using a hand blender. Place the paneer kulfi mix in a Pacojet beaker and freeze. Once frozen solid, spin in the Pacojet.

Finish
Melt the dip and keep it at 40°C in a large enough container to dip the kulfis. Set up your dipping station with the dip and garnishes. Once the mixture is fully frozen, demould the kulfis and dip them twice in the chocolate. While the chocolate is still runny, garnish with crystallised pistachios. Store in an airtight container in the freezer until needed.

BiBi Essentials

These are the heartbeat of the restaurant; beyond a well-stocked pantry full of spices, it's almost impossible to cook the recipes in this book without having at least a handful of these essential bits of *mise en place* prepared and ready to go in your kitchen.

Pastes and Bases

Tamarind Paste

Makes 400g

100g dried tamarind, broken into chunks
300g water

Put the tamarind chunks in a pan with the water, bring to the boil and simmer for 5 minutes. Remove and leave to soak overnight. Once cool, pass through a fine sieve to remove the seeds and fibres.

Store in an airtight container in the refrigerator for up to 10 days.

Cashew Paste

Makes 300g

100g cashews
200g water

Preheat the oven to 160°C. Roast the cashews on a baking tray for 12-16 minutes, stirring them every 4 minutes, until light brown. Put them in a pan with the water and bring to the boil, then remove from the heat. Blend the nuts with the cooking water, while still warm, in a high-speed blender or Vitamix until a very smooth paste is formed. Pass it through a fine chinois.

Store in an airtight container at room temperature for up to 5 days.

Walnut Paste

Makes 200g

100g walnuts
100g water

Preheat the oven to 160°C. Roast the walnuts on a baking tray for 12-16 minutes, stirring them every 4 minutes, until golden. Place the walnuts on a perforated gastro and break them roughly, then put a lid and shake it vigorously in order to remove the skins. Put the skinned walnuts in a pan with the water and bring to the boil, then remove from the heat. Blend the nuts with the cooking water, while still warm, in a high-speed blender or Vitamix until a very smooth paste is formed. Pass it through a fine chinois.

Store in an airtight container in the refrigerator for up to 5 days.

Ginger and Garlic Paste

Makes 100g

50g peeled garlic
50g peeled ginger

Blend the garlic and ginger to a smooth paste in a high-speed blender or Vitamix. Store in an airtight container in the refrigerator for up to 3 days.

Truffle Paste

Makes 185g

20g shallots, finely diced
10g MSG Oil (page 221)
60g frozen ceps, defrosted and sliced
40g chestnut mushrooms, sliced
40g black winter / autumn truffle paste or truffle trims
10g truffle water
1g MSG
4g Pre-Hy (page 212)
kosher salt

Sweat the shallots slowly in the MSG oil in a frying pan over a medium heat for 5-6 minutes or until soft and translucent. Add both mushrooms and cook until brown and all the liquid has evaporated, then blend all the ingredients together in a Thermomix or food processor until they form a smooth paste. Season with salt.

Store in an airtight container in the refrigerator for up to 5 days.

Yoghurt

Makes 1kg

1kg full-fat milk
50g milk powder
20g live yoghurt culture (from a previous batch)

Slowly heat the milk and milk powder in a pan to 90°C to denature some of the milk proteins. Cool the mixture in an ice bath to 45°C, then add the live culture and pour it into a container. Hold the mix at between 40 and 45°C, and the yoghurt will be ready in 4-6 hours.

Store in an airtight container in the refrigerator for up to 5 days.

Cultured Cream

Makes 1kg

1kg whipping cream
20g live yoghurt culture (from a previous
    batch)

Slowly heat the cream in a pan to 90°C to
denature some of the milk proteins. Cool
the cream in an ice bath to 45°C, then add
the live culture and pour the mixture into a
container. Hold the mix at between 40 and
45°C, and the cultured cream will be ready
in 10–12 hours.

Store in an airtight container in the
refrigerator for up to 5 days.

Hung Yoghurt and Yoghurt Whey

natural yoghurt

Place a double layer of muslin cloth over
a bowl. Stir the yoghurt and place it on the
muslin cloth. Tie the muslin cloth and hang it
in the refrigerator with the bowl underneath.
Leave it hanging for 3 days. Keep both
the whey and the hung yoghurt to use in
recipe such as the Cashew Yoghurt and the
marinades on page 215.

Store in separate airtight containers in the
refrigerator for up to 5 days.

Tepache

Makes 500g

500g filtered water
90g light brown sugar
160g pineapple trims
20g fresh peeled ginger, sliced
3g cinnamon sticks
2g cloves
3g green cardamom pods, crushed
3g mace blades
2g star anise

Put all the ingredients in a sterilised non-
reactive (ceramic or glass) container and
mix until the sugar has dissolved. Cover
with a muslin cloth, making sure it is tightly
secured to avoid anything from getting in,
and place in a warm place (22–28°C) to
ferment. After 5 days of fermentation,
check if a frothy white foam has formed
on the surface. If there is no foam, leave
it to ferment longer, until mildly alcoholic
and slightly fizzy. Pass the tepache through
a fine chinois, discarding the solids. Store
the liquid in an airtight container in the
refrigerator for up to 1 month.

Chicken Stock and Reduced Chicken Stock

Makes 2–2.5kg

3 litres filtered water
1kg chicken feet
1kg chicken wings, bones and trims

Put all the ingredients in a stockpot and
slowly bring to the boil. Once it boils, turn
down to a low simmer and skim every 5–10
minutes for 2 hours. Pass through a fine
chinois. Put the stock in a container and
chill over ice. Once cool, store in the
refrigerator in an airtight container.

For the reduced chicken stock, keep simmering the stock after passing it through
the chinois and reduce it by two thirds.

Store in an airtight container in the
refrigerator for up to 5 days.

Fish Stock

Makes 2–2.5kg

2kg fish bones, ideally monkfish or turbot
3 litres filtered water

Put the fish bones in a large container and
wash them under cold running water for
20 minutes, or until the water runs clear.
The bones should look white, without any
blood in them.

Put the bones and filtered water in a stockpot and slowly bring to the boil, then turn
down to a low simmer and cook for 40
minutes, skimming every 5–10 minutes.
Take the pot off the heat and allow to infuse
for another 20 minutes. Pass through a fine
chinois. Put the stock in a container and chill
over ice.

Once cool, store in an airtight container in
the refrigerator for up to 5 days.

Vegetable Stock

Makes 2kg

500g white Spanish onions, cut into chunks
150g carrots, cut into chunks
100g fennel, cut into chunks
45g celery, cut into chunks
25g turnip, cut into chunks
150g celeriac, peeled and cut into chunks
7.5g peeled garlic
250g dried chickpeas, washed and soaked
    overnight
2.5g bay leaves
2.5g cumin seeds
5g fennel seeds
5g coriander seeds
5g black peppercorns
2.5 litres filtered cold water

Put the vegetables in a stockpot along with
the garlic cloves, drained soaked chickpeas
and spices. Add the cold water, bring to the
boil, then reduce the heat and simmer for
2 hours. Pass through a fine chinois.

Once cool, store in an airtight container in
the refrigerator for up to 5 days.

Tomato Water

Makes 250g

1kg datterini tomatoes
10g kosher salt

Pulse the tomatoes with the salt in a Thermomix or food processor, just enough to
break the tomatoes (do not blend smooth,
otherwise the consommé won't be clear).
Put the tomatoes in a superbag and leave
to hang over a container in the refrigerator
for 2 days. Set the pulp aside for another
use. Simmer the tomato water until reduced
by half. Chill immediately.

Store in an airtight container in the
refrigerator for up to 5 days.

Roasted Besan Flour

besan flour

Preheat the oven to 160°C. Spread out the besan flour on a baking tray and roast for about 30 minutes until slightly brown, mixing it every 10 minutes.

Store in an airtight container at room temperature for up to 3 months.

Dashi Resting Butter

Makes 250g

250g unsalted butter, cubed
5g milk powder
5g roasted ajwain seeds
12.5g lemon juice
5g katsobushi
5g dashi concentrate
2% kosher salt

Heat a frying pan over a medium-high heat. Add the butter and milk powder and cook for about 10 minutes, or until the milk solids turn dark brown. Take off the heat and add the ajwain seeds and lemon juice to stop the cooking. Leave to cool until it reaches 80°C, then add the katsobushi and dashi concentrate and leave to cool to 50°C. Pass the mixture through a fine chinois lined with muslin cloth. Weigh out the final infused brown butter and add 2% of its weight in kosher salt.

Dosa Batter

Makes 1kg

600g ponni rice, rinsed
200g split white urad dal, rinsed
50g chana dal, rinsed
5g fenugreek seeds
10g kosher salt
8g white caster sugar
200g filtered water

Soak the rice and dals separately in tap water overnight.

Drain both dals and put them in a Thermomix or food processor with the fenugreek seeds, salt and sugar. Blend until smooth. If necessary, add 50g of filtered water. Add the soaked rice and filtered water and keep blending until you have a slightly grainy batter. Place the mixture in a container with a lid and let it ferment at room temperature of 26–28°C for about 8 hours.

Once fermented, store in an airtight container in the refrigerator for a maximum of 2 days.

Pre-Hy (Pre-hydrated Xanthan Gum)

Makes 1.2kg

1 litre water
20g xanthan gum

Put the water in a blender and slowly add the xanthan until the water turns to a gummy texture.

Masalas and Marinades

Awadhi Masala

Makes 385g

10g dried fenugreek leaves
5g cinnamon stick
30g cumin seeds
60g coriander seeds
6g green cardamom seeds
3g mace blades
9g cloves
12g black cardamom seeds
45g Garam Masala (page 213)
45g black pepper
60g Kashmiri red chilliies
100g kosher salt

Blend all the spices to a fine powder in a spice or coffee grinder. Store in an airtight container for up to 1 month.

BiBi Chaat Masala

Makes 200g

22g cumin seeds
22g black peppercorns
22g black salt
12g dried mint
1g citric acid
1g mace blades
6g green cardamom seeds
2g cloves
1g cinnamon stick
2g ajwain seeds
4g asafoetida
62g amchoor
22g kosher salt
12g ground ginger
9g yellow chilli powder

Blend all the ingredients to a fine powder in a spice or coffee grinder. Store in an airtight container for up to 1 month.

Chettinad Masala

Makes 145g

60g coriander seeds
15g cumin seeds
15g fennel seeds
5g star anise
1g green cardamom seeds
1g cloves
10g cinnamon sticks
5g mace blades
5g black peppercorns
3g fenugreek seeds
10g dagad phool
15g Kashmiri chilli powder

Preheat the oven to 160°C. Spread all the spices, except the dagad phool and Kashmiri chilli powder, out on a baking tray. Roast in the oven for 4 minutes, then remove and allow to cool to room temperature. Add the roasted spices, along with the dagad phool and Kashmiri chilli powder, to a spice or coffee grinder and blend to a fine powder. Store in an airtight container for up to 1 month.

Garam Masala

Makes 250g

15g green cardamom seeds
9g black cardamom seeds
15g cloves
23g cinnamon stick
15g mace blades
8g royal cumin seeds
56g cumin seeds
30g black peppercorns
15g dried ginger
3g freshly grated nutmeg
27g coriander seeds
12g fennel seeds
3g dagad phool
15g rose petals
8g bay leaves

Preheat the oven to 160°C. Spread all the spices, except the dagad phool, rose petals and bay leaves on a baking tray and roast in the oven for 4 minutes, then remove from the oven and allow to cool to room temperature. Blend the roasted spices along with the remaining ingredients to a fine powder in a spice or coffee grinder. Store in an airtight container for up to 1 month.

Jawahari Masala

Makes 41g

4g coriander seeds
4g cumin seeds
2g royal cumin seeds
2g pippali (long pepper)
2g cubeb pepper
4g black peppercorns
1g Garam Masala (page 213)
4g Kashmiri chilli powder
8g kosher salt
2g black salt
8g BiBi Chaat Masala (page 213)

Blend all the spices to a fine powder in a spice or coffee grinder. Store in an airtight container for up to 1 month.

Jeera Chaat Masala

Makes 265g

50g cumin seeds
30g royal cumin seeds
150g Bibi Chaat Masala (page 213)
25g amchoor
10g black salt

Blend all the ingredients to a fine powder in a spice or coffee grinder. Store in an airtight container for up to 1 month.

Kurkure Masala

Makes 95g

45g tomato powder
5g roasted cumin
10g BiBi Chaat Masala (page 213)
1g black peppercorns
20g onion powder
1g garlic powder
2g citric acid
5g deggi mirch
3g caster sugar
3g amchoor

Blend all the ingredients to a fine powder in a spice or coffee grinder. Store in an airtight container for up to 1 month.

Lime Leaf Chaat Masala

Makes 185g

60g royal cumin seeds
30g black salt
30g amchoor
5g citric acid
20g black peppercorns
10g vegetable charcoal
10g lime leaf powder
20g mint leaf powder

Blend all the ingredients to a coarse powder in a spice or coffee grinder. Store in an airtight container for up to 1 month.

Maggi Masala

Makes 625g

210g coriander seeds
140g cumin seeds
25g fennel seeds
12g fenugreek seeds
6g bay leaves
21g cinnamon stick
4g green cardamom seeds
3g cloves
12g black peppercorns
100g deggi mirch
15g ground turmeric
15g garlic powder
15g onion powder
32g amchoor
15g kosher salt

Blend all the ingredients to a fine powder in a spice or coffee grinder. Store in an airtight container for up to 1 month.

Maggi Tastemaker

Makes 443g

210g coriander seeds
32g cumin seeds
25g Garam Masala (page 213)
6g ground turmeric
32g deggi mirch
15g garlic powder
15g ground ginger
20g onion powder
32g amchoor
12g ground black pepper
32g kosher salt
12g icing sugar

Blend all the ingredients to a fine powder in a spice or coffee grinder. Store in an airtight container for up to 1 month.

Malai Masala

Makes 195g

20g mace blades
20g green cardamom seeds
5g freshly grated nutmeg
10g white peppercorns
20g yellow chilli powder
100g Maldon salt
20g citric acid

Blend all the ingredients to a fine powder in a spice or coffee grinder. Store in an airtight container for up to 1 month.

Pav Bhaji Masala

Makes 213g

30g coriander seeds
6g black cardamom seeds
30g cumin seeds
30g fennel seeds
15g black peppercorns
2g cloves
10g cinnamon stick
50g Kashmiri chilli powder
10g ground turmeric
30g amchoor

Blend all the spices to a fine powder in a spice or coffee grinder. Store in an airtight container for up to 1 month.

Rassam Masala

Makes 175g

100g coriander seeds
25g cumin seeds
10g dried long red chilli
5g fenugreek seeds
10g asafoetida
10g curry leaf powder
15g black peppercorns

Blend all the spices to a fine powder in a spice or coffee grinder. Store in an airtight container for up to 1 month.

Sharmaji Masala

Makes 465g

50g cumin seeds
50g black peppercorns
50g black salt
30g dried mint
20g dried fenugreek leaves
4g citric acid
2.5g mace blades
15g green cardamom seeds
5g cloves
3g cinnamon stick
5g ajwain seeds
5g asafoetida
125g amchoor
50g kosher salt
30g ground ginger
25g yellow chilli powder

Blend all the ingredients to a coarse powder in a spice or coffee grinder. Store in an airtight container for up to 1 month.

Ver Masala

Makes 350g

5g royal cumin seeds
50g fennel seeds
3.5g cinnamon stick
0.5g cloves
2g black cardamom seeds
1g green cardamom seeds
50g peeled garlic
50g shallots, chopped
25g rapeseed oil
100g Kashmiri chilli powder
50g ground ginger
7.5g ground turmeric
125g water

Preheat the oven to 160°C. Spread the royal cumin and fennel on a baking tray and roast in the oven for 4 minutes, then remove from the oven and allow to cool to room temperature. Blend the roasted spices along with the remaining whole spices to a fine powder in a spice or coffee grinder.

Put the garlic and shallots in a blender and blend to a smooth paste. Heat the oil in a saucepan over a medium-high heat, add the shallot and garlic mixture and cook until translucent. Take off the heat and reserve.

Mix the ground spices with the garlic and shallot paste and the rest of the ingredients, then shape into 100g doughnuts (the mix should make about 3½ doughnuts) and de-hydrate at 40–50°C for 24–48 hours until completely dry. Store in an airtight container for up to 1 month.

First Marinade

Makes 100g

33g peeled garlic
33g peeled ginger
33g lemon juice
1.5g kosher salt

Blend all the ingredients to a smooth paste in a high-speed blender or Vitamix. Store in an airtight container in the refrigerator for up to 5 days.

Awadhi Marinade

Makes 315g

16g Awadhi Masala (page 213)
16g mustard oil
2g kosher salt
8g garlic
15g ginger
20g double cream
240g Hung Yoghurt (page 209)

Blend the masala, mustard oil, salt, garlic and ginger to a paste in a high-speed blender or Vitamix until smooth. Mix the paste with the cream and yoghurt until homogeneous in colour. Store in an airtight container in the refrigerator for up to 5 days.

Barra Marinade

Makes 360g

9g Kashmiri chilli powder
1g dried fenugreek leaves
2g royal cumin seeds
4g kosher salt
16g peeled ginger
40g Indian onion
10g Fried Onions (page 225)
40g mustard oil
4g deggi mirch
240g Awadhi Marinade (above)

Blend all the ingredients, except the awadhi marinade, in a blender to a smooth paste. Mix the awadhi marinade with the paste until mixed thoroughly. Store in an airtight container in the refrigerator for up to 5 days.

Achari Marinade

Makes 350g

25g red bell pepper, roasted
125g Garlic Achaar (page 224)
25g mustard oil
25g rice wine vinegar
50g anchovy paste
13g green bird's eye chilli
13g Kashmiri chilli powder
50g ssamjang
6g kosher salt
25g gochujang

Char the bell pepper over a flame. Once fully black, wrap in a cloth and let it cool down. Peel the pepper, then discard the stem, seeds and charred skin. Blend all the ingredients along with the red pepper pulp in a high-speed blender or Vitamix to a smooth paste. Store in an airtight container in the refrigerator for up to 5 days.

Red Chamba Chukh Marinade

Makes 96g

30g lemon juice
6g kosher salt
60g red chamba chukh masala

Mix all the ingredients together. Store in an airtight container in the refrigerator for up to 5 days.

Malai Marinade

Makes 357g

14g Malai Masala (opposite)
15g garlic paste
15g fresh peeled ginger, finely chopped
3g green bird's eye chilli, very finely chopped
10g coriander stem, very finely chopped
250g Hung Yoghurt (page 209)
50g crème fraîche

Mix all the ingredients together. Store in an airtight container in the refrigerator for up to 5 days.

Imli Miso

Makes 400g

20g neutral vegetable oil
100g Indian onion, thinly sliced
30g fresh peeled ginger, chopped
2.5g curry leaves
15g green bird's eye chilli, chopped
1.5g kosher salt
40g jaggery, grated
100g Tamarind Paste (page 208)
25g water
12.5g Chettinad Masala (page 213)
100g white miso

Heat the vegetable oil in a frying pan over a medium-low heat. Add the sliced onion and caramelise to a dark brown colour. Add the chopped ginger, curry leaves and green chilli and cook for 2 minutes until fragrant and the curry leaves splutter. Add the salt, grated jaggery, tamarind paste and water. Take off the heat and add the Chettinad masala and miso. Blitz everything together in a Thermomix or food processor until homogenous.

Lemon Fish Cure

Makes 100g

70g kosher salt
30g caster sugar
1g lemon zest, grated with a microplane

Combine all the ingredients and store in an airtight container at room temperature for up to 1 month.

Vinegar Bath for Fish

10% rice wine vinegar

Fill a container big enough to cover the fish with water and add 10% of the water weight with vinegar. Wash the cured fish in the solution. Pat the fish dry.

Indian Lemon Dressing

Makes 120g

100g Indian lemon juice
15g kosher salt
5g chaat masala

Mix all the ingredients together.

Chutneys and Emulsions

Coconut Chutney

Makes 400g

For the base
150g freshly grated coconut
15g ginger
7.5g green bird's eye chilli
1g curry leaves
5g kosher salt
25g grapeseed oil
160g water
10g coriander leaves

For the tempering
20g grapeseed oil
2g urad dal
2g black mustard seeds
1g curry leaves
1g dried red chilli

Base
Put all the ingredients except the coriander in a high-speed blender or Vitamix and blend to a paste. Add the coriander and blend until smooth.

Tempering
Heat the oil in a frying pan to 180°C. Add the urad dal and cook for 1-2 minutes until it starts turning golden around the edges. Add the mustard seeds and cook until they crack, then add the curry leaves and cook till they splutter. Remove from the heat, add the dried chilli and let it cook in the hot oil for 2 minutes, then remove the whole dried chilli and fold the tempering into the chutney.

Store in an airtight container in the refrigerator for up to 3 days.

Jalapeño Emulsion

Makes 250g

20g egg white
10g dashi vinegar
40g jalapeño juice
grated zest and juice of ½ lime
3g kosher salt
5g Pre-Hy (page 212)
165g grapeseed oil

Put all the ingredients except the grapeseed oil in a high-speed blender or Vitamix and blitz at full speed until smooth, then slowly stream in the grapeseed oil until emulsified.

Store in an airtight container in the refrigerator for up to 3 days.

Curry Leaf Jalapeño Emulsion

Makes 255g

5g curry leaves
neutral vegetable oil, for deep frying
250g Jalapeño Emulsion (left)

Heat enough neutral vegetable oil for deep frying to 180°C in a deep fat fryer (two-thirds to three-quarters full). Fry the curry leaves for 5-10 seconds until crispy. Drain on kitchen paper to absorb excess oil, then blend the curry leaves to a paste. Mix through the jalapeño emulsion.

Store in an airtight container in the refrigerator for up to 3 days.

Green Chutney

Makes 330g

60g silken tofu
10g green chilli
15g ginger
10g garlic
35g Indian onion, cut into chunks
3g Maldon salt
3g black salt
3g BiBi Chaat Masala (page 213)
15g lemon juice
ice cubes, to blend
100g coriander leaves
35g coriander stems
35g mint leaves
15g grapeseed oil

Blend all the ingredients except the herbs and oil to a paste in a high-speed blender or Vitamix, then refrigerate the paste. Wash the herbs in iced water, then strain well, ideally using a salad spinner. Blitz everything in the high-speed blender or Vitamix, emulsifying with the oil until very smooth.

Store in medium and small bottles in the refrigerator for ideally no longer than 24 hours (maximum 3 days).

Green Pepper Sauce

Makes 200g

neutral vegetable oil, for deep frying
50g long Indian chillies
25g poblano peppers
10g spinach
10g turnip tops (cime di rapa)
2g amchoor
1g BiBi Chaat Masala (page 213)
3g Pre-Hy (page 212)
2g Maldon salt
1g black salt
2g roasted cumin seeds
30g silken tofu
20g ice cubes
kosher salt
25g coriander (leaves and stems)
5g mint leaves
24g grapeseed oil

Heat enough vegetable oil for deep frying
to 180°C in a deep fat fryer (two-thirds
to three-quarters full). Fry the long Indian
chillies and the poblano peppers for
2 minutes. Transfer to a bowl and cover
them. Let them rest for a few minutes,
then peel and set aside.

Blanch the spinach and turnip tops in boiling
salted water for 30 seconds, shock in iced
water, remove and squeeze out excess water.

Place all the ingredients except the herbs
and grapeseed oil in a high-speed blender
or Vitamix and blend to a paste, then add the
herbs and blitz again until smooth. Gradually
add the grapeseed oil to emulsify. Cool over
ice and adjust seasoning.

Store in an airtight container in the
refrigerator for up to 3 days.

Mango Chutney

Makes 4kg

125g golden raisins
20g melon seeds
250g filtered water
1.5kg unripe mangoes, peeled, washed
    and destoned
1kg demerara sugar
125g Indian onion, finely diced
75g fresh peeled ginger, finely diced
20g Kashmiri chilli powder
10g Garam Masala (page 213)
10g nigella seeds
5g freshly ground cassia bark
250g white wine vinegar
20g black salt

Soak the golden raisins and melon seeds in
the water and leave to soak overnight in the
refrigerator.

Grate the mango flesh with a coarse box
grater. Heat a heavy-based saucepan over
a medium-low heat, add the sugar and
mango and cook for 30-45 minutes until all
the water comes out of the mango and all the
sugar dissolves and you have a thick, sweet
mango mix. Add the remaining ingredients
except the vinegar and black salt and cook
until the mix has a jammy consistency, or
until it reaches over 105°C. Add the vinegar
and salt and remove from the heat.

To store the chutney, place the hot chutney
in sterilised jam jars, cover with wax paper
until cool, then screw the lid on tightly. Store
in an airtight container in the refrigerator
for up to 1 month.

Tamarind Chutney

Makes 1kg

30g deggi mirch
300g jaggery, grated
600g Tamarind Paste (page 208)
30g fennel seeds
25g ground ginger
20g roasted cumin seeds
20g roasted coriander seeds
15g black salt

Put the deggi mirch, jaggery and tamarind
in a large, heavy-based saucepan or pot
and bring to a rolling boil, whisking constantly. Remove from the heat and add the
remaining ingredients. Blend with a hand
blender while hot, adding filtered water as
required, to achieve a consistency similar
to double cream.

To store, place the hot chutney in sterilised
jam jars, cover with wax paper until cool,
then screw the lid on tightly.

Store in an airtight container in the refrigerator for up to 1 month.

Walnut Chutney

Makes 300g

20g Indian onion, cut into chunks
6g garlic
0.5g dried mint
10g red chukh masala
10g fresh ginger
10g coriander (leaves and stems)
3g mint leaves
4g rice vinegar
10g ice cubes
200g Walnut Paste (page 208)
10g grapeseed oil
30g Hung Yoghurt (page 209)
black salt
kosher salt

Put the onion, garlic, mint, masala, ginger,
herbs, vinegar and ice cubes in a blender
and blend until smooth. Add the walnut paste
and stream in the the oil while blitzing. Fold
in the hung yoghurt. Season with both salts.
Pass through a chinois if needed.

Store in an airtight container in the refrigerator for up to 3 days.

Oils and Pickles

Fennel Oil

Makes 70g

100g fennel fronds
100g grapeseed oil

Blend the fennel fronds and oil in a high-speed blender or Vitamix until the mixture reaches 63–69°C and the oil starts to split. Chill over ice immediately. Store in the refrigerator overnight.

Strain the mix through a fine sieve, and then through a superbag.

Store the oil in an airtight container in the refrigerator for up to 1 month.

Green Curry Oil

Makes 300g

25g mint leaves
25g Thai basil leaves
25g basil leaves
100g coriander (leaves and stems)
10g lemongrass (15cm pieces), trimmed and thinly sliced
40g fresh peeled ginger, roughly chopped
8g garlic, roughly chopped
10g kosher salt
340g grapeseed oil

Wash the herbs in iced water.

Put all the ingredients in a Thermomix and blend between 63°C and 69°C until the mixture starts to split. Place the split mixture in a container and cool it down over ice. Once cool, let it infuse for a night in the refrigerator.

The next morning, strain the mix through a superbag, or pass it through a fine chinois and then a coffee filter. Put the liquid in a large piping bag, then tie and hang for 2 hours in the refrigerator to allow any sediments and water to separate from the oil.

Prepare a container and a squeezy bottle to store the oil. Once the oil has decanted, grab the piping bag by the top, place it over the container and cut the very end of the tip with a pair of scissors. The sediments and water will start to come out of the bag. As soon as the oil starts to come out without impurities, pinch the tip, place it over the bottle and fill it with the green oil.

Store in the sealed bottle in the refrigerator for up to 1 month.

Lapsang Oil

Makes 200g

20g lapsang souchong tea leaves
200g grapeseed oil

Wash the tea leaves in iced water.

Place the lapsang and the oil in a container and cook at 70°C in a combination oven, water bath or dehydrator overnight. Pass through a fine chinois.

Store the oil in an airtight container in the refrigerator for up to 1 month.

Lemon Oil

Makes 100g

30g pared zest of unwaxed Amalfi lemons
100g grapeseed oil

Place the lemon zest and the oil in a container and cook at 70°C in a combination oven, water bath or dehydrator overnight. Pass through a fine chinois.

Store the oil in an airtight container in the refrigerator for up to 1 month.

Lemongrass Oil

Makes 100g

100g grapeseed oil
1 lemongrass stalk

Put the grapeseed oil and lemongrass in a container and infuse overnight at 70°C in a combination oven, water bath or dehydrator overnight. Pass through a fine chinois.

Store the oil in an airtight container in the refrigerator for up to 1 month.

MSG Oil

Makes 700g

700g rapeseed oil
0.2g black peppercorns
0.15g cloves
0.25g black cardamom seeds
0.15g green cardamom seeds
0.15g bay leaves
150g spring onions, roughly chopped
100g shallots (skin on), roughly chopped
15g fresh ginger (skin on), roughly chopped
40g coriander (leaves and stems), roughly chopped
4g MSG

Heat the oil in a pan to 130°C, add the whole spices and cook for 1 minute until fragrant. Add the roughly chopped onions, shallots, ginger and coriander and herbs to the oil, heat to 160°C and cook for 20-30 minutes until the onions and shallots are golden and caramelised. Remove from the heat and pour into a container on top of an ice bath to cool the oil down quickly. Leave to infuse in the refrigerator overnight.

The following day, pass through a fine chinois and mix in the MSG with a hand blender.

Store in an airtight container in the refrigerator for up to 1 month.

Peanut Oil

Makes 200g

1g cumin seeds
0.5g coriander seeds
7g dried long Indian red chillies
10g white sesame seeds
13g garlic
7.5g kosher salt
2g deggi mirch
5g gochugaru
10g jaggery
20g white miso
250g grapeseed oil

Preheat the oven to 160°C.

Place the cumin and coriander seeds on a tray and roast in the oven for 1 minute, then add the dried chillies to the tray and roast for 3 more minutes. Remove the toasted spices from the oven and set aside. On a separate tray, place the sesame seeds and roast in the oven for 15 minutes until golden.

Put all the ingredients except the oil in a food processor and blend until finely minced, then add the oil and blend for another minute until emulsified. Put the mixture inside a vacuum pouch and seal.

Set up a dehydrator or a steam oven to 70°C and cook the oil for 15 hours.

Pass the oil through a fine chinois. Keep the pulp and oil in separate airtight containers in the refrigerator for up to 1 month.

Tomato Oil

Makes 400g

200g tomato pulp (leftover from the tomato water - see page 212)
50g tomato purée
500g grapeseed oil

Blend all the ingredients in a Thermomix or food processor until incorporated. Transfer the mixture to a pan, place over a medium-low heat and heat the mixture to 100°C. Cook at 100°C for 30 minutes, then pass the mixture through a fine chinois lined with muslin cloth. Keep the liquid and discard the pulp.

Put the liquid in a large piping bag, then tie and hang for 2 hours at room temperature, to allow any sediments and water to separate from the oil.

Prepare a container and a squeezy bottle to store the oil. Once the oil has decanted, grab a piping bag by the top, place it over the container and cut the very end of the tip with a pair of scissors. The sediments and water will start to come out of the bag. As soon as the oil starts to come out without impurities, pinch the tip, place it over the bottle and fill it with the tomato oil.

Store in an airtight container in the refrigerator for up to 1 month.

Truffle Oil

Makes 110g

10g black truffle
100g grapeseed oil

Put the truffle and oil in a Thermomix and blitz until it reaches 60°C. Let it infuse in the refrigerator overnight.

Pass through a fine chinois lined with muslin cloth.

Store the oil in an airtight container in the refrigerator for up to 1 month and use the leftover truffle paste to make the truffle paste on page 208.

BiBi Essentials

Garlic Achaar

Makes 550g

9g fennel seeds
3g black mustard seeds
1g fenugreek seeds
360g garlic
100g mustard oil
16g whole green chilli
30g fresh ginger
17g salt
12g Kashmiri chilli powder
2g ground turmeric
1g asafoetida

Preheat the oven to 160°C. Dry roast the fennel and mustard seeds on a roasting tray for 4 minutes. Add the fenugreek and roast for a further 1 minute, then remove from the oven and allow to cool.

Grind the roasted spices to a fine powder in a spice or coffee grinder.

Blanch the garlic in boiling water for 2 minutes and refresh in cold water. Repeat two more times (three in total).

Mix all the ingredients and seal in a vacuum machine. Cook in a water bath at 75°C for 18 hours. Cool in a blast chiller.

Store in an airtight container in the refrigerator for up to 1 month.

Green Chilli Pickle

Makes 1.1kg

125g yellow mustard seeds
7.5g fenugreek seeds
25g fennel seeds
10g black mustard seeds
500g Indian green chillies
350g mustard oil
20g kosher salt
3g ground turmeric
120g white rice wine vinegar

Dry roast the whole spices in a frying pan over a medium-high heat until the mustard seeds crack and the mixture is fragrant. Remove from the heat and allow to cool, then grind to a coarse powder using a pestle and mortar.

Thoroughly wash and pat dry the Indian green chillies. Discard the stems and cut them into 1cm pieces.

Heat the mustard oil to smoking point in a saucepan over a high heat.

Mix the ground spices, salt and turmeric with the chopped chillies in a heatproof container and pour the hot mustard oil over it. Mix thoroughly and add the vinegar.

Allow the mixture to cool and once it reaches room temperature place in a sterilised glass jar, making sure that the chillies are fully submerged in the oil. Leave the chillies to mature for at least 1 month before using. Alternatively, after 1 month, transfer the pickle to sterile vacpack bags and seal under full vacuum.

Store in an airtight container in the refrigerator for up to 3 months.

Pickling Liquor Base

Makes 325g

150g rice wine vinegar
100g water
50g white caster sugar
10g green bird's-eye chilli, split
15g garlic

Put all the ingredients in a saucepan and bring to the boil, stirring until all the sugar is dissolved. While still warm, pour it over whatever you want to pickle. Let it cool.

Store in an airtight container, preferably glass, in the refrigerator for up to 1 month.

Tendli Pickle

Makes 150g

kosher salt
150g tendli
325g Pickling Liquor Base (above)

Make a brine with cold water and 3 per cent salt. Add the tendlie and brine overnight in the refrigerator, then strain. Bring the rest of ingredients to the boil in a pan, then pour the liquid over the brined tendli. Allow to cool.

Store in a sealed glass jar in the refrigerator for up to 3 months.

BiBi Essentials

Garnishes

Boondi

Makes 300g

200g besan flour
30g rice flour
5g ground turmeric
5g Kashmiri chilli powder
3g ajwain seeds
8g kosher salt
400g cold filtered water
neutral vegetable oil, for deep frying

Put all the dry ingredients in a bowl and whisk until evenly distributed. Slowly add the water to the dry mix while stirring, to avoid the formation of any lumps.

Heat enough vegetable oil for deep frying to 180°C in a deep fat fryer (two-thirds to three-quarters full). Place a slotted spoon over the hot oil and slowly pour one ladle of the mixture through the slotted spoon.

Small balls of batter will form and rise to the surface of the oil. Stir the boondi around the oil to ensure they colour all over and fry for 3 minutes until crispy. Remove from the oil and place on a tray lined with kitchen paper to absorb excess oil.

Store in an airtight container at room temperature for up to 1 month.

Fried Curry Leaves

neutral vegetable oil, for deep frying
curry leaves

Heat enough vegetable oil for deep frying to 180°C in a deep fat fryer (two-thirds to three-quarters full). Fry the curry leaves until they become crispy and translucent and stop spluttering. Drain on a tray lined with kitchen paper to absorb excess oil.

These are best used straight away, but can be stored in an airtight container at room temperature for up to 5 days.

Fried Moong Dal

100g split yellow moong dal, rinsed and
    soaked for minimum 4 hours
neutral vegetable oil, for deep frying
2g kosher salt

Drain the soaked dal and place them on a kitchen towel to dry them thoroughly.

Heat enough vegetable oil for deep frying to 160°C in a deep fat fryer (two-thirds to three-quarters full). Add the dal to the oil in small batches and fry for 2-3 minutes until they crisp up and turn golden. Remove from the oil and place on a tray lined with kitchen paper to absorb the excess oil.

Season with the salt and store in an airtight container at room temperature for up to 1 month.

Fried Onions

neutral vegetable oil, for deep frying
Indian onions, thinly sliced with a mandoline

Heat enough vegetable oil for deep frying to 160°C in a deep fat fryer (two-thirds to three-quarters full). Deep fry the sliced onions in small batches for 3–5 minutes per batch until they start turning golden (they will carry on cooking for a couple of minutes after you remove them from the oil). Remove from the oil with a slotted spoon, lay flat on a tray lined with kitchen paper and let them dry out under a hot lamp or a dehydrator while you fry the remaining batches.

Store in an airtight container at room temperature for up to 1 week.

Peanut Podi

Makes 1kg

500g peanuts (skinned)
10g BiBi Chaat Masala (page 213)
25g deggi mirch
1g coriander seeds
1g fennel seeds
0.5g cumin seeds
450g freshly grated coconut
10g black salt
5g kosher salt

Preheat the oven to 160°C. Roast the peanuts on a baking tray for about 12 minutes, mix in the spices, coconut and both salts while hot, then grind to a crumb in a Thermomix or food processor. Dehydrate overnight in a dehydrator or an oven at 75°C for 12 hours. The next day, blitz to a fine crumb consistency.

Store in an airtight container at room temperature for up to 1 month.

Puffed Grains

Makes 100g puffed grains

100g quinoa or buckwheat
300g cold water
neutral vegetable oil, for deep frying
kosher salt

Put the quinoa or buckwheat in a pan with the cold water and bring to the boil, then reduce the heat and simmer for 15 minutes. Remove from the heat and drain, discarding all the water.

Set up a dehydrator or an oven to 60°C. Once the dehydrator is ready, place the grains on a tray inside the dehydrator for 45 minutes.

Heat enough vegetable oil for deep frying to 190°C in a deep fat fryer (two-thirds to three-quarters full). Fry the dehydrated grains in small batches for 1–2 minutes until the grains are fully crispy. Remove from the oil, drain on a paper-lined tray to absorb excess oil and season to taste.

Store in an airtight container at room temperature for up to 5 days.

Thin Sev

Makes 250g

240g gram flour
1g asafoetida
1g freshly ground black pepper
2g ground turmeric
2.5g Kashmiri chilli powder
6g kosher salt
90g room-temperature water
neutral vegetable oil, for deep frying
    and greasing

Sift the gram flour into a bowl and add all the spices and salt.

Gradually add the water while mixing it by hand, and knead until a smooth dough is formed. Take a sevai machine and lightly grease the interior with oil. Use the disc with the thinnest holes – around 1mm diameter – and fill the machine with the dough.

Heat enough vegetable oil for deep frying to 160°C in a deep fat fryer (two-thirds to three-quarters full). Press the sevai machine on a slotted spoon and shape the noodles into a nest shape. Place the noodles in the oil and fry for 2 minutes, flip the nest and fry for 2 more minutes until crispy. Remove the noodles from the oil with a slotted spoon and rest for 10–15 minutes on kitchen paper to absorb the excess oil.

Bread, Rice and Dal

Ghee Dal

Makes 1kg

For the base
300g split red lentils
1g ground turmeric
5g neutral vegetable oil
12g kosher salt

For the masala
50g neutral vegetable oil
4g cumin seeds
2.5g asafoetida
30g garlic, finely chopped
15g fresh peeled ginger, finely chopped
150g Indian onion, finely diced
1 whole Kashmiri chilli
2g deggi mirch

To finish
100g San Marzano tomatoes, diced
80g grass-fed ghee
20g coriander leaves, cut into a chiffonade

Base
Soak the red lentils in water for 30 minutes. Discard the soaking water and rinse until the water runs clear.

Add all the ingredients to a large pot and cover with water by at least 5cm. Place over a medium heat, bring to the boil, then turn down to a simmer and cook for about 30 minutes or until the lentils are fully cooked. Skim the foam produced by the lentils every 5-10 minutes. Take off the heat.

Masala
Heat the oil in a frying pan over a medium-high heat. Add the cumin and asafoetida and cook for 30 seconds until the cumin seeds crack, then add the garlic and ginger and fry for 2-3 minutes, stirring constantly, until they turn deep golden brown. Add the chopped onion and Kashmiri chilli, reduce the heat to medium-low and cook for about 15 minutes until the onion is soft and starting to colour. Add the deggi mirch and cook for 1 minute, then take off the heat.

To finish
Add the masala to the base along with the diced tomatoes. Melt the ghee and top the dal with the ghee and coriander before serving.

Ladi Pav

Makes 20 ladi pav

For the tangzhong
120g full-fat milk
25g April bearded flour

For the ladi pav
145g tangzhong
45g April bearded flour
200g strong white bread flour
20g full-fat milk
8g kosher salt
6.3g fresh yeast
25g white caster sugar
115g eggs
25g grapeseed oil
75g unsalted butter, softened, plus extra melted butter for brushing

Tangzhong
Combine the milk and April bearded flour in a saucepan over a low heat and cook until the mixture is well blended and reaches 65°C. Remove from the heat and leave to cool to room temperature.

Ladi pav
Put the tangzhong in the bowl of a stand mixer fitted with the dough hook attachment along with the rest of the ingredients except the oil and butter and start mixing the dough at medium-low speed. When the dough starts to come together, gradually add the oil. Mix the dough at medium speed for 1 hour.

Slowly add the softened butter and mix for a further 15 minutes, then remove the dough from the mixer and allow to rest in the refrigerator for at least 4 hours before portioning it.

Preheat a combination oven to 170°C and 90% humidity. Spray the moulds (we use ten 9 x 6 x 4cm non-stick tins) with oil spray, roll the chilled dough into 20 x 30g balls and put two in each mould. Steam-roast in the oven for 13 minutes, then turn the ladi pavs around in the oven and bake for another 6 minutes, or until brown. Remove and brush them with melted butter while hot, then transfer to a wire rack to cool.

Store in an airtight container in the refrigerator for up to 3 days.

Papdi

1 Roomali Roti (right)
neutral vegetable oil, for deep frying
Lime Leaf Chaat Masala (page 214),
    for dusting

Using a round pastry cutter, punch out
7–8cm-diameter circles of roomali.

Heat enough vegetable oil for deep frying
to 160°C in a deep fat fryer (two-thirds
to three-quarters full). Fry the discs for
1–2 minutes until they start to become
golden. Transfer them to a paper-lined
tray to absorb the excess oil.

Dust liberally with lime leaf chaat masala.

Gol Gappa

Makes 20–30

200g fine semolina
200g plain flour, plus extra for dusting
1g baking powder
6g kosher salt
10g rapeseed oil
230–250g filtered water
rapeseed oil, for deep frying

Mix all the dry ingredients and oil in a bowl.

Add 60g of the water and knead the dough
for 10 minutes until fully incorporated and
a smooth dough is formed. If the dough is
too dry, add more water in small increments.
Cover the dough and leave to rest in the
refrigerator for at least 20 minutes and
up to 30 minutes.

Heat rapeseed oil in a deep fat fryer (two-
thirds to three-quarters full) to 160°C. Roll
the dough on a slighty floured surface to
a thickness of about 2mm. Using a round
cutter, punch out discs around 4cm in diameter. Gently place them in the hot oil and
keep turning them around with a slotted
spoon.

Remove from the fryer once puffed, golden
and crispy. Transfer the gol gappa to a
tray lined with kitchen paper to absorb the
excess oil, then they will be ready to use.

Store in an airtight container at room
temperature for to 3 days.

Roghani Kulcha

Makes 8

150g self-raising flour
50g wholemeal chakki atta
5g kosher salt
8g white caster sugar
4g fresh yeast, crumbled
80g full-fat milk
20g whipping cream
20g eggs
20g natural stirred yoghurt
neutral vegetable oil, for greasing
plain flour, for dusting
salted butter or chicken fat, melted,
    for brushing

Put all the dry ingredients and the yeast
in the bowl of a stand mixer fitted with the
dough hook and mix on medium-low speed.

Heat the milk and cream in a pan to 35°C.
In a separate bowl, combine the eggs and
yoghurt.

Add the milk and cream to the dry mixture,
while mixing. Once incorporated, add the
egg and yoghurt mix and knead on medium
speed for 15 minutes. Place the mix in
an airtight container and transfer to the
refrigerator for 6 hours to prove.

Transfer the dough to a floured surface,
remove all the air from it and portion it into
40g balls.

Heat a tawa or plancha to a medium-high
heat. Using the palm of your hand and a
rolling pin, flatten the dough to 5mm-thick
discs. Cook them on the tawa for 30–40
seconds per side or until puffed slightly, with
the sides taking on some colour. Brush with
melted butter or chicken fat before serving.

Roomali Roti

Makes 8

300g organic Shipton Mill plain flour, plus
    extra for dusting
100g wholemeal chakki atta
4g kosher salt
280g full-fat milk
20g ghee

Put all the dry ingredients in a stand mixer
fitted with the dough hook attachment.

Warm the milk to 60°C. Pour the warm
milk into the dry mix while mixing a medium
speed, and keep mixing on medium-low
speed for 20 minutes. Add the ghee and mix
for another 5 minutes until incorporated.
Place the mixture in an airtight container
and let it rest in the refrigerator for at least
4 hours before dividing it into 8 x 75g balls.

Heat a tawa or plancha to about 250°C.

Dust a worktop with flour and, with the help
of a rolling pin, stretch each piece of dough
to an oval shape of 1–2mm thickness. Cook
over the tawa – 10–15 seconds on the first
side, 5–10 seconds after flipping – and serve
immediately.

Sourdough Pao

Makes 1 large loaf or multiple pao

285g strong white flour
6g fresh yeast, crumbled
30g active sourdough starter
150g full-fat milk
30g honey
36g eggs
6g kosher salt
60g unsalted butter, cubed and softened
neutral vegetable oil, for greasing
salted butter, softened, for brushing

Mix the strong flour, yeast and sourdough starter in a stand mixer fitted with the dough hook attachment.

Warm up the milk and honey just enough to melt the honey, then add the eggs. Add the milk mix to the dry ingredients and beat the dough with the dough hook for 10-15 minutes. Once it comes together, add the salt and butter until incorporated. Set the dough in the refrigerator and leave there for up to 24 hours, or until needed.

Portion and shape the pao according to the recipe:

To make mini pao, portion the dough into 25-35g balls and form into mini loaf shapes. Grease mini loaf moulds with oil, add the dough and allow the dough to prove at 24°C until doubled in size. The shape and weight might vary based on the mould used. We use 80 x 30 x 30mm mini loaf moulds.

For a full-size loaf, shape the dough into one large loaf. Grease a standard brioche tin and place the dough in the tin. Allow the dough to prove at 24°C until doubled in size.

Preheat a combination oven to 160°C, 60% humidity. Bake mini pao for 14 minutes, rotating the tray halfway through the baking time. Bake the full-size loaf for 30-35 minutes, until golden brown. Brush the tops with soft salted butter while still warm.

Store in an airtight container in the refrigerator for up to 3 days.

Yahkni Pulao

Serves 8

For the yahkni stock
30g rapeseed oil
9g fennel seeds
9g coriander seeds
2g green cardamom seeds
3g black cardamom seeds
4g black peppercorns
2g cloves
1g whole nutmeg
3g mace blades
3g cassia bark
15g garlic, crushed
45g fresh peeled ginger, smashed
7g green bird's eye chilli, roughly chopped
150g Indian onion, sliced
1.5kg Chicken Stock (page 209)

For the pulao
500g kaima or jeerakasala rice
10g chicken fat
7g royal cumin seeds
1.1kg yahkni stock
20g kosher salt

Yahkni stock
Heat the oil in a pot over a medium-high heat, add all the spices and cook for 5 minutes until fragrant. Add the garlic, ginger, chilli and sliced onion and cook for 5-8 minutes until the onions are soft and translucent. Add the chicken stock and bring the mixture to the boil, then simmer over a low heat for 20 minutes. Pass the stock through a fine chinois and return it to the pan.

Pulao
Wash the rice under cold running water for a minimum 5 minutes. Once the water runs clear, strain the rice and cover with fresh cold water for at least 30 minutes and up to 2 hours. Strain the rice just before cooking.

Heat the chicken fat in a saucepan over a medium-high heat. Add the royal cumin and cook until it crackles, then add the yakhni stock and salt and bring to the boil. Add the strained rice and cook, uncovered, over a medium-low heat for 10-12 minutes until most of the stock has been absorbed by the rice and the rice starts to come to the surface. Cover the pan with a clean tea towel and a lid, remove from the heat and rest for 10 minutes before serving.

Pastry

Coconut Sorbet

1kg Boiron coconut purée
100g prosorbet
90g caster sugar
10g lime juice

Mix the purée, sugar, prosorbet and juice together and hand blend until incorporated. Portion in 500g Pacojet beakers and freeze at -20°C until solid. Process in the Pacojet as required.

Crystallised Garnishes

100g desired garnish
100g caster sugar
20g water

If you need to crystallise a nut or a seed, they will have to be roasted in the oven at 160°C beforehand until they achieve the desired colour.

Mix the sugar and the water in a large saucepan until it has a wet sand texture. Melt the mix until it reaches 114°C. Add the garnish of your choice and gently stir until crystallised. Take off the heat and place your crystallised garnish on parchment paper until cool.

Some garnishes will have to be chopped in a food processor to break them into smaller pieces. Store in an airtight container at room temperature.

Flavoured Meringues

50g egg white
50g caster sugar
5g albuwhip
50g icing sugar
15g yoghurt powder or fig leaf powder

Whisk the egg white and sugar in a heat-proof bowl over a bain marie until it reaches 45°C.

Transfer to a stand mixer fitted with the whisk attachment, add the albuwhip and icing sugar and whisk to stiff peaks. Dust liberally with yoghurt powder or fold the fig leaf powder through.

Put in a piping bag and pipe in kisses for the Alphonso Mango Lassi (page 164) or in straight lines for the Amrood Ka Meetha (page 166) using the k11 nozzle. Dehydrate overnight at 65°C.

Once cool, store in an airtight container in the refrigerator for up to 3 days.

Passion Fruit Gel

100g Boiron passion fruit purée
50g caster sugar
2g agar agar

Put the purée and sugar in a saucepan, bring to the boil, then add the agar agar and simmer for 2 minutes, stirring to avoid lumps. Blend with a hand blender, then decant into a container and let it set in the refrigerator. Once solid, blend in a high-speed blender or Vitamix and pass through a fine chinois. Remove excess air in a vacpack.

Store in a piping bag or squeezy bottle in the refrigerator for up to 3 days.

Passion Fruit and Mango Gel

50g Boiron passion fruit purée
50g Kissan alphonso mango pulp
50g caster sugar
2g agar agar

Put the purée, pulp and sugar in a saucepan, bring to the boil, then add the agar agar and simmer for 2 minutes, stirring to avoid lumps. Blend with a hand blender then decant in a container and let it set in the refrigerator. Once solid, blend in a high-speed blender or Vitamix, pass through a fine chinois. Remove excess air in a vacpack.

Store in a piping bag or squeezy bottle in the refrigerator for up to 3 days.

About the author

Raised in Berkshire, Chef Chet Sharma's journey into kitchens was far from typical. Immersed in a world of two cultures, his maternal grandmother was from India, his paternal from London, and he spent much of his early life split across two continents. Chet spent his childhood in the kitchen, watching and learning from his grandmothers' cooking. They were both resourceful cooks and, like many of their generation, advocates of retaining their heritage through their food. He also became a voracious reader (he now has a library of over 1,200 volumes), using books to learn and discover and ultimately as a form of escapism.

Chet excelled academically at school and, with a natural curiosity for science, secured a place at UCL (University College London) to read Chemistry. At the same time, he hosted and DJ'd at events to help fund his studies with a late-night residency at the Ministry of Sound in London and performed on stage with, among others, Kanye West, 50 Cent and Sean Paul. He also explored his love for cooking and began working initially at Benares under Atul Kochhar in Mayfair, all the while continuing with his degree. When Giorgio Locatelli released his book, *Made in Italy: Food and Stories*, in 2006, Chet inhaled the words, drawing parallels with his own heritage, family and community. He applied for a position at Locanda Locatelli in Marylebone and within days of arriving, Giorgio had recognised not only a willingness to learn but also a skill for considered precision in execution. He commissioned Chet to the pastry section. During his time working with Giorgio, Chet revelled in the informality of family-orientated dishes, coupled with a dedication to fine dining. By now, his academic progress had taken him to a Master's in Neurology at UCL. His formal studies were also now running in tandem with an eagerness to experience as much as he could from professional kitchens. He embarked on the first of a total of 16 stagiaire positions that lasted from 2005–2013, under great chefs including Pierre Gagnaire, Tom Kerridge, Raymond Blanc, Heston Blumenthal and Ollie Dabbous.

After graduating from UCL with a completed Master's, his attention turned to Oxford University and a second Master's in Physics, followed by a doctorate in Condensed Matter Physics. An intense period followed and, remarkably, he successfully achieved his doctorate in just over three years. Now freed from his formal studies, Chet moved to San Sebastián in Spain where his knowledge of science secured him a position under the tutelage of Chef Andoni Aduriz at Mugaritz. This would be a formative period for him where he learned how to work within and later motivate a team, and manage the finer elements of developing food at this creative level. On his return to Britain, Chet joined the team at Simon Rogan's Umbel Restaurant Group as Director of Research and Development, overseeing development for all of Simon's restaurants, including L'Enclume, Roganic and Fera. From there, he consulted for various restaurants, including with Brett Graham at The Ledbury, before joining Mark Birchall at Moor Hall in West Lancashire as part of his opening team. Chet was then approached by JKS Restaurants to work with them as Group Development Chef. He was already friendly with their co-founder, Karam Sethi, who over the years had become in part a mentor to him, and they both shared an outlook for creativity and guest satisfaction.

Chet's focus turned to developing his own culinary style and he experimented and began to create dishes in his home kitchen on days and weekends off. He researched single-origin spices and the health benefits of heritage grains and continued to push his produce-led cooking, albeit with more attention on ingredients and stories from the Indian subcontinent. He adopted the analytical skills he had learned in academia to drive his recipes forward using a strong ability to think abstractly and creatively. All of which he combined with the craft he had honed over many years working in professional kitchens.

In the summer of 2019, they found and signed a site in Mayfair for a restaurant in North Audley Street. Then the pandemic hit. Like for so many others, this was a period of self-reflection and, as the country moved in and out of lockdown, the project slowly came together as Chet refined the menus, the concept and the overall identity of the restaurant. In September 2021, BiBi opened its doors to huge critical acclaim. Named after an affectionate term for 'grandmother' in Urdu, Chet's restaurant is an ode to the two women who helped inspire his career and elements of whose influence is now interlaced throughout his menus and the restaurant's interiors.

Acknowledgements

Jyo, Karam, Sue. JKS. You've always stood behind me and helped me realise a dream I didn't even know I had. Thank you. And a huge thank you to all those at JKS who have played their part as we've gone on this very long journey together.

Lois, it's an understatement to say this book wouldn't have happened without you. We joke that I'm the voice of flavour and you're the voice of reason, but you have been the sane ying to my crazy yang throughout this project. For any chefs out there hoping to write a cookbook – please, trust me, it's a whole load of work. At least three times more than you would expect. You need a Lois to make it happen. You just can't have my one.

To my team in the restaurant, past and present, thank you for helping me (us) to tick one off the bucket list – our own cookbook! Ash, Ale, Irene, Telis, Nicole and many, many more. You freed me up from the day-to-day running of the restaurant whenever I needed (or Lois told me) to write. Hannah before, and now Mira, thank you for your near-unlimited patience with my ludicrous lack of organisation.

Emilia, Laura and the Phaidon team. Now that we're at this stage I can be honest. There was no chance I was doing this book with anyone else. And you've shown me so many times along the way that I made the right call. Your knowledge, experience and unflappable nature has steadied this ship through some choppy waters.

Anton – you're pretty good at this photography gig. Maybe you should give up the pizza chef life and give it a proper go (!). Thank you for bringing the dishes to life in a way that only someone with a trained eye and supreme skill behind the lens could.

Dr Stephen Tucker – the last person to have read and guided me through the last 'book' I wrote. If you made it to this point of the book, I'm sorry, this isn't a physics thesis so it's inevitably a bit 'wishy washy'. But if you hadn't supported me through my time at Oxford, I would have never made it here. Thank you.

I will be forever indebted to my family – both new and old, past and present – for their unwavering support as I embarked on a uniquely haphazard path in opening a risky restaurant, in the most expensive neighbourhood in Britain, during the height of a global pandemic. While recovering from a life-changing illness. Actually, why did you let me do it?!

Firstly, my parents, Shushant and Promila Sharma. Thank you for both being such uninterested cooks that I had to learn from my grandmothers. But also thank you for the most amazing childhood that let me experience the world and India in a way few others could. I would be nowhere and nobody without you.

Raj – thanks for being a lawyer, getting married young and having so many kids so that all the pressure was taken off me. You supported me by depositing money in my account when I was off travelling the world learning to do this thing which has done nothing but taken me further away from you and your ever-expanding family. You are in every way the best older brother anybody could ask for. Especially because you'll always be shorter than me.

My extended family – from my nieces and nephews, cousins, sisters-in-law (who are both like the sisters I never had) – Dadda, B.C. (not short for what it's usually short for), Renu massi and more – it takes a village to raise a child, and for you all I am eternally grateful. Mani, you helped this kid from Slough realise that the road most often taken isn't the only one. Neelam Uncle, you're not with us anymore but you are forever etched in mind as the picture of true Punjabi hospitality; I'd need another book just to write the stories you left us with.

Sabreen. I'm not sure I can ever make up for being the often-absent husband I've been over the past four years. Can I even begin to express my deepest gratitude to the one who has been my rock, my inspiration and my best friend throughout this entire journey? You've lived up to the true meaning of your name – patience – and your love of great hospitality has also opened my eyes to a completely different viewpoint, the benefit of which is felt by every guest that steps through the door. Thank you for being my partner in life and in this creative endeavour. There simply is no BiBi without you. I'm not even sure there is a 'me' without you.

Finally, of course, my bibis, Kamal and Ranjana. Thank you. You are the spark that ignited this flame in me. And you are still the most generous people I've ever been fortunate enough to know.

Recipe notes

Many of the recipes in this book require advanced techniques, specialist ingredients, professional equipment and years of experience to achieve the best results.

Please exercise a high level of caution when following recipes involving any potentially dangerous activity, including when using charcoal and an open flame, as well as when deep frying. As professional chefs, we always carry out these activities with the right equipment and appropriate clothing – an apron doesn't just keep your clothes clean, it is also the first line of defence against scorching charcoal or oil splashes.

The cooking times suggested here are tuned for our commercial kitchen. We have, among other things, three-phase powered induction and combination ovens which heat up and maintain temperatures far quicker and with far more accuracy than an oven in a domestic kitchen. If you are using a standard fan or convection oven at home, please follow the manufacturer's instructions with regards to oven temperatures.

Some recipes include raw or very lightly cooked eggs, meat or fish. All eggs in the restaurant are pasteurised, but these are less readily available for domestic consumption. For your own safety, we recommend that preparations that involve raw or lightly cooked eggs, meat or fish should be avoided by the elderly, infants, pregnant women, convalescents and anyone else who may be immunocompromised. For further information, please consult your GP or physician.

Please exercise caution when making any of the fermented or pickled products, ensuring that all equipment is clean and sanitised. Seek expert advice if in any doubt.

When no quantity is specified, for example of oils, salts and herbs used for finishing dishes, or for deep frying, quantities are discretionary and flexible.

All herbs, shoots, flowers and leaves should be picked fresh, from a clean source. In particular, when foraging for any products, please avoid busy areas as car pollutants can be seriously injurious to your health. Ensure that ingredients are thoroughly cleaned before use. If you have any doubts about any of the less familiar ingredients, please consult an expert to ensure that they are safe to eat.

Glossary

achar – pickle
adrak – ginger
amchoor – green mango powder
bhindi – okra
elaichi – green cardamom
ghee – clarified butter
gucchi – Kashmiri morel mushroom
gur – jaggery
haldi – ground turmeric
hing – asafoetida
imli – tamarind
jaifal – nutmeg
javitri – mace
jeera – cumin
kala jeera – black cumin
kala namak – black salt
kalunji – nigella seeds
kasundi – Indian mustard
khus khus – black poppy seeds
kodra – kodo millet
laung – clove
masoor dal – red lentils
methi – fenugreek
saunf – fennel seeds
saunth – dried ginger
tej patta – bay leaf

Index

Phaidon Press Limited
2 Cooperage Yard
London E15 2QR

Phaidon Press Inc.
111 Broadway
New York, NY 10006

Phaidon SARL
55, rue Traversière
75012 Paris

phaidon.com

First published 2025
© 2025 Phaidon Press Limited
ISBN 978 1 83729 050 5

978 1 83729 119 9 (signed edition)

A CIP catalogue record for this book is available from the British
Library and the Library of Congress.

Commissioning Editor: Emilia Terragni
Project Editor: Laura Nickoll
Production Controller: Adela Cory
Design: Hyperkit

Printed in China